Thunder
& sunshine

alastair humphreys

From your front door, it's a long ride home.
Alastair Humphreys

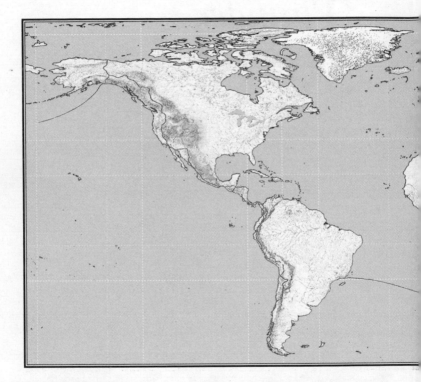

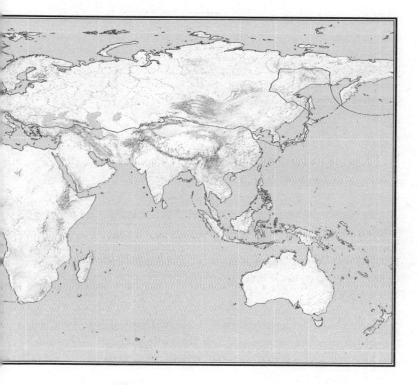

Souls… that ever with a frolic welcome took,
  The thunder and the sunshine.
   – 'Ulysses,' Alfred Lord Tennyson

Thunder & Sunshine, second edition, reprinted 2009

Published by Eye Books Ltd 2007
7 Peacock Yard
Iliffe Street
London
SE17 3LH

Tel. +44 (0) 207 708 2942
www.eye-books.com

Typeset in Bembo and Bodoni

ISBN-13: 9781903070543

Cover design and creative direction by David Whelan for Eye Books,
with editorial assistance from Laura Chastney.

The events and opinions in this book originate from the author. The publisher
accepts no responsibility for their accuracy.

Printed and bound in Great Britain by J F Print Ltd., Sparkford.

The main focus of Eye Books has always been tales of travelling and journeys – but the stories resulting from these are not only geographical and physical, but relate also to the emotional and human reactions that these journeys have on the individuals involved. The reason why the expeditions were considered and the effects of carrying them out.

Life is not a competition. Those who do not achieve major feats are certainly not failures, and those who DO achieve great feats are not all heroes. However, the story that this book tells must surely rank high, not just for the achievement but also for human courage and inspiration. It tells of challenges that would have destroyed most people, and of a 4 year endurance test – both of these by someone to whom a secure and conventional future was an option.

Alastair's decision to do what he did – to test himself (in the fullest sense of the word) – involved him confronting not only outside challenges, but being challenged by so many different values and cultures and realities. His decision was also taken as a result of his awareness of other people and his desire to help others – not just with the considerable amount of money that he raised for *Hope and Homes for Children*, but his reaction to the many strangers he met along the way and their undoubted reaction to meeting him. This will certainly have left an impression on him and on them.

Whatever strengths Alastair needed during this trip, he remains essentially human, both feeling and expressing all the frailties of fear, despair, loneliness, homesickness, exhaustion ... as well as genuine wonderment of all the goodness that he saw. It is definitely 4 years of living on the brink. Perhaps it is only by getting so close to the brink that enables people to view and experience the things that go unnoticed by most.

In publishing this story, I hope we have played a small part in helping others share the experience and will have given the readers a chance to glimpse the greater horizon on life, and in the honesty of the writing we have seen not just the journey of a man with a bike, but the journey of a man who saw, as Louis Armstrong sang, 'a wonderful world'.

Details of other books written by Alastair Humphreys and other Eye Books authors may be found at the back of this book or on the website below.

Dan Hiscocks
Publisher Eye Books

www.eye-books.com

For Sarah, my wife

After all it is only a book and no worlds are made or destroyed by it. But it becomes important out of all proportion to its importance. And I might just as well get to it because putting it off isn't going to help a bit.
– John Steinbeck

Foreword

Alastair is a man who has earned the title of, 'a man,' the hard way. He is one of the few who understands that the romance of high adventure is but a mirage, and that the reality of such an epic journey as his is one of loneliness, aching muscles and of being at times both humbled and intimidated under the vast expanses of our planet's wildernesses.

Alone, with only his bike as companion, Alastair tells in brutal honesty the often grim reality of cycling the globe. At times the journey is furious with bustling cities and bureaucratic checkpoints and at other moments he gives a very moving sense of what solitude does to us. He struggles to answer what it is that makes him punish himself under the scale and burden of this once-in-a-lifetime challenge. The answer is always the least important part. It is the journey that matters, and what that journey does to us.

I think it is fair to say that if Alastair had had any idea of how hard and long the road would have really been he might well have thought twice about taking on such a challenge. But thinking twice doesn't always lead down the road of achieving something monumental. Sometimes to make something of our lives requires us to dream, and then to shun the doubts and fears and grasp that dream with both hands and get out there and just start making some steps towards that dream. We need to commit, deep inside ourselves, not to rest until the job is done. My mother often told me, "when a job is once begun, leave it not till it is done; be it big or be it small, do it well, or not at all." Alastair sure did this job well, and I am full of admiration for this remarkable man and his epic journey. Oh, there is one other quote that sums him up, "commitment is doing the thing you said you would do, long after the mood in which you said it in has left you." Alastair: I bet that romantic mood had long left you on that lonely road as you headed into the wind and rain winding your way to the start of the Andes, eh?! But that's why you are special.

Bear Grylls, 2007

…mesmerising story. You can almost feel the sand being kicked up in your face as you turn the page… This book is a literary match to his physical achievement.
– Geographical

…if a lad from Yorkshire can overcome international terrorism, dysentery, a crushing Siberian winter and a month without showering… then there's not really any reason why we all can't. He may not have meant it, but Humphreys' engaging, sometimes brutal, sometimes comic style is above all a call to arms… documented with unflinching honesty. Humphreys conveys his loneliness, wanderlust, grit and despair in a manner reminiscent of the great tradition of British explorers. He may have spent many hours asking why the hell he was doing this; anyone reading his book may, in the great tradition of watching British explorers, be more curious as to whether this man was insane or not.
– The Guardian

Wonderful…
– Midweek, BBC Radio 4

An Epic Adventure
– Benedict Allen

An incredible journey of distance, strength and determination
– Josie Dew

Contents

Prologue

I had come so far. I could barely comprehend that I had not finished, that I still had so much further still to go. Over a year ago I had cycled away from home, bound for Australia. I had pedalled out of my village in Yorkshire, out of sight of my watching family, and out into the world. I did not know what I would find, nor whether I would cope. I knew only that it was a significant moment. I knew that, in the unlikely event of success, that I would probably categorise things for ever more as taking place either before or after that day I began my ride.

Riding to Australia was to be the first part of my dream to cycle the whole way around our planet, but, just a fortnight into my journey, the events of September 11th 2001 changed everything. As a new world exploded into the vacuum of our post Cold War complacency and war brewed in far away Afghanistan, my planned route through Central Asia was under threat. So I paused in Istanbul and concocted a new plan. I began riding through the Middle East instead, towards Africa. I arrived in Cairo and steeled myself to begin riding south. I did not expect to get far. To my surprise I managed to stick it out, overcoming massive self-doubt about my suitability for such an expedition. I pedalled all the way down Africa to Cape Town, to the ocean, to the end of the road, and to the end of Africa. I could ride no further.

But I had to ride further. I had set out to cycle round the world and Africa had been an incredible experience, but my journey was only really beginning. I still had so far to ride.

Part 1

'The sea on my left'

THE AMERICAS

Patagonia to Alaska

Gotta do what it is that I do,
Then I'm coming back.
Got the sun in my face,
Sleeping rough on the road,
I'll tell you all about it,
When I get home.
– 'Long Way Round,' *Stereophonics*

San Blas
Islands
Cartagena
Panama City
Medellin
Manizales
Popayan
Quito
Cuenca
Loja
Cajamarca
Huamachucho
Cusco
Copacabana
La Paz
Nazca
Oruro
San Pedro de Atacama
Pumamarca
Salta
Rio de Janeiro
Cape Town >
Santiago
Mendoza
Concepcion
Villa O'Higgins
El Chalten
Ushuaia

Cape Town to Panama

Gone to Patagonia

Dreams have only one owner at a time.
That's why dreamers are lonely.
— Erma Bombeck

At home, above the fireplace, since I was a child, hung a painting. A maelstrom of slate green waves and leaden troughs, a wild and savage ocean, heaved and pounded and shattered. In the thick of the fury, unmoved and constant, the rain-shrouded, craggy black outcrop of Cape Horn looms, the southernmost tip of South America and, amongst sailors, the most feared and revered spot on our planet. Incredibly, ludicrously, alone in the midst of such power and fury, is a little boat. Just 53 feet of mahogany, sailed by one man. This painting of the yacht *Gipsy Moth IV*, sailed by Francis Chichester, was my first introduction to Patagonia and the deep south of the world, 50 degrees below the equator, past the 'Roaring 40s' and into the 'Screaming 50s.' Sailors said, "Below 40 degrees, there is no law. Below 50 degrees, there is no God."

Patagonia, spans both Argentina and Chile. Mountains plateau and plains taper down to the rocky southern tip. South across the Straits of Magellan is the island of Tierra del Fuego, and at the far tip of that island, Ushuaia, the most southern town on the planet.

The names, *Patagonia* and *Tierra del Fuego* and *Ushuaia,* had thrilled and lured me for years. As I stepped off the bus in Ushuaia, I discovered that my yearning for *el fin del mundo* was not particularly original. A six-foot tall fluffy penguin demanded two *pesos* to pose for a picture with me to celebrate my arrival among the tourists at the remote end of the world. Ushuaia is a colourful hotchpotch of pink, blue, green and orange corrugated metal buildings in the lee of dark mountains on the tranquil shore of the Beagle Channel.

Tourism flourishes in Ushuaia, but probably not for the guided city tour, highlights of which included the old house of Mr. Pastoriza's, who worked in a sardine canning company. The project failed because the sardines never appeared. Or Mr. Solomon's General Goods store which became famous for the variety of its products, and which closed in 1970. No. People went to enjoy the beautiful ruggedness of Patagonia, to look out to sea, knowing that only Antarctica lay beyond the horizon. I looked in the opposite direction. I looked north, up the road I meant to follow to its very end, in Alaska.

The morning I began riding, I found it even harder than usual to get up. How do you persuade yourself to leave a nice warm sleeping bag and begin cycling, with 17,848 kilometres between you and your destination? Staying in bed seemed a far more attractive option. All the riding I had done counted for nothing now. I was back at the beginning, a brand new start at the bottom of a continental landmass, whose top was one third of the circumference of the globe away.

I pedalled south out of town, and down to the seashore where the road to Alaska truly began. I looked across the slate-coloured Lapataia Bay. Patches of white snow were on the upper scree slopes of the sharp grey mountains behind me. To welcome me back onto the road, a headwind was brewing. A clean green stream wound through the boggy fields and blended into the clean, pebbly shallows of the bay. My ears were cold and a light mist pearled tiny droplets over my fleece jacket and eyelashes. I stood still and felt small in the silence, and in awe of the phenomenal distance ahead of me. The bike was heavier than I was accustomed to, loaded with clothes I hadn't needed in Africa, like a fleece jacket, a hat and a pair of gloves. The gaffa tape was peeling from one of the holes in my faded bags. I needed to fix that; I was probably in for a few weeks of rain. Far away, a chainsaw started up and amplified how quiet the little cove was. My hand swirled through the cold water, I was intimidated by the road ahead. The old self-doubt rose through me, but I was determined not to cry. This runaway expedition had dragged me along and stampeded me. I was just managing to cling on. I was going to enjoy this ride up the Americas. I was determined. *Come on, Al, let's go have some fun!*

I climbed onto my bike and began to pedal, away from one sea towards another, far distant one. The first pedal strokes of millions, turning up the crunching dirt track through the lichen covered forest, away from the sea, back into Ushuaia and out the other side. It was mid-February. I hoped to reach Alaska by the end of summer next year.

My ride up the Americas was under way. I planned to cross to Asia and cycle back to England. This leg of my journey had begun months before, thousands of miles away, on another distant shore.

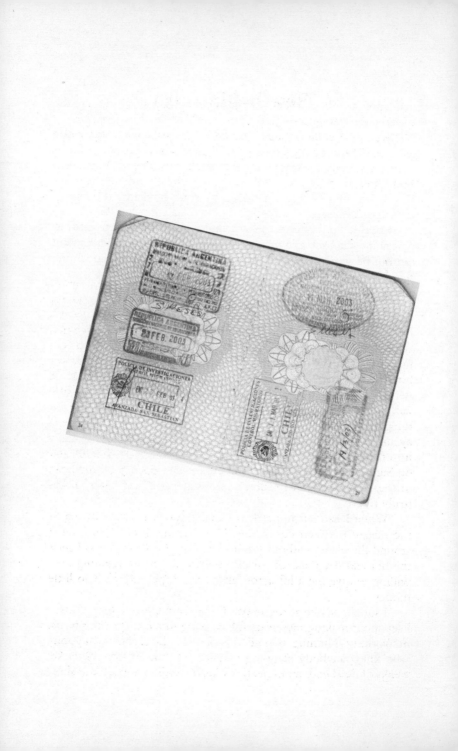

New beginnings

Every new beginning comes from some other new beginning's end.
– 'Feeling Strangely Fine,' Semisonic

Strange that South America should begin under South Africa's Table Mountain. I was aboard *Maiden* bound for Rio de Janeiro yet, as I gripped a halyard on the yacht's foredeck, it felt more like a start than a farewell. Table Bay teemed with all the glamour and excitement of the triennial Cape to Rio race. Amongst the racing yachts were sailing boats, jet-skis, power boats, canoes, press boats, gin palaces and bathtub rowing boats. A dramatic horizon of spears of masts, and bird-wing curves of white sail. Television helicopters swept low over the fleet, swooping for the perfect shot. Beneath the rotors water fretted in a circular frenzy and sailors panicked as their sails crashed from filled efficiency into flapping maelstrom. The shoreline was lined with people and on Signal Hill scores of binoculars flashed. I tipped back my head in the warm breeze to squint at the sun and I was happy. I was ready to go.

When I had left home I had assumed that I would fly across the oceans between continents. However the idea of making it around the planet without leaving its surface germinated as I rode the hot and dry roads of Africa. How would I find a sailing boat willing to give me a lift across an ocean? Especially with so little money...

I sought advice at the Royal Cape Yacht Club in Cape Town. I set about making myself useful, crewing in races, cleaning boats, networking, phoning people to ask if anybody knew anybody who knew anybody planning to sail across the Atlantic. After six weeks of dead ends and rejections, Terry Nielsen, owner and skipper of ocean-going yacht *Maiden*, offered me a ride. He was competing in the Cape to Rio race, had a spare berth and was happy to give me a ride.

I loaded my bike and gear into a freight container that was taking the fleet's spare sails and anchors to Rio de Janeiro, and I lived out of a tiny rucksack for another month until departure. I fixed my bike, gave talks, partied, sat on the beach, made friends and tried to get my head round the fact that, contrary to everything I had been telling myself, Cape Town was not actually the end of the road. I had cajoled and dragged myself down the length of Africa only by convincing myself this would be the end. I had refused to think further ahead than Cape Town. If I was to cycle around the world though, Cape Town was not even half of the journey. I seemed to be on an ever-lengthening, ever-ascending path. Once a way across the ocean had come my way, and the departure date set, the reality and the implications sank in. If I continued to South America I would be putting myself, once again, at the beginning of a very long road. A new horizon would open up, demanding to be crossed, challenging me to try.

My aim was to cycle round the world, to complete a circumnavigation, crossing the length of the world's three greatest landmasses. I had ridden the length of Africa. Now I planned to ride from the bottom of South America to the northern coast of Alaska, and then search for a boat to cross the Pacific, and ride across Asia, back to Europe and home.

After Christmas and New Year and only just before the start of the race, a badly delayed *Maiden* reached Cape Town. As crew flew in from around the world we prepared her for the race. An ocean-crossing novice, I tried to make myself useful, and at the same time not get in the way. Two hours before the race began I doubted we would make it to the start-line on time. I was stuck in a supermarket checkout queue with one trolley full of bananas and another of bread, last minute additions to the three weeks food supply for 15 people. Grannies fumbled in their purses for the exact change while I fretted about missing my escape from Africa.

I sprinted down the jetty with the shopping bags, the bowline was thrown off, I jumped aboard and we were away. The friends I had made in Cape Town waved and walked down the jetty. More fragile, precious connections broken. I was on my own again, in motion once again, and I had left Africa.

As the spectators turned for home the 30 or so competing yachts faced 4000 miles of ocean. Our crew of 15 had just come together and only now, at sea, was there time for proper introductions. My new companions were English, German, South African, Zimbabwean, Canadian, American and Spanish. We were students, business men, professional sailors, oil-workers, shop owners and architects. We were men and women, from 18 to 50-ish. We were a shambles. We were happy. Alberto, the second in command, was a charming Spanish Casanova who had been sailing his way round the world for three years on various yachts. He stood at the stern playing his guitar and singing, Bob Marley style, "Every little wind, is gonna be alright." Retired lawyer Terry set about turning the rabble into a team. Hen, a city girl in a dinky little Union Jack crop top, looked towards the empty horizon and declared cheerfully, "Well, at least we are out of sight of land now." Everyone laughed and turned her round; there were pedestrians on the shore just a few hundred metres away. Spirits were high although the wind was not and our boat had already stopped. The on-board GPS gave us an ETA for Rio de Janeiro of October; the finish line was ten months away on current progress. Perhaps I should have bought more bananas.

As our first night at sea approached, the breeze stiffened and the yacht stopped wallowing and began to heel. As *Maiden* came to life, she cut through the waves and I felt a thrill to be travelling again. I was totally free, and I was a lucky man for that. I sat with my legs dangling over the rushing water. I had not cut my hair since leaving home, and the sun-bleached dreadlocks whipped around my face. We chased the sunset, bearing west, heaving across the planet by the pure force of wind in our sails. The yacht ahead of us silhouetted dark against a late orange sky, the one behind us glowed peach on green waves. *Maiden's* hull thumped the waves, and spray leapt up to my face. I was soaked, frozen, nauseous and grinning like an idiot.

Seasickness caught me and I spent that first night hanging

over the side of the boat. In my cycling clothes and shoes I was soaking wet and cold. I had no sailing gear. But by sunset on the second day I had found sea legs and I set to learning about life aboard a 58-foot yacht. We were divided into two four-hour watches. The on-watch cooked, cleaned made repairs and sailed the boat. The off-watch slept. Our life slipping into our new tiny little world revolved on the sequence of watches. Each yacht in the race had by now diverged on its own chosen route searching for the best possible winds across the vast spread of ocean. We were alone on the vast blue canvas. Nothing else was in sight.

It took 24 days to sail across the Atlantic. Think how many people you talk to, how many miles you drive and how many phone calls you make in 24 days. Weeks in the office, weekends at home. Ever-changing horizons. Hours of television, reams of newspapers. Text messages, emails, changes of pants. But, for us, at sea, the world was reduced to blue water, 58 feet of boat and 14 other people who, until the starting cannon, had not known each other. There was nowhere to go. It was a massive simplification of my life, already simplified when I pedalled away from my past life and priorities and cares. I loved crossing the ocean, it was so different to a cyclist's life. On the bike I had grown sensitive, literally, I had become so aware of all that was around me, of the sights and sounds, smells and tastes, and the feel of the wind on my face. As the miles of sea crept by, I read seventeen books, drank countless cups of tea, daydreamed of sailing around the world, snoozed in the sail lockers and nattered like a granny with everybody.

Small events broke up the days: Pete being smacked in the head by a passing flying fish one night, and exacting his revenge by frying the fourteen he found on deck for breakfast; hilarity over a version of clay pigeon shooting involving a tray of rotten eggs; Terry's angry shouts of, "Only admirals and arseholes stand in the hatchway"; Sparky, our Mr. Fixit genius, trying heroically to repair the water de-salinator; an increasingly vocal campaign amongst the rest of the crew to cut my hair; the clamouring race for second helpings at dinner with the greediest of us on deck sitting right above the kitchen hatch for rapid access to leftovers; the stillness as we sat together and shared the sunsets.

Helming duties rotated hourly and occasional frenzies of activity were needed when the sails were changed, but generally there was not a lot to do. We were becalmed and barely moved for several days. Cabin fever escalated. The heat was getting to us all and the unusual wallowing motion of the boat was far harder to sleep through than the severe, but constant, heeling of the boat in a strong wind. So we covered ourselves from head to foot in soap and leapt from the bow for a swim and a wash, surfacing in a fizzing cloud of soap bubbles and hoping that there weren't any sharks nearby. It was an uneasy feeling to jump from my tiny island of sanctuary into water five kilometres deep with thousands of kilometres to the nearest landfall and God only knows how many millions of kilometres of emptiness above me. I felt very small.

Music blasted constantly through the speakers on deck and arguments flew about music preferences. Ken, the broad, strong Canadian oil worker with a handlebar moustache who I shared my bunk with, would put on one of his CD's and emerge on deck declaring, "There's only two types of music worth listening to, boys and girls, and that's Country, and Western!" before launching into one of his surprisingly camp dance routines. Minutes later the CD would be abruptly changed by a Country Music hater, of which there were 14, and the arguments would begin again. Every dawn the on-watch people would debate what tune to pick to welcome the sunrise with. My favourite was the morning when our watch lined up in the stern at the first golden sliver of sun and moshed to full-volume *Come as you are* from Nirvana before waking the other watch with a cacophony of banging pans. They were not best pleased.

We spent hours fishing as dorado circled beneath the boat, mocking our attempts to catch them. Eventually we hooked one, our only one, and hauled the 10kg of slippery muscle on board, watching its incredible death display as its entire body changed colour, shimmering through blue and gold and green and crimson until death drained all the colour and we sliced the beautiful fish into strips and ate the poor thing.

We all cheered as we crossed the Greenwich Meridian. The GPS rolled over to 0.00.000, and Alberto made the first tea of the Western hemisphere. I only had 360 degrees to travel.

I lay on shaded parts of the deck trying to mentally prepare myself for what lay ahead. I studied my map of South America and grew excited as I looked at the roads and mountains and cities and tried to imagine what lay in wait. I looked forward to turning the red lines of the roads and the yellow dots of towns into real memories. I reminisced about Africa, already remembering it as a wonderful experience, for 'one always begins to forgive a place as soon as it's left behind.'

The days blazed beneath a pale blue sky and above an incredibly clear blue ocean streaked deep with shafts of white light. The world felt a simple and pure place. Sunset brought relief from the heat, leaving the world to darkness, us and the comforting glow of the GPS and compass. When there was no moon the black sky was crowded with so many stars and shooting stars that they seemed to spill over into the ocean, where showers of phosphorescent sparks streamed in our wake like a bonfire, a wake of churning white water that stretched back to Africa and the end of the thin tyre tracks beginning from my home. We began the race with a fat cream moon in a golden halo, dead ahead of us. We made bets on the precise time of moonset. Silver clouds shone as we cruised down the yellow carpet of moonlight. The helmsman heaved on the wheel as we surfed the heavy, fast black waves. Eternal motion, racing ever onwards towards South America. The fair wind was flying now and we excitedly crowded over the GPS hoping to beat speed records set by the other watch.

Behind us, morning caught the boat; the water mauve, the pallid sky orange and blue and the clouds still grey. Only the strong stars survived. Eventually even Venus faded.

"Land ahoy!" At long last South America edged above the horizon. Excitement rippled amongst us, all craning for a better view on the starboard side of the boat. My first thought was 'wow it's hilly!' as I switched seamlessly back into cyclist mentality once again. I was nervous but excited to see folds of rock and vertical lines once again after weeks on a horizontal flat blue disc. The water turned to a shallow, muddy green as we hugged the coast southwards, turtles drifted by and the passing of large ships once again prompted renewed vigilance on watch. The rich smell of earth and trees gripped me like a pheromone, until, in the last hours before reaching Rio, all natural scents were obliterated by the breaking out of deodourant and aftershave, and clean but crumpled T-shirts, specially preserved for the occasion, were donned.

We arrived in the bay of Rio de Janeiro in the dead of night, beneath the outline of Sugarloaf mountain and the iconic illuminated statue of Christ that appeared to hang in the dark sky above us. It was so exciting to see them with my own eyes. A claxon from the yacht club sounded to welcome us across the finish line and a small launch with race officials chugged out to meet us. The race meant little to any of us. Crossing the Atlantic Ocean, on the other hand, was an achievement we were all thrilled with. The officials welcomed us with a gift of a large case of beer but informed us that we would have to stay at anchor for the night until the immigration office opened in the morning. Those Brazilian girls would have to wait another day for the pleasure of our company. The anchor was dropped and after the handshakes, hugs and congratulations, we sat on deck to savour our first beer in weeks and the unusual stillness of being stationary. Around us was the sweep of the bay, the streetlights, palm trees, tower blocks, buses and taxis of the city. It was so exciting to have arrived on the other side of an ocean, under sail. I could not wait to set foot on this new world. Celebratory cigar smoke and laughter wafted in the tropical night air. Amid the joviality I sat alone, perched on the boom and hugging my knees. I was nervous.

Poor Cape Town! It had been the most beautiful city I had ever seen, but Rio now cast even her into the shadows. Looking down from Sugarloaf mountain to all the yachts in the harbour I could not believe how lucky I was to be there, and to have arrived by sea. I relished the insane atmosphere of the Flamengo-Fluminense football derby in the gigantic Maracanã stadium and the beaches and the edgy, exciting *favelas*. Add samba, football, bikinis, painfully tight fluorescent Speedos, unfortunately, and a permanent party, to the most beautiful cityscape on Earth and you have Rio de Janeiro. Rio walked with a bum wiggle, sang, danced and never slept.

I loved it.

I considered riding away from the yacht directly towards Alaska. It would have been the simple and logical step, maintaining the purity of stepping onto my bike in Cape Town and getting back onto the bike at the other side of the ocean. However I also wanted to ride the complete length of the Americas, from Southern Patagonia to Northern Alaska. Unfortunately I could not find a boat to take me from Rio down to Cape Horn. So I had to decide what I wanted most: to ride an unbroken trail away from Rio or to ride the full length of the Americas.

After being brutally parted from 17 months of hair growth by our crew at the post-race party, for the entertainment value I was paid £50, I decided that I wanted to ride the full length of the continent. I loaded my bike and bags onto a bus and headed south. Five and a half days later, with a new respect for the endurance capacities of bus-travelling backpackers, I arrived in Ushuaia, and set about pedalling back north again.

My road

It may be your village, but it's my road.
    – Ffyona Campbell

The first day back on the bike I rode over a low pass through the black, jagged mountains into a landscape of peaceful blue lakes and forest. I camped early, in a field of clover overlooking a still lake. The evening was warm and at those latitudes the sun would not set for three more hours. It felt good, as always, to be camping and self-sufficient and free, but I was anxious at how I would stiffen my sinews and summon the perseverance to keep myself going.

Outside the tent I re-arranged the equipment in my bags, packing things into their proper places. Organising myself helped me to believe that I was serious about this ride. I sat down to cook, grinding fresh peppercorns with the pliers on my Leatherman tool into the boiling pasta and a stock cube. This was the first pan of pasta in a bubbling chain of hundreds, fuelling me on towards the north.

I awoke to the lovely rattle of rain on the taut tent, and rolled over to sleep some more until it stopped. A couple of hours later I was riding through the dripping beauty of lichen-stringed forests, skirting lakes and crossing sinuous trout rivers with curves of perfect camping spots. Patagonia, like Mr. Kipling, really does make exceedingly good lakes. Compared to Africa, I felt comfortable here. Fells and dew-soaked clover fields were carpeted with daisies and dandelions. I enjoyed the cold nights and wan sunsets, and despite being further from England than I had ever been, I felt quite at home.

I moved on to classic Patagonian *pampas*; flat, soggy moorland beneath an enormous sky. The distances in Patagonia are virtually unimaginable to anyone raised in the efficient compactness of Europe. Only occasionally was there a solitary farmhouse, red roofed and white walled. Stopping to refill my water bottles at these *estancias,* I would often be invited in and treated to a bowl of the mutton soup that bubbled constantly on old kitchen stoves. At one *estancia,* a father, son and grandson galloped home on dappled brown horses for lunch, three generations of *gaucho,* hungry after a long morning tending the cattle and sheep. They dropped their cowboy hats on the massive kitchen table as they shook my hand and welcomed me to Argentina, jovially asking when they were going to get their Falkland Islands back. They did not seem surprised to find me sitting at their table and tucking into their lunch. I told them they could have *Las Malvinas* back when Maradona apologised for his cheating. "*Touché!*" they laughed, or whatever the Spanish equivalent is.

The wild winds from the north were my nemesis for the next couple of months. At their worst, they made me pedal hard, in first gear, on flat tarmac, just to keep a speed of 3mph. The only two options to deal with the wind were to ride or to hide. There was no point hiding and waiting because the winds of Patagonia never end, so that left two other options: to ride or to quit. I rode, and fought for every kilometre. Often the winds were so strong that I had to walk and push the bike. Pushing a bicycle downhill is a singularly depressing experience. Vehicles stopped to offer me lifts, but there was far too far to go for me to take the easy option.

Tierra del Fuego is sliced into Argentinian and Chilean halves. Historically there was not much love lost between the two, and they have spent a lot of time bickering over possession of pieces of Patagonia. I crossed over the Magellan Straits to the South American mainland at Punta Arenas, and over the next few weeks bounced back and forth between Argentina and Chile, and between rain and sunshine as I wound my way northwards. Border crossings were simple, thankfully, but the countries are very different in speech, outlook and attitude.

Argentina had endured decades of military rule, with paramilitary death squads crushing opposition and a 'dirty war' resulting in 30,000 'disappeared' people. This internal conflict and military rule ended after the Falklands War in 1982. The next two decades were far more pleasant for Argentina until she defaulted on the largest loan repayment in history. The economy crashed, and political chaos ensued.

An unknown Patagonian governor, Néstor Kirchner, became president with a mere 22% of the nation's vote while I was in Argentina. It did not bode well in a country that had six presidents in the last couple of years. Yet he was very successful, and Argentina has bounced back superbly. Chileans will no doubt be less pleased about their neighbour and rival's recovery.

Chile's own economic crisis led to General Pinochet's violent coup, encouraged by the US in 1973, which ushered in years of purges and exiles. Around 80,000 people were tortured, murdered or 'disappeared.' Right-wing Pinochet suspended all opposition parties and democracy did not return until 15 years later. Since then Chileans have worked hard to redeem their country's human rights reputation, and it has become one of the continent's most developed, stable and economically successful countries.

In both countries I was invited into homes for food and *maté*, the favourite drink of the South. *Maté* is a hot infusion of what looks, and tastes, suspiciously like grass cuttings, drunk through a silver straw from a calabash. *Maté* is a drink to share, a social event, an excuse to idle away time and talk for hours. The locations and people changed each time I drank it, the *maté* and the conversation rarely did. We talked of Maradona and *Las Malvinas*, Pinochet and Beckham, England and bicycles, family, work and lifestyles. We wondered whether war would start soon in Iraq and we all hoped that it would not.

Both countries shared the wild landscapes and the mad headwind. In Chile, the *Torres del Paine* were cupped in a chaos of shattered rock, whipped by an angry wind. A steep gorge held a murky pale green triangular lake, the wind thrashing spray from the surface. Above this bleak scene rose the *torres* or towers, three majestic needles of pale orange rock hundreds of metres high, with grey cloud fussing around the peaks. A faint white sun failed to warm me as I stared at the imposing glory of the towers of rock.

Equally magnificent, Argentina's *Perito Moreno* glacier is a massive wall of blue ice, 18-storeys-high, advancing across Lake Argentina. The glacier was only a tiny finger at the distant end of one of the many arms of the enormous *Hielo Sur*, the largest icefield outside Antarctica or Greenland. Nevertheless, a 60 metre wall of contorted blue ice is still a fine old sight. Weakened by the warmth of the afternoon sun, the front of the ice wall constantly crumbles. Enormous chunks, as big as cars, as big as buses, break away from the wall and teeter and crack and then, almost in slow motion, crash into the lake in a magnificent thunder of rumbling echoes and huge waves of water. I was transfixed for a whole day.

In Africa, I had promised myself that I would never again complain about being cold, so delicious had the prospect seemed. So I murmured, "how delightful," as I surfaced from my warm sleeping bag into dark dawns, with numb hands and feet, and donned two woolly hats to begin cycling early before the morning wind became too strong. My bike laden with a week's supply of food, I enjoyed the independence and the freedom of the empty spaces. Unfortunately, my rear wheel could not cope with the weight of the bike on the rocky track, and spokes were beginning to break. I was used to this, and replacing them was simple, but the latest spokes I had bought were a couple of millimetres shorter than the old ones. If I replaced one spoke, I would need to replace them all. Back in Africa this would have stressed me, but I was a more relaxed rider these days and felt confident that I would muddle through somehow.

I knocked on the door of a remote machinery depot to ask for water. Ramón, a small, wiry, middle-aged man with an oil-smeared face and cigarette-stained teeth shook my hand and invited me inside. At the kitchen table, his face broke into a smile as I fretted about my broken wheel in my improving Spanish. He insisted that I stay the night.

"*Escuchame ché,* Listen pal, *todo lo que necesitás en la vida es paciencia o plata!*" he said, "All you need in life is patience or money!"

Permanently short of both, I laughed, promised to strive for patience at least, and thanked him for his invitation to stay. He lived alone in the depot for a month at a time, guarding the machinery, before returning to town on leave to his wife and three children who he missed badly during the long, lonely weeks maintaining and guarding a handful of tractors. Neither of us could imagine who would steal a steamroller in that empty wilderness, but we were both glad for some company.

Ramón had been cooking as I arrived, and my nostrils hinted that dinner was almost ready. I protested that I did not want him to give up half his dinner for me, and assured him that I had my own food. He said nothing, just smiled, walked out the back door, and staggered back inside with a barbecued slab of lamb large enough to feed at least a dozen people. The table shuddered with the weight of meat, steaming magnificently and smelling wonderful as Ramón sprinkled homemade seasoning over it from an old Coke bottle with small holes stabbed through the lid. "*Chimichurri,*" he called the sauce, dreamily.

"Eat!" he commanded, and he plonked a plate heavy with meat onto the table in front of me.

"Back home my wife makes me eat all this *comida sana*, healthy food," complained Ramón, his mouth full of meat. "It is not good for a man! *Aqui estoy libre:* out here I am free, free to eat like a man, like an Argentinian. Free to eat meat!"

A couple of days later my wheel was unrideable, and I camped in a wood near the village of El Chaltén to completely rebuild it. I bought a box of rough red wine for 40p in the village to compensate for my mechanical phobia and returned to my tent. Storm clouds swirled around the beautiful yet ferocious Mount Fitzroy above me. The wind was strengthening by the minute, and I added extra rocks to the guy ropes supporting my tent before I climbed inside to start building the new wheel.

Hours later, a dismembered confusion of cogs and rim and a tangle of bike spokes were strewn about the hunched gloom of the tent. My back was braced against the tent wall that bucked and thrashed in the punishment of the storm, screaming and pummelling down from the mountain. The beam from my head torch was the only light, a feeble glow over the chaos. Wet canvas flapped and cracked around my face. Puddles were growing on the floor and everything was wet. The sour wine was half-finished but my back wheel was not nearly so advanced. Frustration boiled: at my inadequate, lightweight tools, at the cramped workspace, at my incompetence, at the weather, at the brutally wearing roads and at the whole bloody silliness of this escapade. 'What am I doing here?' I tried to remember.

But, before I slept that night, I finished the task and I was proud. Slightly egg-shaped it may have been, but I had a wheel that would keep me moving. In the morning, the tent was dusted with snow and the wind had not eased, but the sky was bright and clear. Mount Fitzroy looked incredible above me, its vast massifs of rock powdered in snow and gleaming in the dawn.

I wanted to ride the 750 mile *Carretera Austral*, the Southern Highway, a stunningly beautiful yet terribly corrugated gravel road running north through Chile. I had heard rumours of an adventurous, alternative border crossing that would take me to Villa O'Higgins where the *Carretera Austral* began. The crossing was not open to vehicles, and it did not appear on my map. It would require cross-country travel and a boat ride, but information on the route proved elusive. Even a helpful police station, after much noisy telephoning and gesticulation, could only advise me that "there is no road, and there are only two boats a month."

I asked when the boats departed.

"Perhaps around the 5th and the 20th of the month?" they suggested, without much confidence.

Thanking them for their help, I rode past Lago del Desierto with lots of food in my bags. I was prepared for a long wait for the boat. I rode away from the towering peaks of Fitzroy towards a broad blue glacier, the egg-shaped wheel bouncing me up and down. A few bridges were down and the river crossings were cold, but the sun shone as I approached the remote border post, where the guards were under-worked and walking around in their socks.

I had crossed into 30 countries now, but this was the first time that a customs officer had offered me a cup of tea as he toasted his slippered feet beside a wood fire. I was concerned about finding my way through the forest and over the pass to the Chilean fron-

tier, so one of the guards pulled on some boots and walked outside with me, laces flapping, to show me the way. At a narrow gap
in the trees he pointed out a skinny, muddy path, dotted with
horse manure. "You want to get to Chile, *amigo*?" he chuckled,
"Just follow the shit. It'll take you right there!" He clapped me on
the back, wished me *buen viaje*, and turned back to the warmth of
his hut.

I set off feeling that Hansel and Gretel were luckier with
breadcrumbs to show them the way, rather than piles of poo. I
hiked up the steep footpath, axle-deep in mud. I had to shuttle my
bike and bags because the path was too jumbled with rocks and
roots to push the bike, and it was all too heavy to carry in one
load. There were cold streams to cross too. The five miles up to the
pass in the damp green forest took five hours to complete. Only
my huffing and puffing, slipping and cursing broke the silence of
dripping drops of water from the trees. At the top of the pass I
found a tall pole, like a lamppost. On one side a plaque read
'Argentina', the other 'Chile.' I amused myself for a short while
hopping backwards and forwards between nations before re-
mounting my bike and pedalling down into Chile.

Below me was Lago O'Higgins, turbid grey with floating
hunks of blue ice. The mountains beyond the lake were slabs of
bare rock, the peaks topped with permanent snow and fields of
ice. White waterfalls plummeted in slow motion down the cliffs
from the ice-fields. The lower slopes were only dusted with snow,
which somehow made them look more cold and bleak than a
thick icing of fluffy whiteness. Summer was fading fast, and I
needed to outrun it northwards. I had foolishly lost my raincoat,
shoving it too hastily under the bungees on my rear rack, and was
now sporting a very stylish bin bag, with holes cut for my head
and arms.

The track improved as I rode the ten miles downhill to the
Chilean checkpoint, but the road surface and a large plodding bull
that I was too scared to overtake meant that the descent took two
hours. By the time I reached the lake it was evening and the handful of Chilean officials there decided that my arrival was a good
enough reason to stop work for the day, fire up the barbecue and
get some lamb cooking. As I was the only person who passed

north in the entire month I suppose that it had constituted a stressful day at the office for them.

I set up camp above the jetty in a small cove and waited for the boat. The lake and the blue icebergs shone in the evening sun. All around was a ring of mountains. I hoped that the boat would arrive sometime...

I was relieved in the end to be waiting on the lakeshore for just two days. The two days of porridge, popcorn and coffee, lying in my sleeping bag and struggling with a hoarded crossword puzzle were relaxing. Two weeks may have become a little dull, but on the other hand, I may have finished the crossword by then.

Before I saw it, I heard the tap, tap, tap of a diesel engine that had me scampering from my tent. The small boat, yellow and blue, came into view soon afterwards and I waited for it on the jetty. A ruddy, cheery woman of indeterminate age hurled me the stern line as the fishing boat nudged towards the jetty. I was rather proud of the slick clove hitch I threw around a bollard to secure the boat, but the woman laughed and called me a "*gringo*" as she jumped down from the boat with a graceless thud to replace my hitch with a traditional Chilean granny knot.

The crew of five, in old woolly hats and rakish berets, welcomed me aboard with big smiles and handshakes. I was then left to strike my tent and load my bike aboard as the crew climbed the grassy hill to the police hut. I settled down for a snooze on a bench below decks while I waited, assuming they would be back soon. The crew, by now very drunk, made their slurred return at 5am, and I was awoken by the engines cranking up. We were off.

In that rainy darkness, as the ferry puttered along Lago O'Higgins, I found out that my country was at war. That Britain had invaded Iraq. The middle-aged captain, stout in knitted pullovers, with a dashing blue beret crumpled above his enormous sprouting ears and radish red nose, made me uncomfortable as he told me. His tone was cordial enough, but his use of the word '*you*,' suggesting that I had personally invaded Iraq, cut deep, and I realised how much of a representative for my country I was. Many people I encountered had never met a real-life Englishman, and I knew that my opinions and actions would be generalised as typical of the whole nation. Any traits of my own, like rarely showering, riding a bicycle round the world, or not taking sugar in my tea, were liable to become standard terms of reference for all my country-folk in the minds of the people I met. I do apologise.

I was not the only passenger on the boat. As well as the crew were a couple of shivering dogs, their tails tucked between their legs, a wriggling sack of quietly clucking indignant chickens, three relaxed sheep, and four sleepy children. The children were heading for school in Villa O'Higgins. They would stay there for six months, until the next summer, when they would cross the lake again to work on their family farm.

As morning came the cloud was lower than ever, the water an oily grey. The engine punched at the silence and the chickens seemed to have resigned themselves to their fate as we drew up to the jetty at Villa O'Higgins. It was a silent, empty world, a balm for the soul. I thanked the crew for the ride, paid my fare, lowered my bike down onto the jetty and began cycling once more.

The village of Villa O'Higgins is the southern-most point of the *Carretera Austral* not, as it sounds, a faux Irish pub in Ibiza. An advantage for cyclists is that despotic dictators seem to like to building symbolic roads. The *Carretera Austral* was General Pinochet's little project, a plan to unite the isolated far south of Chile with the rest of the country.

The *Carretera Austral* proved to be the most beautiful ride of the world so far. I revelled in the mountains, forests, clear lakes, waterfalls, glaciers, uncannily bright blue rivers, log cabins and lush green alpine pastures. Mountains and glaciers stood sentry as I edged my way between them. At the source of the vividly turquoise River Backer, I sat in a wooden cart with solid wooden wheels and drank *maté* with three *gauchos*. The horse stood dolefully in the shafts and tore noisily at the damp grass while we chatted. It was easy to become blasé about such magnificence and the freedom to enjoy it, in the same way that people living in our civilisation take beds, showers and electric lights for granted. I filled my water bottles from the clean streams, doused my head under waterfalls so cold they hurt my skull, and camped safely and peacefully wherever I wanted.

Camping beside rivers was torture: as my revolting pasta boiled on the stove, smug trout rose lazily for flies, taunting my incompetent angling. My improvised night lines of hook, line, bread and flip-flop float were not successful either. One evening, as my clothes and gear hung drying on the trees, an armadillo strutted hastily past my tent. I had been told that armadillo tasted very good in a casserole. It certainly sounded a lot better than what I was eating, but I let him trot on home undisturbed.

Autumn was overtaking summer and sharp, misty mornings of flaming colours jumbled with warm afternoons and sunsets. I stopped in villages to buy pasta, small earth-covered vegetables, bread rolls and *manjar,* condensed milk boiled to caramel, eaten in place of jam. Log cabins plumed ribbons of smoke and men worked among yapping dogs and fretting chickens to pile chopped wood against their homes in readiness for winter.

I was chased by an angry dog that sank its teeth into my panniers and refused to let go, despite my kicking it in the head as I rode. I jumped off my bike. The dog ran off but, feeling vindictive, I sprinted after it. The poor dog looked very surprised and fled into a garden. I did not give up the chase and I ran, hot on the dog's heels, straight into the garden. I pulled up quickly as a family stared at me from their breakfast table. I gave them a big smile, waved a cheery *"Buenos días!"* and strolled nonchalantly back out of their garden, feeling like Basil Fawlty.

Approaching Argentina once more, and the end of this magical highway, the land opened up into fenced pastures and smallholdings. The sun shone through clouds along curving rivers and above creases of mountains. It reminded me of the Eastern Cape of South Africa. I always enjoyed reminders of other happy memories, other beautiful roads and other campsites. They helped me pin reference points on the timeline of all my riding and gave me confidence for having come so far.

The next few thousand kilometres blurred in my mind. There were days with volcanoes, conical and white, breathing a thin curl of smoke with James Dean nonchalance and an insinuation of waiting menace. There were exiled Welsh towns with dragons and cream teas, and forests of monkey-puzzle trees, spiky and dark with pale fruit that tasted like chestnuts. There were enough days of dirt road to remind myself that I was in an adventure, yet not so many as to make me think fondly of how much I could be earning in an office in London.

There were miles of empty coastline with pelotons of pelicans, gliding in formation inches above the noisy Pacific waves. But those days could not match the majesty of the *Carretera Austral* and besides, I still had more than 20,000 kilometres of noisy Pacific waves to watch, so I did not linger. There was a sad moment when I crossed the first river in Chile where the water was too polluted to drink and I realised that I was entering a new phase of South America, a region less idyllic for those who lived there than the fairytale, carefree wilderness I had been so fortunate to experience.

I passed through edgy towns that were no more than collections of liquor stores flogging cheap *pisco* and gloomy wooden shops spacing their wares out to fill the shelves. Those rough towns told of a South America where so many still live in poverty, with streets of cheap breeze block buildings, blowing rubbish, dirt roads and eroded footpaths on brown grass winding around wrecked old cars, *gomerias* (tyre repair shacks) and burnt out rings of car tyres. All around was unemployment and unattainable dreams.

But being amongst people was a good thing. In Concepción I gave a talk at a school to a young class, where the children felt sorry for my not having had a birthday party for two years. On my last day in town there was a knock on the door of the house I was staying in. I opened it and saw nobody. Then, adjusting my view from my eye level to my knee level, I saw Class 5a on the doorstep, grinning. They were armed with hotdogs, cake, fizzy drinks and enough chocolate to see me half way to Bolivia. They were ready to party!

One evening I pulled up to a roadside house on a quiet country road to ask for water. Several hours later I was alone and half-drunk inside the house, on a soft sofa and listening to Ella Fitzgerald. The man who answered the door had replied to my request for water with, *"no prefieres cerveza?* Wouldn't you rather have beer?"

He ushered me inside, poured two beers and we sat down at

his kitchen table. David told me that he was 42 and waiting nervously to go out on a date. He downed his beer, got sad about his father's recent death, downed another beer and cursed me for giving him the idea of moving to England and starting a new life. He ate half a Viagra pill, "I'm not so old that I need a whole one yet!" and headed out to meet his young girlfriend. I was alone in a total stranger's house, trusted to spend the evening relaxing on his sofa with a spare bedroom and a comfy bed to sleep in. I felt flattered that he had not allowed me to meet his girlfriend in case my youth and dashing good looks swept her off her feet.

One afternoon I slogged up and down very steep spurs between beaches and inlets as the road paralleled the coast. At the bottom of the hills, beside the crashing waves, were little single street fishing villages. I was tired and looking forward to stopping for the evening. A car passed me, then turned and came back to warn me that I must stop for the night in the next village. To continue, they said, was too dangerous. I wondered what the danger could be.

"*Ladrones?*" I asked. "Thieves?"

"No," the driver shook his head.

"Pumas?"

"No."

The grave danger was that there was '*nada*' ahead, 'nothing.' No people, no houses, no thieves, no pumas and no psychopathic murderers. Nothing but beaches and forests. Assured of a very safe night I thanked the man for his kind concern and rode on to camp alone in the *nada*.

Almost every human spends every night inside a building with the comfort of enclosed familiarity and security. I could understand how 'nothing' could be a frightening concept, combined with our other primitive fears of night and darkness. But I had grown used to being outside. I welcomed the darkness as an ally. I felt fortunate to not know where I would camp, to live my days by the hours of the sun and to sit watching the lonely sea and the sky, listening to the flung spray and the seagulls crying.

Here or there

When I was here, I wanted to be there.
When I was there, all I could think of was getting back.
— Willard, 'Apocalypse Now'

It was a sinking feeling to wake from a sweet dream and realise that, yet again, I had to tear myself from new friends and security, leave it all, and ride away. My stomach lurched and I screwed my eyes in prayer, or rather a stern talking to myself, before getting out of bed. I loaded my bike and returned to the road after saying another heartfelt thanks to another kind family who had been incredibly generous and welcoming to me and who I would never be able to repay. Three months into this South American ride, yet the moving on never became any easier.

After a hot day's slog on busy roads out of Santiago, I camped at sunset in a grassy field beneath the massive white Andes. In the blue sky a passing plane glinted. I wished that I was on that plane. I had felt deflated all day. The boyish thrill of Patagonia gone, I was too stuck in this life to be able to say, "Stop", but no longer finding it fun or exciting. I began to realise how far it was to Alaska. I was growing bored with my own company, my high-volume singing of half-remembered songs, daydreams of home and devilish little voices saying how nice it would be to stop riding.

Rita, my bike, looked as glum as I felt. Spokes were snapping, punctures popping, brakes breaking and gears grinding. A tyre split and I repaired it with the Achilles of an old rubber boot that I found rummaging on a village dump. It made an effective, if bumpy, protective sleeve.

I had always said that if I were to wake one morning and realise that the journey had become mere routine then I would stop and go home. To continue just for the sake of getting right round the world, in order to impress people, to confound doubters, or to not disappoint supporters were not the reasons that I wanted to keep me going. I had finally been able to accept that what other people thought of me was not nearly as important as what I thought of myself. It had taken a lot of pedalling to get there, but I was at last able to reflect on my triumphs and disasters without the unhelpful complication of wondering what others would think.

I knew that I was lucky. My Mondays were like most people's Sundays. Every day my horizons were beautiful, changing and new. I slept where I wanted, when I wanted, in solitude and silence. I recognised the stars. I knew if the moon was waxing or waning, and I noticed as the seasons slowly changed. I listened to birdsong and when I saw something beautiful I stopped to appreciate it. Everyday I met new people and learned new things about them, their lives and myself. But, perhaps, it is not good to be too free for too long.

It sounded daft, but I began yearning for unreasonable deadlines, for a jammed diary, for more work than I could manage and the pressure to get it done, for a quick game of squash after work with a mate, and the companionship of a cold, wet, muddy football team on Saturday morning. I was disillusioned with the steadiness of my life, the comfort of its routine. Which was precisely what I had been trying to get away from.

I came across a prayer once, which resonated because it suggested that I was not alone in my inability to be satisfied with comfortable satisfaction. The prayer asks the Lord for "What one cannot demand from oneself." It doesn't ask "for rest, or quiet, whether of soul or body." It continues, "I don't ask You for wealth, nor for success, nor even health perhaps. That sort of thing You get asked for so much that You can't have any of it left. Give me, Lord, what you have left over, Give me what no-one wants from you. I want insecurity, strife, and I want You to give me these once and for all so that I can be sure of having them always, since I shall not always have the courage to ask You for them."

But I was also growing to believe that there was more to life than seeking new experiences. I wanted to live as well. There is a great difference between existing and existentialism, and I began to feel that the middle ground of the life that I aspired towards was to combine the harvesting of experiences with the time and stability to put their lessons into practice.

The biggest problem with my mood was that everything had become routine. Everything felt simple and obvious: planning a route across continents, riding over mountains, finding food and water, hiding well in order to sleep safely, arranging visas, communicating with strangers without a common tongue. My adventure felt mundane. I had lost my grip on the purpose of my ride. Oddly, I also lost the sensation of travel. Every day felt normal to me. Because I moved so slowly from one environment to the next, I felt at home in whatever land I was crossing. I had lost that wonderful thrill of travelling, the sensation of being dumped in a strange land where everything is new. The crux of thinking that the time had come to concede defeat was that I was bored with myself. It seemed that I wasn't such an interesting person to spend time with as I had thought I was. I was a slave to the tarmac and the Sisyphean challenge of an unending road. I thought that I was free, but I was not. But there were mountains awaiting me now: it was time for climbing not for whining. After Santiago, a long duel with the Andes and the *altiplano* awaited. Apart from the tedium of my own company and the worry of failing equipment, I was looking forward to the challenge.

A signpost cautioned '*Gradiente Fuerte* 55 km' as I followed the Aconcagua River up towards the highest peak in the Western hemisphere. Climbing hard from the warm lowlands of acacia trees and prickly pears into the mountains, I spent a night at an army sentry post. The snow outside was waist deep, so I was happy to be inside by the fire. I watched Chilean Big Brother and chatted with the Lance Corporal and two scruffy National Service soldiers. Their job was to keep an eye on the ferociously steep wall of hairpin bends that snaked up to the border post at the summit, and to make sure that the road was kept clear of snow. The black road furled like a ribbon in the wind, twisting ever higher. The hut, ringed by peaks, felt as though it was at the bottom of a cauldron of mountains and snow. Condors soared high above and mocked my gasping attempt to creep over their mountains.

Looking out of the frost-covered window of the hut after a breakfast of instant coffee, rolls and *manjar*, the switchbacks seemed almost to fold on top of each other. It looked a brutal climb, and the soldiers were certain that it was impossible to ride up. They offered to whisk me to the top in their jeep. I don't think that they had anything else to do that day. I thanked them but assured them that I was actually looking forward to the climb. They promised to watch me through their binoculars and rescue me if I waved my surrender. I grinned at their pessimism and set about ticking off the 45 hairpin bends.

Before long I was steaming in only my shirt sleeves, sweating in the freezing morning air. I climbed higher into the sunrise, relishing the fitness I felt in my legs and lungs, and wishing only that I had a friend to share the climb with. The bright sun felt fabulous on my face, though there was little warmth in it. Up, down, up, down, up, down went my legs. Up, up, up crept the bike. On and on and on I pedalled. Down, down, down fell the distance to the summit. Cars and buses hooted and waved their encouragement. Hours later I reached the border post at the summit, dragged off my damp shirt and shivered in the bitter wind, almost four kilometres above the comfy bed that I had left so reluctantly in Santiago. I tugged from my pannier a dry shirt, a couple of fleeces, a windproof jacket, a balaclava and thick gloves, and prepared for the descent into Argentina. All around me the mountains gleamed, and the sky was a flawless blue. In the silence I watched a white fox flop its way through a snowdrift as I tucked in my clothes and fastened shut my bags.

Determined to ride every inch of the road, I ignored a series of very clear 'no cycling' road signs and pedalled on into the long road tunnel between Chile and Argentina. Within moments speakers in the tunnel started yelling at me. Frightening echoes thundered round the dark tunnel. I pedalled faster into the gloom, but a pick-up truck, all sirens and flashing orange lights, was already chasing me down. I had the feeling that someone was about to be very cross with me. Sure enough a security guard in overalls and helmet jumped out of the truck yelling at me for my idiocy. I smiled a lot, said, "no speaka Spanish" a lot and was escorted in silence and the back of the pick-up to the bright daylight and snowy freshness at the end of the tunnel and Argentina. The pass was perfect for cycling: ferociously steep but short and sweet on the ascent, then a gradual, gentle descent for 60 kilometres down the other side. I freewheeled alongside Mount Aconcagua, at 6,962 metres, the highest peak in South America, down past an alpinists graveyard, and eventually down below the snowline once again.

After the tough and beautiful day, I lay in my sleeping bag that night and my emotions were a jumble. I loved the mountains, the battle to climb them, the rhythmic hammering at the pedals and the slow but constant erosion of the distance ahead of me. I thrived on being fiercely fit and pushing myself hard. But I was also tired of not having anyone to share all these experiences and challenges and emotions with. 'Too many highways, too many byways, and nobody's walking behind.' I felt sure that I would give up soon.

Riding to Mendoza, I was trying to come to terms with feeling ready to quit my ride. I pulled into a service station to refill my water bottles. Blasting out over the forecourt from massive speakers, at a ridiculous volume, was The New Radicals' song *You've Got the Music in You*, a song that always reminds me of riding the length of Britain, from Land's End to John O'Groats, with friends from university. We had made the ride in nine days, and the final day was a brute. Freezing Scottish winter wind mocked our attempts to fight it, but we finally wobbled into John O'Groats together, and it was a wonderful, communal triumph. Far better than the transient pleasure and relief that giving up would bring.

I found the outside tap and filled my first bottle when the next song began, another dose of soft rock that I often listened to while riding: Nickelback's *How You Remind Me*, 'this is how you remind me of what I really am.' Right then I did not like to be reminded. I had no idea who I really was or what I was trying to get out of my life.

Unsure once again of what I wanted to do, I rode hard, covering the remaining 90 miles to Mendoza in six hours. I checked into a cheap backpackers' hostel to take a couple of days off and sort out my head. I woke in the morning with stiff legs and took my time to prepare a pancake breakfast. I decided that I was at peace with my decision to go home. Not necessarily quitting for ever, but postponing it all for a while.

Hearing those songs in the petrol station had helped me to realise that I still felt trapped. Ever since my first major crisis of confidence back in Damascus, so many thousands of miles ago, the feeling of being trapped had shadowed much of my journey. I had bitten off far more than I could chew. I had taken on something that required more strength and persistence and positive thinking than I could manage. I had wanted something hard, and I had got that, but I had wanted it hard because I had thought that 'difficult' would be fun, satisfying and rewarding. I had not intended to subject myself to two years of masochistic introspection and self-flagellation. I also knew that if I gave up, I would be throwing away something unique, and the best memories of my life.

I don't know where it sprang from. One minute three Brits, a Kiwi and a Frenchman were enjoying a box of low budget wine with dinner, the next we were on a boisterous tour of Mendoza's bars, and I woke up, to my surprise, in a Love Motel on a round red bed with frilly red pillows. There were also flashing red heart-shaped lights, and an unidentified Argentinian girl. I did an undignified early morning runner, dashed out the door with the free chocolate bars and scampered back to the hostel. After a few more days and nights of similar intelligent introspection, I caught myself studying the Asia route of my trip on a world map and weighing up various options. I also convinced a French backpacker, Fabien, that cycling was a better way to experience a country than sitting on a bus, and he decided to join me for a couple of weeks on the road. It was a bold decision for him to take and we both buzzed with excitement as we trawled the shops of Mendoza for a cheap bike and what equipment we could find. The bike cost less than he would have spent in two weeks of bus fares and accommodation. We laughed and joked, and my heart was happy as I eulogised about the magic of the open road and the freedom of a bicycle. It seemed as though I was ready to ride again.

The wine-drenched city, reputedly home to Argentina's most beautiful women, had snapped me out of my self-pity and returned the compulsion of the road. I made a note in my diary, *Today is the first day of the rest of my life and I am going to enjoy it.* Fabien and I loaded up our bikes and rode north.

A final postscript to this latest dalliance with quitting: A few weeks after I left Mendoza, I was sitting alone on a mountain pass at sunset. I would have loved to have had someone to share the moment with, the girl I had loved but left behind or a good friend and accomplice bonded together in the forge of physical endeavour with hoops of steel. But, I was alone. I listened to David Gray's *Babylon* as I looked ahead to where the sun sat pale and low beneath the fat white clouds above the mountains. I was running wild, seeing it all so clear as the road glided down to yet another vast, empty valley. I could see about 50 kilometres up the deserted valley that the road would take me through tomorrow. Nothing constrained me, nothing constricted me, no red lights would slow my progress. I could do what I wanted, I could be what I wanted, I would make my choices and I would stand or fall by them. It was all up to me. To become who I wanted to be, to be as happy as I wanted to be, to be as fulfilled as I wanted to be. It was all up to me. I had no excuses. "Healthy, free, the world before me, the long brown path before me, leading wherever I choose," the *'Song of the Open Road.'* I thought of everything and everyone I had left behind, and everything that may lie ahead, and as I looked forward I knew for sure that beginning this ride was the best decision I had ever made.

My first inkling of worry about my new companion had been as we left the hostel, when Fabien strapped on a heart rate monitor. I had never met a backpacker with a heart rate monitor before. He exploded up the road out of Mendoza with the sunrise on his right and the passion of a Tour de France breakaway. Surprised, piqued, and stubborn, I put my head down and gave chase, struggling to keep on his wheel. The road was flat and the miles screamed by as we burned up the continent. The road was empty and eerily beautiful. A white eagle looked down scornfully from a telegraph pole. I had no time to stop and look back, I was hanging on by my fingernails to keep up with Fabien.

We camped that night on a barren, sterile plain dotted with scrub and cacti. I was knackered. On our left and waiting ahead of us was a ridge of rocky hills. I hoped that they would slow my new pace maker down. The moonscape we were in continued for a few more days. Thankfully the Frenchman's bold chat about heart rate monitors, the ease of cycling and his great fitness, did not. He emerged from his tent on the morning of the second day, bleary-eyed and bow-legged. He was in pain and I saw in his face that the competitive machismo was over. We continued at a very gentle pace through impressive, mountainous emptiness. A cruel headwind blew up a sharp sandstorm. Snakes of orange sand writhed across the road and our eyes, noses and mouths filled with swirling dust. We wore sunglasses and wrapped our faces with bandanas. Our teeth crunched sand whenever we ate. I told Fabien a joke to try to take his mind off his aching bum: "why do you not get hungry in the desert? Because of all the sand which is there!" He was not amused.

When we began riding together, Fabien was thrilled to be liberated from the constraints of buses and to experience the sights and sounds and smells and people of Argentina more thoroughly. However, he soon grew frustrated by how slowly the thrills came, how hard he had to work for each highlight, and how long the horizons took to reach across empty plains where villages on my map often proved to be figments of a caffeine-charged cartographer's over-fertile imagination.

On a particularly bad run of fictitious villages we ran out of water. Fortunately we eventually came across a commemorative shrine to Difunta Correa. According to legend, María Antonia Deolinda Correa died of thirst in the desert in the 1840s as she followed her conscript husband across the country in the Argentine civil wars. When her body was discovered, her baby son was miraculously alive, feeding at her still-flowing breast. Difunta Correa became a legend and an unofficial saint for those on the road, and those in need of a miracle. Her shrines, decorated with nik-naks, model cars, photographs, number plates, coins and plastic flowers can be seen all along the roads of Argentina. Piles of plastic bottles of water are stacked around each shrine as offerings for the thirsty miracle worker. We thanked her politely and helped ourselves to eight much-needed litres.

Nobody that I rode with could endure my grinding menu of banana sandwiches, and bland pasta for long, but for a Frenchman it was unthinkable. Fabien quickly decided that I was mad and loaded his bags with salamis and jams. Willing, with company, to compromise my miserly shopping regime we bought bread loaves which looked like cannon balls but were warm and soft inside, and potatoes and llama steaks to cook on our evening campfires. Shirts off, bare feet, we'd build our campfires at sunset below weird rock shapes, wind hewn or piled together in the red gorges we were riding through. We ate well and slept under the stars, curled in sleeping bags beside the glowing embers. As dawn broke we gathered the embers from the fire, blew them back to life and made toast and coffee. Frenchmen do not tolerate bad eating.

I think Fabien enjoyed his two weeks' riding. I know he does not regret it, he certainly felt he had seen more of Argentina in those two weeks than in the rest of his travels. It was interesting to watch Fabien on his debut ride; his reactions to situations and how he dealt with them gave me an idea of how I had changed and adapted imperceptibly, but massively over the past two years.

On the last evening of our fortnight together, before we reached Salta, Fabien looked out of his tent, dirty, hungry, and exhausted. He said, "If I had known it would be this hard I would never have begun."

"*Moi aussi,*" I murmured. "Me too."

Feeling and understanding

Si no lo sientes, no lo entiendes
(If you don't feel it, you won't understand it).
– motto of 'The Strongest,' Bolivian Football Club
and eight-times national Champions

As Bolivia and the Andes approached, I felt that I was in another new South America, and once again I was excited. Fabien and I rolled down into Salta, surrounded by hills with cacti silhouetted like sentinels on top. Olive trees grew in the villages and sheets of tobacco dried in the fields amid frothy billows of heady yellow daisies. The sun was just starting to touch the hilltops as it set for the night. Evening was my favourite time of day on the road, when the sun lost its wrath and mountains dissolved from harsh light to gentle blues. At home it was midwinter but here I was free and freewheeling down a valley bathed in warm sunshine.

South America is a theatre of dreams for fair-haired *gringos*, high on testosterone with an eye out for girls, and with dreams of glory on the giant playing fields of the world. The exit road out of town and trouble was always so sweetly accessible and recrimination and commitment so easily avoided. Fair hair, a foreign accent and a fertile imagination to elaborate the realities of the road into grand escapades, were all that was needed to give one an inkling of what life must be like as a very handsome man. Fabien disappeared to a Love Motel with a pretty girl. He was unsure how he felt when the girl produced a membership card to the Motel, but it secured them a nice discount, and when he reappeared the next morning he said that he would delay his departure from Salta.

Before I left town, though, we persuaded yet another backpacker to buy a bike and hit the road with Fabien. My bicycling evangelism was going well. The two of them set about organising to ride north together up to Bolivia, and I was on my own again.

I headed towards 4,500 metre high mountain passes *en route* for San Pedro de Atacama in Chile, alone but recharged, with a sketch map on a piece of paper to guide me over the mountains to Chile. It felt good to be on the road, if a little lonely as I curved down a fabulous, sinuous downhill through old growth forest. Mist hung across the horizon, a lake sat beneath the silver blue mist, and it felt more like South East Asia than Argentina. In a few days, I would climb high into the Andes, to a cold, saline, gravel plateau miles above sea level.

I was now into the tough north, where rural peasants subsist with their llamas and tiny vegetable patches. Coya Indian women stared out from beneath wide-brimmed black bowler hats, their shining hair bunched in long plaits and babies bundled on their backs beneath red shawls.

Dawn brought a killer headwind as I pedalled up the steady gradient. My bike was the heaviest it had ever been, laden with ten days worth of food, 18 litres of water and enough clothes, I hoped, to cope with the temperatures of -20°C that awaited at the top of the climb. I had never experienced such cold, and I was not looking forward to it. The track was too rocky and rough to ride, and all day I walked, up one switchback after another. By nightfall, I had covered less than 30 kilometres.

Above 4,000 metres, I started to feel the altitude. A thumping headache pounded the back of my eyes, I felt sick and listless and I struggled for breath. I felt weak, feeble and drained. I had to stop and rest every few minutes, doubled over my bike, gasping for air and wanting to vomit. Weak and nauseous I felt like a granny with a hangover.

Eventually I reached the pass and before me lay *Salinas Grande*, a broad expanse of shimmering salt. It was a relief to be working with gravity rather than fighting it. I freewheeled down the track, squeezing hard on the brakes and concentrating on trying to choose the least bone-jarring, bike-wrecking route. Down on the plateau I veered off the impossibly corrugated track to ride across the shimmering *salar* itself. The dumb faces of llamas and alpacas stared at me, their wool titivated and identified with ribbons. I never saw their owners. Snowy peaks and volcanoes were all around and flamingos stood uninterested as I passed their salt-rimmed lake. The white horizon shimmered and wobbled weirdly in the bright, cold light.

The scenery was desolate. Sparse yellow coarse grass whipped in the gale that blasted unimpeded across the flat gravel plateau. The track was corrugated sand, and for days on end I did nothing but push the bike into a freezing gale. My face was chapped and raw and my lips dried and split and oozed pus and blood. Mornings got off to a bad start with a shower of ice crystals on my head as I yanked the frozen tent zip open. Any water bottles not kept inside my sleeping bag would be frozen solid. Dawns were beautifully calm, so I rose early to get some miles behind me before the wind picked up. I was on a great grey gravel plain resembling the world's biggest carpark. There was nowhere to go but on, and I pushed the bike slowly through the numbing wind.

After days in the emptiness with no human interaction, I came across a mud hut. It was an extraordinarily harsh place to live. I stopped and asked at the hut for water. Three Indian ladies in traditional bowler hats cackled at my huffing, puffing, wind-wrecked appearance, a fish out of water, and they took my bottle, finding the whole thing hilarious. They laughed excitedly and chattered about me whilst I stood in the doorway too tired to care or to respond. One lady began filling my bottle from their bucket in corner. The water was the muddy colour of carrot juice, and when my bottle was just half full I lied that it was sufficient, and I thanked her.

Two snot-nosed children stared at me from the bed in the corner of the hut, the walls blackened by smoke from a small twig fire. On a box by the door were a few crusts of bread and a couple of gnawed bones. There was no other furniture. The tough world of rural poverty made a mockery of my naïve belief that I was leading a frugal, hard, simple life. Outside, a young boy in rags was tending about 30 llamas, 30 goats and 20 cows. It was quite a herd for a ten-year-old. The boy was called Sergio, and he explained to me that his mother did not speak Spanish, that his father was away working in Salta for several weeks and that he was not looking forward to returning to school after the holidays!

Sergio was very inquisitive about my bike, and his mother smiled at me, showing her coca-stained teeth and gums as I answered Sergio's stream of questions. I told him where I had been, and that I carried everything I needed for my life in my bags. He translated excitedly to his mother and, judging by the length of his sentences, elaborated a great deal on what I had said.

They were all disbelieving as I explained that I (ultra-rich weirdo *gringo*), slept alone in a tent, even in those frozen and wind-ravaged heights. They invited me to spend the night with them instead, but I declined. I often spent nights in the homes of very poor families and, no matter how hard I protested, they would invariably give me more of everything than they could spare. I would sometimes lie awake for a while in their cramped homes, listening to snores and the hacking coughs of ill children, and my mind would spin at the disparity between their lives and mine. I would fret at my inability to see a solution to their struggles. At other times small incidents would change my thoughts to positive ones about the resilience, versatility and optimism of us all; a child running into the house howling with laughter, a mother rolling over to comfort the coughing child who would relax and soften into sleep again, or the dignified, proud, contented handshake of a father as I said goodbye to his family.

That night I camped on the plain, sheltering from the wind behind a roadworkers' dry-stone windbreak. In the night, the wind blew a brick-sized stone off the top of the wall. The stone landed on my head and I was momentarily able to marvel that I really did see electric blue swirling stars, before the pain arrived. The wind, the sand, the cold, the terrible road, a massive headache… there was only one solution: turn over and go back to sleep for a few more hours.

Eventually, after ten long days, I reached the lonely Argentinean customs point, my head-bump blossoming nicely. On entering the building I realised how shattered I was. I was wobbly on my feet and speechless from exhaustion. Fortunately these Argentineans were as friendly as all the others had been. They sat me down in an armchair with a bowl of hot soup and said that I could stay as long as I wanted to. They turned on the satellite TV for me to watch some English football. Minutes later I was fast asleep.

A hot dinner, a shower, and a night in a warm, windless bed sorted me out, and by morning I was ready to complete the crossing to Chile. The actual frontier, I was told, was another five kilometres up a very steep dirt road. After that there was another 80 kilometres of climbing, up to 5,000 metres, before swooping – on tarmac no less! – down to the Chilean customs point. As I thanked the guards for their hospitality and prepared to take on the gale once more they warned me that a German cyclist had once dropped dead attempting this pass. Then they smiled and waved me a hearty cheerio.

I camped beside a beautiful dark blue lake crusted with ice and salt beneath stark orange hills. As the sun set, the sky turned crimson, reflected in the lake, and the very white salt contrasted. A full moon slowly eased into the sky, shining upon a magical, mystical scene. Shame it was bloody freezing. I climbed and climbed, my head thumping as I walked up the road, stopping to rest every few minutes.

Next morning, a tour group of intrepid middle-aged, bird-watching Brits passed me in a minibus, travelling the opposite way towards to one of the flamingo lakes I had passed. The bus stopped and out poured a clean-smelling collection of zip-off trousers and Goretex to chat, chuckle at me and take pictures. They kindly gave me some much-needed biscuits and clean water, but best of all was the news they gave me about the road ahead,

"There's only six or seven kilometres more climbing, ten tops, then it's flat for a while and then you're going to love the downhill into San Pedro! You've almost done it now! You're almost at the end: well done!"

Forty five kilometres of climbing later I finally reached the proper summit. Forty Five Kilometres. *FORTY BLOODY FIVE.* It took me an entire day of lung-wrenching slog. I was often angered at the directions from people in vehicles. They see and feel so little of the land that they are not even aware of where they have been. Eventually I did enjoy riding downhill, a beautiful hour of freewheeling into the sunset. Below me lay the emptiness of the *Salar de Atacama* salt plain and beyond it lay the border with Bolivia. All the hardships of the last days were whooped away in jubilation and zest at this extraordinary highland of red and green lakes, flamingos and steaming geysers as I swept downhill into the village of San Pedro de Atacama, knowing that the mountains were over, for a few weeks at least.

Bolivia's *Salar de Uyuni* was the shining jewel that had lured me on this slog through the mountains from Salta. Days of hauling the bike, laden with water, through sandy nonsense and colourful lakes brought me to this morning at the edge of the salt lake, a surreal and fantastical landscape stretching far into the distance. I could see nothing but white salt. Rimming the horizon were volcanoes, red, golden and purple in the dawn before the high-altitude sun rose higher and bleached away the colours. As I rode across the 4,000 square miles of salt, the crisp crunch of my wheels over the hard pentagons of white salt was the only sound. I was well-stocked with food and water, and pleased that I remembered to carry a large stone with me; the salt is so hard that you need a stone to knock in your tent pegs and, there are no stones in sight for days once you ride out onto the salt flat.

I had worried about navigation in that emptiness, but quite a number of tourist jeeps were to-ing and fro-ing between San Pedro and Uyuni, so it was easy, although the sense of wilderness was a little spoiled. I followed the biggest jeep tracks until I saw the blue volcano that I knew would direct me towards the town of Uyuni. Then I headed straight across the pure, wonderful whiteness towards the volcano. I rode northeast: aiming slightly left of the sunrise, well right of the noon sun and to the left of my afternoon shadow. I was riding on a flat disc of utter purity, simplicity and beauty. Feng shui perfected by nature. Surrounding the horizon the volcanoes shimmered and seemed to sit on a bed of blue air.

After some hours the *Isla de Pescadores* began to appear over the horizon 40 kilometres away and I adjusted my direction to head towards it. The 'island' is a lone outcrop in the empty ocean of salt, spiked with hundreds of magnificent cacti. The cacti grow a mere centimetre a year, yet some of them are 12 metres high.

Finding ways to occupy my mind for long hours in the saddle was always a challenge and on the *salar* I had more time than usual to amuse myself. The next day I pulled my woolly hat down over my eyes and rode in total darkness for a while. Where else could you do that without crashing into something? When I emerged from my hat I discovered that I was heading in completely the wrong direction. Later, three tourist jeeps appeared as minute specks on the distant horizon. I decided, in the student tradition, that a naked fly-by was in order. So, when the jeeps drew closer I stripped butt-naked (except for hat, shoes, and gloves) and streaked past them as fast as I could. The sight of a very white streaker on a bicycle on a salt lake in the highlands of Bolivia drew much surprised laughter and pointing from within the jeeps. I got my own surprise when one of the jeeps wheeled round for another look at me. Embarrassed, I swiftly dressed (sub-zero + wind chill = not looking my best), to greet the amused *gringos* who climbed out of the jeep to stretch their legs.

"You must be English," was their first comment.

Sod's law states that 'If anything can go wrong, it will.' It encompasses a whole world of woes such as 'Toast will always land butter side down' and 'When naked on a salt flat in Bolivia, jeeps passed will always contain a teacher from the school in Lima, thousands of kilometres away, where you are due to give a talk.' You can imagine the reception I received in Peru when I walked, a few weeks later, (fully clothed) into the staff room of that school.

Camping on the *salar* was the best part of all. The tourists had driven away to their hotels and I was alone, banging the tent pegs into the salt with my trusty stone. The night was bitterly cold, the stars were so bright and thick that I felt as though I could reach up and grab armfuls of them. My friends at the Argentinian customs post had given me a small bottle of contraband Bolivian liquor and I took a good warming gulp before hunkering down into my sleeping bag for another night at -20°C.

Two miles above sea-level, it was strange to ride over coral, remnants, like the *salar*, of an enormous ancient lake. I was riding now across the *altiplano*, the vast high plateau that stretches through Argentina, Chile, Bolivia, Peru and Ecuador. I passed through single-street villages with rough, mud-brick homes about 50 metres back from the dirt road. In Bolivia, away from the tourist spots and internet cafés, the *altiplano* was a dusty, windy gloom of adobe houses with straw roofs, rickety doors and hard lives. It seemed like a bleak life but above every village primary school the red, green and yellow Bolivian national flag flew. People were proud of their lives and their country. In every village that I passed through for several days, I heard brass bands practicing for Bolivia's national day. Hearing the chaotic practice sessions, I hoped their big day was a long way off.

The rutted dirt road became so awful that I chose instead the cross-country route of an old railway line across the dry spiky grass, cropped short and prickly by llamas and alpacas. At times I pedalled across the flat, rough grass. At others I walked along the old railway, my bike rattling from sleeper to sleeper. Barefoot I waded through broad, shallow rivers that were phenomenally cold. I had acquired three maps of Bolivia, all rather different. At any place one map may not show a river, another omitted a railway, and the third suggested that where I was there should have been a nice paved road. I had to use my imagination to form a vague mid-value from all three maps, season with imagination, then treat it, along with most of the advice from locals, with a hefty pinch of *salar*. I asked one man how far it was to a town that I knew was at least 40 kilometres away. He assured me that it was only three kilometres.

People's lives were so localised that there was no point in telling anyone that I had ridden to Bolivia from Patagonia. Mentioning the name of a town a day or two's ride away would provoke sufficient reaction of surprise and disbelief. Anywhere further than that was beyond their imagination. One little girl was excited to hear that I had been in an aeroplane. She had only ever seen them, tiny and slow, high in the blue sky above her. She was struggling to visualise them, and I told her that the planes she saw were actually about as long as five buses put end to end, and that the wings would stretch from where we were standing to those men talking by the liquor store over the street. She asked, "Do the animals still go *arriba*, on top?" because nobody would take a long journey without a bag of irate chickens or a miserable piglet.

I moved onto a new fold of the map, which always boosted my spirits. This page stretched all the way from where I was up to the northern hemisphere and Central America. No longer was I looking back at where I had been; I was looking forward once again. New roads, new places, new experiences, new excitement. When the mighty 6,000-plus metres of Mount Illimani emerged above a row of lesser peaks I knew that La Paz was not far away.

From nothingness into a city once again. Through the enormous migrant slum that is El Alto, the traffic crazier by the minute, past all the usual characteristics of developing world cities: car-repair shacks, brick makers and sellers, laundry being washed in stagnant streams, prowling dogs, minibus taxis, potholes, women with lurid fizzy drinks in buckets of ice, then, suddenly, there it was! Dropping away below me was the magnificent cauldron of red bricked chaos that is the city of La Paz, with the four snow-caped peaks of Illimani standing guard. I zipped jubilantly down into the centre of La Paz and I found the address of Anthony, a friend of a friend, with whom I had been invited to stay. There I would rendezvous with my friend Rob who was flying out from England to ride with me to Peru.

In our first year at university it was Rob who suggested we spent our summer holidays cycling over the Karakoram mountains from Pakistan to China's Xinjiang province. It was my first serious expedition. The gigantic mountains, the magical madness of Kashgar's famous Sunday market, the freedom that travelling by bike granted; it had been an eye-opening, life-changing summer. When I decided to try to cycle round the world I asked Rob to do it with me. Although he came up with a number of wimpish reasons why he did not want to come along for the whole thing, he promised to fly out and ride with me occasionally.

Rob is one of the world's good guys, someone who always tries to do the right thing. He thinks hard about life and what we are doing on Earth. He is also so chaotically disorganised and clumsy that I had invented a verb from his surname, "to lilwall," (Lilwall: /*lillwawl*/ verb. To utterly, irrevocably yet accidentally break, crumple or lose everything you touch. For example "I can't believe you lilwalled my book: I only lent it to you five minutes ago"; "please don't lilwall this.") Despite this, Rob is a great travel companion. He is patient, thoughtful, interesting, curious, funny and tough, and I looked forward to riding with him.

The steep bowl of central La Paz, the world's highest capital city, is one of the world's great cityscapes. Its steep, cobbled markets intrigued and delighted me. The famous witches' market is a ghoulish, gripping place where talismans and ingredients for elixirs and potions are sold. Dried llamas foetuses, shrivelled and gruesome, are bought to be interred in the foundations of new homes as bringers of luck. There are dead armadillos, incense for funerals and the translucently pale tourists in sandals bayonet bowler-hatted locals with their telephoto lenses. Grubby children sit and watch over sackloads of carrots, chillies and sweet potatoes piled on the pavements. Stout women in colourful ponchos and bowler hats sit on boxes by sacks of grain, piles of clothes, boxes of toothpaste, *Durapell* batteries, *Reedok* caps and pirated DVD's.

At lunchtime, rows of stalls appear on the streets to sell bits of meat fried on paraffin stoves, served with chunks of potato and slices of corn on the cob. After lunch those stalls disappear and another set of people take their place, selling a weird kind of banana ice-cream that is not cold. After sunset, burger stalls appeared, and their bright light bulbs lured me moth-like to the temptation of more gluttonous grazing. The small portions of burgers and chips were offered with a range of sauces to smother them.

When Bolivia began the 20th Century, its entire coastline was lost to Chile, and Peru, Argentina, Brazil and Paraguay helped themselves to bits of the country too. It floundered through decades of instability and changing regimes, and ended the century poor, unsettled and drifting. Like Argentina, Bolivia was even more politically chaotic than usual while I was there, having already got through four presidents since the millennium. *Campesinos*, the rural Indian peasants who make up the majority of Bolivia's population, were fed up with their position as the underpaid, unheard underclass of the country, still dominated by a small elite of European descent. Street protests and murmurings of revolution became daily events and governments changed more regularly than my underpants.

As Rob and I hauled ourselves over the ten mile climb out of La Paz and rode towards Lake Titicaca, we found the road blocked by rocks, a large crowd of angry protesters and a long line of vehicles, their journeys interrupted. We rode past the stationary traffic to the front of the queue and, to our relief, the protesters we spoke to snapped briefly from their anger to smile. They wished us, "*Buen viaje,*" and allowed us to pass on our way. I was impressed at their rationality: their problems were not caused by us and so they had no axe to grind with us. I called out, "*Suerte!* Good luck!" as we pushed our bikes round the barricade and rode on.

Lake Titicaca, 3,800 metres above sea level, is a burst of blue among the white Andean peaks and dry brown fields, terraced over centuries up the steep hillsides. Women with babies strapped to their backs spun wool on spindles as they walked behind their flocks of sheep. The shore was fringed with reeds, drying in the sun and used for building reed boats. Lake Titicaca is also the base for the Bolivian Navy, an odd concept in a landlocked nation. Bolivia still celebrates the annual '*Day of the Sea*' and televises the '*Miss Coastline*' beauty contest.

There are two Copacabanas in the world. One has sunshine, music, dancing and gorgeous girls playing beach volleyball. We were at the other Copacabana. The cold one with squat women in bowler hats and thick woolly tights. On the shore of Lake Titicaca, Bolivia's Copacabana is a town renowned for religious miracles. It was busy with taxi drivers paying to have their vehicles blessed. Outside the gold-filled cathedral, destitute beggars watched the blessing ceremonies of the confetti-covered taxis parked in a line. A priest sprinkled holy water on the bonnets, firecrackers popped as the priest murmured his imprecations, and the drivers toasted the show with lots of beer. I thought that the blessing had better be good to get the drunk drivers home safely.

In the year since I had last seen him in Ethiopia, Rob had been teaching back in England. I was interested to notice how much our preferences in eating venues had diverged. Normally it was difficult for me to identify whether the ride was changing me, because I was permanently moving and always among strangers. I had no constants to measure myself against. Rob and I had always enjoyed eating cheap and cheerful food from street stalls on our travels, but the year of civilised, salaried living in England had seen Rob's standards rise and he no longer wanted to frequent the grubbiest of dining establishments. In the same time frame, I had grown used to a hugely restrictive budget and descended to new depths of street café choices, cheaper and muckier than ever before. These backstreet places were so dirty and hard to find that the owners were invariably astonished to see a *gringo* at their door. They would be eager to chat, make friends, and show off their best food. I often found two chicken's feet, rather than the usual, one, floating in my soup. During our few weeks together Rob and I ate upmarket, at cafés with plastic tablecloths and two or three variations of chicken and rice. Perhaps even a cold Pepsi.

Having a friend along was a relaxing dilution from spending every minute with myself and my journey. With Rob I could alternate between enjoying Peru and escaping to chat about home, friends, or whatever took our fancy. As Rob acclimatised to the altitude and the cold we rode hard and fast, as is our wont together, on the road to Machu Picchu.

We rode up and down passes, and one night climbed up 4,300 metres by the meagre light of a thin moon. We had no good reason to be riding long after sunset in plummeting temperatures but when riding together we had a tendency to push ourselves and each other harder. We eventually reached the summit, surely a stunning view by day, but rather less so late at night. We wrapped up warm at the top and prepared to descend. Whizzing down the pass in complete darkness we could only trust with hopeless naïvety that the road would be free both from potholes and from vehicles driving without lights, an alarmingly common habit in many of the countries I had ridden.

Dropping low again after weeks at altitude, I enjoyed the sight of green trees and inhaled the oxygen-rich air greedily. In a misty dawn, we swept down a wooded valley alongside a trout river that flowed into the Amazon. After the bleakness of the highlands it was invigorating. A green valley, a small quick river, trees, black and white cows, even the veil of dew and clouds of vapour when you exhaled: it was just like home.

I entertained myself by riding up behind Rob and barking like a dog. It never failed to make the London boy jump with fright and never failed to amuse me. Cruising cheerfully into Cusco that afternoon Rob gave a big jolly cheer of celebration as we passed a marching brass band. Then he spied the coffin, and the procession of mourners that the band accompanied.

We rode out from Cusco's weird international world of Guinness, pizza, dope and dollars. Cusco is the nerve centre of the South American backpacker route, known as the Gringo Trail. The road from Cusco to Nazca was beautiful but unrelentingly mountainous.

From low, warm green valleys, we pedalled up to bleak summits and back down again. And again, and again. We cheered and whooped, freezing but thrilled, on reckless descents then huffed and sweated and crept our way for hours up endless hairpins back up to the altitude we had just enjoyed hurtling down from, on the other side of the valley. Occasionally we managed to grab hold of the back of lorries as they overtook us, to be hauled up the mountains. Our arm muscles and shoulder sockets screamed for us to let go, but our legs and lungs warned, 'Don't even think about it! Hold on! This pain is easier than pedalling.' Truck-surfing, as we called it, was a real thrill and an exciting variation on riding slowly up another massive climb. We debated whether truck-surfing went against our riding ethos of covering every inch of the route under our own power, but we concluded that it was so much fun that we didn't really care. Besides, being dragged by one arm behind a smoky, noisy truck up 1,000 metres of steep Andean hairpin bends, dodging potholes and oncoming traffic at uncomfortably high speeds, is not as easy as it might sound.

At 4,500 metres the world was stark and silent. Vicuñas stared at us dumbly and the nights were freezing on the scrubby, hard earth. Down in the valleys streams gurgled and villagers called out to us as we passed. In one village, somebody in the gathering crowd asked if we wanted to buy a small child to take home with us. I said that I would be delighted to since, in my country, eating small children was a real treat. The crowd laughed and two terrified children burst into tears.

After yet another gruelling 100 mile day through the mountains, we arrived at the summit of the final pass. In front of us remained only a 50 mile descent down to Nazca and the Pacific Ocean, making a grand total of 150 miles for the day; a new record for me. We raced down the road from up high, down towards a fiery red sunset. Hills rolled forever below us and stretched on and on towards the distant shore. Darkness came as we descended, and the temperature soared as we cruised effortlessly by moonlight down the steep-sided lunar valley into Nazca. Side by side on the edge of the sand, we rode in the light of the moon, the moon. We rode by the light of the moon.

The sound of your wheels

Don't let the sound of your own wheels drive you crazy.
– 'Take it Easy,' Glen Frey and Jackson Browne

Year three of my journey began on the morning I said goodbye to Rob, and pedalled north out of Lima, alone. I had all my usual nerves and anxiety and insecurities, but compared to how I felt two years ago I felt good. I was positive about the year ahead.

It was a damp Monday morning on the crowded Pan American highway. I passed through 40 kilometres of cheap, grubby housing before I reached the dreary grey sand and grey sky of the coastal desert. The land and sky blurred together in a miserable smudge of fog, the desert's expanses dotted with lines of long tents, all crammed with intensively-farmed chickens that were fed on crushed, stinking fishmeal. I thought about the year ahead as I rode along in autopilot. Where would I be a year from now? Alaska perhaps? Australia? Asia? What would I have seen? What a weird way to spend a year! The unknown potential of those 365 days was intriguing and exciting. Would I have achieved anything? What would be the point of it all? How could I make the most of my too few allotted days? What was I looking for?

During the first two years of my attempt to cycle around the planet, it became apparent in many ways that ours is a very small world. The internet, global music and western popular culture followed me wherever I went. From the seat of a bicycle, though, the world seemed massive. The differences in lifestyles and opportunities of people around the world were immense. Not being even halfway back to where I had begun was a daunting prospect, yet the further I rode, the more I felt at home in our world.

If I had known at the beginning all that I knew the day I left Lima on the third year of the expedition, I would not have dared to begin. After years of reading glossy travel magazines and watching Michael Palin on the telly, I had entered the project with my eyes shut, dreaming of adventure and exotic locations. What I had not considered was the 5,000 miles between London and the pyramids, the 7,500 miles between Cairo and Cape Town or the 5,000 miles from Ushuaia to Machu Picchu. I had not imagined the months of slog and the demoralisingly improbable distance, in both time and space, to the next destination. I had learned that the real travelling is all the stuff in between. The destinations merely added direction to the journey, acting as the frame upon which I could weave the colourful fabric of my experiences.

Slowly the journey had come to be the reward. The thousands of miles amongst the ordinariness of the thousands of people I encountered in all the villages and towns I rode through blended into one giant, rolling memory. Everywhere I had ridden was somebody else's normality, their ordinary world. Extraordinary sights like the pyramids and Machu Picchu are marvellous, but these wonders do not represent the reality of the normality of the people who you want to learn about when travelling.

This is perhaps the biggest difference between cycling and forms of tourism like backpacking. For many people travelling, the destinations are what their experiences are primarily about, moving swiftly and isolated in vehicles from one place to another. By bike, travel is so slow that it becomes the dominant aspect of the journey. I had passed through deserts and mountains and mad Arabian melées and Latin fiestas and African funeral parades. I witnessed strange and extravagant sights and sounds and unfathomable animated conversations on street corners and market stalls. Yet I was always just looking in to other people's ordinary days. The reverse effect also applied. I, a normal, middle-of-the-road English guy on a bike gradually became an exotic, extraordinary spectacle to the people and places I was seeing, merely by riding a long way from my own natural environment. The ride thus far had not been how I had pictured it would be. The battles had been against loneliness, boredom and apathy rather than against corrupt officials, gun-toting child soldiers or enormous mountains. My journey round the world was actually a study of the magic of humankind's normality.

The damp-skied desert and fish-stinking chicken farms were so depressing that I was relieved to head back into the Andes for more vertical punishment. Away from the Pan American highway the sky was blue once more and, before I climbed too high, the sun was hot on my back. I followed a rocky riverbed that climbed steadily and unforgivingly towards the mountains. The valley walls were steep, and as the sun wheeled across the sky, the shadows changed constantly on the hills around me.

Climbing one afternoon towards a 4,100 metre pass, I was struggling. I felt weak and sick, and I was craving a sugary, fizzy drink from one of the roadside shacks that cater to portly lorry drivers on their way to and from the copper mines in the mountains. After hours of resisting temptation and with diminishing energy levels, eventually I succumbed and treated myself to a drink of additive-filled sugary fizz. My mood leaped instantly and I wondered, as I watched tiny hummingbirds dart above me, about whether my attempt to stretch £7,000 of saved student loans to last for a circumnavigation of the whole globe was realistic. Rationing my sugar intake while I cycled over the Andes, and saving mere pennies, did not seem very sensible. I had acquired a taste for Inca Kola, a bright yellow fizzy drink found everywhere in Peru. I had even heard it referred to as Peruvian champagne. There are only two countries in the world where Coca Cola is not the top-selling drink: Peru and Scotland. Strangely Peru's Inca Kola and Scotland's Irn Bru taste almost identical. Irn Bru is a weird orange to Inca Kola's alien yellow but the artificial bubble-gum-miness is the same.

The people of northern Peru were the most open and friendly that I had met so far in South America. My ride through northern Peru was so mountainous and steep that I often struggled to find flat ground sufficient to perch my tent on, and I camped in friendly villages instead. The down to earth, decent atmosphere in those villages reminded me of home in the Yorkshire Dales. In Peru it seemed that people asked me less about the cost of my bike and my wealth and they sniggered less at my horrible Spanish grammar. Camping one night beside a large haystack in a village I chatted for a couple of hours with a gathering of villagers. They sat around and shared their evening relaxation time with me. They told me about their daily lives, about the standard of the village school and the hopes they held for their children, about their jobs and their thoughts on the war in Iraq (their answers: bad school, high hopes, ill-paid jobs, disagreed with war). They appreciated the concept of my journey, of seeing the world while I was young. They offered their support, asking what they could do to help. I told them that they were already helping me so much, as evenings like those made it all worthwhile. To feel at ease and welcome when you are far from home is one of the sweetest feelings of travelling.

I began to set up my stove to prepare my dinner, but people motioned for me to stop. It had already been taken care of. Minutes later a young woman walked carefully down the field from the houses, carrying a tray with a bowl of soup and a plate of chicken and rice for my dinner. The woman watched me eat until my plate was empty and she was satisfied that the *gringo* had enjoyed her cooking. People who invited me into their homes often worried that I would not be able to eat 'their' kind of food. But an enjoyment and appreciation of food brought us closer together, it was something we could share and enjoy together whatever linguistic and cultural barriers stood between us.

I was riding a scenic shortcut towards Cajamarca, leaving the tarmac behind and taking a network of tracks that linked the small mountain villages. In each village, men discussed the pros and cons of which route I should take before delivering their verdicts to me. Few of them had taken the route themselves as the main paved road up the coast was far quicker, despite being longer. It was hot and the road was terrible. One day I had to pedal down-hill into the wind to make headway. I had no idea where I was. Through a sheer canyon, the road cut through 35 rough-hewn tunnels and clung to the cliff edge a nauseating height above the river. There were no roadside barriers.

There was not enough flat ground to pitch my tent and no villages so I ended up rolling out my sleeping bag to sleep on a

narrow goat path half way down a cliff. As I lay on the path in my
sleeping bag, writing my diary and brewing a cup of tea, a bowler-
hatted lady with a bundle over her shoulder approached. I looked
up at her and said, "hello," as though a *gringo* lying beside his bicycle on a vertiginous footpath keenly anticipating his cup of tea was
entirely normal behaviour. As she edged past me her little dog
yapped furiously at me and she asked if I was going to sleep, here,
on this footpath. I said, "yes, lovely view, *linda vista*, isn't it?" She
agreed that it was indeed a lovely view and wished me goodnight
without registering a flicker of surprise at my strangeness.

Men were panning for gold in a river and I stopped to watch.
I asked one of them if there was lots of gold to be found.
"*Mucho!*" he assured me, with enthusiasm.
For a man dressed in rags and living in a shelter of corrugated metal I admired his optimism.
The track turned away from the river and I set about tackling
a mountainside of hairpin bends, promising myself that when I
reached the top I could stop for the night. Five hours later, and
very tired, I arrived in the village perched on the mountain top. I
instantly fell in love with Pallasca, a sleepy village of old mud
bricks and russet tiles. I felt like Laurie Lee in Andalucía as I
arrived at sunset, dusty and parched in the small central plaza.
The village grapevine was working well, and news of the
gringo's arrival spread quickly. I was still enjoying the warm peace
of the plaza when I was approached by a young man who looked
different to the villagers I had seen in recent days. He was wearing smart jeans, an ironed shirt and even a watch. Juan introduced
himself in good English and explained that he lived in Lima but
that his whole extended family had come back to their family
home for three days to celebrate his grandmother's birthday. He
invited me to stay with them and join in the party.
Juan's beautiful family home was large enough for three generations of an extended Catholic family. There were two storeys of
bedrooms and dining rooms running off from a central courtyard,
but the house's best days were behind it now. The wooden door-
frames and balustrades were dotted with woodworm and on the
drawing room walls hung black and white photographs of richer

times, faded and crinkled with age. I was taken to meet Granny and she seemed very unsurprised that a sweaty European cyclist had gate-crashed her birthday party. I wished her a Happy Birthday. She would call me only, '*gringo*,' to the embarrassment of all the younger generations who welcomed me into their party. She addressed all her questions about me to the party at large.

"Is the *gringo* hungry?"

"Where has the *gringo* come from? Why is he not married?"

An aunt who had grown up in Pallasca but who now worked at a university in Lima wanted to show me around her childhood village. We walked around admiring the enormous views on all sides of valleys and peaks and big sky. She reminisced as we walked, she introduced me to people she knew, and she scolded small children for staring at me, making them say "good morning" to me in English before they fled, giggling and embarrassed.

I relished learning about Pallasca. When you spend time somewhere, you remember that life there is not just limited to your passing. It is not *The Truman Show*. You hear a funny story from someone's childhood. Life happened there before you arrived. You hear how beautiful the flowers are in the springtime. Life will continue once you are gone and forgotten. As always, I was glad I had stayed awhile. I wondered what happenings I would miss when I moved on. I wished that I could be relaxed enough to stop for a few weeks and soak up life, but I was unable to relax sufficiently, to take things easy and let life wash over me. With a tinge of romantic regret, I knew that I was not a carefree wandering spirit. I was bound for Alaska, and its magnetic pull never let me rest for long. Maybe tomorrow I might settle down. Until then, I'll just keep moving on.

Cycling through South America did not pose too many logistical challenges, little more than tracking down spare parts, preparing equipment for the mountains, planning a route, arranging provisions for empty desert stretches and finding my way on roads too small to feature on my map. I did not need visas in South America, a rare luxury when travelling. For the past six months my major logistical pastime had been trying to work out what to do about Colombia. Colombia has a well-deserved reputation for lawlessness and is not known as *Loco*-mbia for nothing.

The modern era has never been peaceful in Colombia; the 19th Century saw 50 insurrections and eight civil wars. The civil war that began in the 1940s, known simply as '*la violencia*,' killed more than a quarter of a million people. From it came a military coup and the birth of several left-wing guerrilla or paramilitary factions. Added to the mix was the violence of the hugely powerful drugs cartels, headed by the notorious Pablo Escobar. Drugs continue to dominate in Colombia, both through the violence the industry spawns and the several billion dollars it generates each year. Although the government is working hard to eradicate the drugs barons and stamp out the violence, Colombia is far from a peaceful land.

To travel overland from Patagonia to Alaska, however, there is no alternative but to pass though Colombia, so I had tough decisions to make. People suggested that I should fly from Ecuador to Panama and bypass Colombia. It would be only a short flight, but a very sensible one. I did not want to do that. I wanted to ride through Colombia and out the other side into Panama and North America. The problem with that plan is simple: there is no road from Colombia to Panama. Instead there is about 100 miles of tropical jungle, known as the Darién Gap. The Gap has never had a road built through it for reasons ranging from economics to ecology and disease transmission to security. It is a wild, exciting place and I wanted to cross it with my bike. Much research over the past months had led me to believe that it would be possible, either by carrying my bike through the jungle or by hopping from village to village along the coast in dugout canoes.

However the Darién Gap is not just a jungle filled with creepy crawlies, scary snakes and smelly swamps. Sadly, it is also a last refuge of scoundrels, guerrillas and drug barons hiding from the law, directing criminal activity or fighting each other. The Darién Gap is currently one of the most dangerous places on Earth.

I vacillated back and forth for months over what to do, about my personal boundary line of risk and recklessness and that fine line between bravery and stupidity. Should I detour round Colombia completely through the Amazon basin of Brazil and into Venezuela and then somehow by boat to Panama? Decision time was drawing closer.

Surrounded by peaks in the gorgeous Cordillera Blanca mountain range, perhaps it was a combination of the awe-inspiring scenery and lack of oxygen that turned me light-headed with life and all its possibilities, but over days of riding and thinking, I decided that I really must have a go at both Colombia and the Darién crossing. The prospect scared me, but it excited me as well.

Crossing valleys was a demoralising business and I seemed to be doing a lot of it. As I dropped hundreds of vertical metres down to a valley floor, the smell of brake rubber burned from my wheels and the rims grew so hot that if I squirted water onto them the water would hiss and boil. By the time I reached each summit I would be exhausted. In each high-perched village I reached I was greeted by pessimistic people telling me that the route I planned to take through Huamachuca to Cajamarca was too rough, too remote and too high. But there was no way I was going to retreat to the main road, not least because I knew how difficult that road had been. One benefit from the villages was that I could definitely get water there; between villages I had to rely on finding streams to drink from.

I pushed my bike up the rocky trail past a small glacier and a tiny lake nestling bright in a fold in the bleak yellow and black landscape that reminded me of Scotland's Highlands. I was on my way up a 4,500 metre ascent, and the altitude hurt more than usual. Eventually cresting the pass and gasping for breath, with a nauseous stomach and a headache punching at my eyeballs, I wrapped up in all my clothes and began getting myself down the other side as fast as possible. It was bleak and cold and deserted. I wanted to get down to warmer parts with some oxygen in the air. Approaching me at speed came a little bus, hurtling up the rocky track, pinging small stones behind it and churning up dust. I hadn't seen a vehicle in ages. The driver slammed on his brakes in front of me and people leapt from the bus. They surrounded me shouting and waving their arms.

Alarmed by their panic I managed to decipher that they had just been held up at gunpoint in an ambush.

"It's very dangerous!" shouted some.

"*Muy peligroso!* Go back! You must go back!"
"They will kill you for sure!"
"*Nos mataran a todos!* They will kill us all!"
Before I could get any sense out of them the driver was leaning on his horn and yelling, "*Vamos!* Let's go!" and everyone piled
back on the bus. I stood alone as the dust drifted away and the
sound of crunching gears ebbed into silence. "Hmmm," I said.

It had taken two days of climbing to reach the mountain summit, and many more days from the main road. Should I now turn
around and go back down and look for an alternative route? Of
course I should, those people had just been ambushed and robbed.
The decision was obvious, but instead I pedalled on. I was too lazy
to retreat and undo all the altitude I had worked so hard to gain.
I was scared now and my view of the mountains had changed in
an instant. Moments before I had been enjoying the emptiness,
confident in my ability to cope with the altitude, the distances and
the cold. But now I was afraid.

The steep descent flattened to a plateau that rolled across desolate fells. I pedalled nervously along the exposed track, berating
my folly for continuing. At each hilltop I got off the bike before
cresting the hill. Moving away from the road I crept forward on
my belly until I could scan the land ahead and check that it was
empty. Only then would I continue riding. Only once that day did
I hear an engine. It sounded like a pick-up truck. I scrambled
quickly from the road into a ditch, dragging my bike in too and
making sure that I was out of sight from the road. I lay still, listening to the vehicle approaching at speed. I could feel my heart
thumping in my chest. To my huge relief the pick-up roared past
in a shower of pebbles. I waited until the sound faded then continued riding. I rode until after nightfall then pitched my tent
under the cover of darkness. I ate the last of my cold food rather
than using my stove which created both light and noise, and I lay
scared and cold in my sleeping bag until I fell asleep. I was packed
and riding again before first light, resolved to ride hard to reach a
village that day, to find good people and an escape from my over-
anxious imagination. The shrill cry of lapwings were the only
sound that day but that too was swallowed up by the beckoning
silence.

Late that afternoon the hills gave way to one or two squalid smallholdings, then to a small village and finally the comforting reassurance of a proper road. Cars passed every few minutes, puncturing the eery silence and my swirling imaginings about the dangers of an empty nothingness. I imagine that the baddies must have scarpered after ambushing the bus. At any rate, I had come to no harm. But, during that anxious 24 hours I had learned something important. This was only a bike ride. It did not really *matter*. It was not important. The integrity of my ride, cycling every single inch of the route, meant nothing compared with getting back home alive. I knew now that I was not going to risk crossing the Darién Gap. Should I be contemplating going to Colombia at all, I wondered.

Within range of Ecuador, the next new country on my route, my mind was filled only with the pessimistic news coming out of increasingly unstable, violent Colombia. I had many well-meaning emails trying to put me off going there. The Andes were behind me now, and I zoomed down to the warm lowlands. The higher boiling point of water at low altitudes meant that I kept scalding my mouth until I remembered to eat more slowly.

My final campsite in Peru was on a swathe of warm sand in a thicket, a few miles short of the border. A warm breeze kept the mosquitoes away. My eyes stung with sweat, my legs ached and my feet stank. It was bliss as the heat seeped from the day and my body. Far away a dog barked and a donkey kept up its stupid, monotonous bray. The hills ahead were silhouetted against a darkening sky and Mars shone bright. A shooting star seared the sky and I made a wish.

I wished to get through Colombia safely.

The last time for first times

When was the last time you did something for the first time?
– Fight Club

The short, steep hills of Ecuador only took about an hour each to climb, but non-stop, they were soul-destroying. Riding forever up, down, up, down, up, with no time to settle to a rhythm and no graceful descents. Although my 33rd country, Ecuador, is beautiful, with some of the most vibrant indigenous cultures and splendid headwear on the continent, I was not planning to spend much more than a month there. I had the end of the continent in my sights now and I was eager to push on. It was a pity, as I appreciated the calorie input of meals of fried pig fat (*chicharrones*), fried rice, fried egg, cheese and boiled potatoes. Delicious! I was less sure about the baked guinea pigs…

Ecuador uses American dollars as its currency. It was more expensive than Bolivia or Peru, but I discovered ice lollies that cost only five cents. In each new country I would scout out the local staple food. I then ate little else until the next country, which would offer up its own budget culinary speciality. As ice lollies were cheaper than bananas, they became my new staple. When I told one lolly vendor that I was trying to cycle around the world he looked me up and down and said, "with a body like that you will never make it."

He gave me another lolly to fatten me up and I ate it as I ped-alled out of town to yet another long climb. That town seemed to do a roaring trade in lollies because after about an hour of riding the road became strewn with discarded wooden sticks. Evidently this was about the distance that a lolly lasted in a vehicle. And, this being South America, everyone had thrown their sticks out of the window when they finished with them. It reminded me of South Africa where, at about eating distance from each town, were piles of jettisoned fast-food wrappings. The wrappings from the more expensive fast-food joints tended to be strewn further from the town than those from the less classy eateries. I formed several hypotheses for this: perhaps rich people eat more slowly, rich people eat more than poorer people or else rich people drive faster cars. Empty musings of empty miles.

A deep weariness had been rising inside me for months. I set my sights on Quito and hopes of mental and soulful recuperation before Colombia. One morning I was grinding the distance to Quito when a overloaded lorry spluttered slowly past and the driver whipped me across the face with a knotted rope. I was knocked off my bike and by the time I got to my feet all I could do was watch the bastard trundle up the hill in the slowest getaway vehicle in history. But still faster than me. I have no idea what provoked him to thump me.

Ecuadoreans were the worst drivers in South America. I feared for my life repeatedly as incompetently handled tonnes of metal skimmed past me, overtaking in wildy inappropriate spots.

In Quito I spent hours watching the best street artist I have ever seen, a mimic who walked behind his targets and copied them to perfection. Everything was perfect: the stride pattern, the way they carried themselves, even their characters seemed to be reflected perfectly by this genius of observation. I am sure that it was no coincidence that he worked on *Calle del Espejo,* Mirror Street. When people realised that they were being followed by him the crowd would laugh and they would often try to flee in embarrassment. Their embarrassment and flight was also copied perfectly, and laughter chased them down the street. How cruel it is to be reflected like that, how excruciating to be mimicked perfectly. I was entranced and eager for him to pick on me, but also scared at the prospect. I did not really know who or what I was at that moment, I certainly did not know what image I was portraying or how the world saw me, and I was afraid to find out.

Enormous storm clouds dwarfed the housing that sloshed up the flanks of Quito's many hills. It is hard to orientate yourself in Quito: all around are steep hills and every view changes as the afternoon rain clouds muster on the hills, shrouding the huge statue of an angel standing guard above the city in the slightly crouched posture of someone desperate for a pee.

Round and round I paced, up and down the streets of Quito. Through plazas framed by fine old buildings, past ambling families eating ice-creams, shoeshine boys prowling for business, toddlers chasing pigeons. I sat and stared at the rooftops from where, at some unseen signal, showers of pigeons suddenly scattered, their shadows racing across the plaza as they swooped and curved in the sky to settle on a new resting spot. I needed time to think. I needed to get moving before indecision froze me. I needed to talk to the people I loved. I needed to be the only person in my life so that I could make a selfish and simple decision. Thoughts of Colombia were driving me crazy.

My mental to-ing and fro-ing about Colombia had a welcome respite when an International School asked if I would substitute for an absent teacher for a week. I would be paid $300 to supervise classes, a colossal sum of money for me. I promised myself that by the end of that week I would have made a decision about whether or not to travel to Colombia. News reports portrayed Colombia as degenerating by the day, with violence escalating. Lawlessness spread, haphazardly. Because of a recent spate of kidnappings, the Foreign Office advice was against all travel to the country. In a high office overlooking one of Quito's parks, staff at the British Embassy tried to persuade me not to go. One of the staff offered to watch from the office window and adjudicate while I pedalled sufficient laps of the park below to equal the distance of the ride through Colombia. He reasoned that I could then hop on a plane to Panama with my conscience clear. I was becoming increasingly glum about my chances of getting through. Car bombs were exploding daily in Bogotá, and I had lunch with a Dutch businessman who had loved Colombia until the moment when he was kidnapped. He had only recently been released. This yin and yang was a common theme in tales of Colombia.

There was a measure of recklessness in my life, of trusting to luck, of hoping for the best and believing in the goodness of people. But there was also a serious soul inside me as well, a worrier who thought too much about the consequences of his actions and did not like trusting to chance something that could be thought through and planned. I lusted for life and the thrilling spontaneity of chance encounters and those luminous moments of lucidity where everything made sense and the pathway through the life of my choice seemed so clear and attainable. But I also thought hard about how to initiate those moments of jubilant impulsiveness. Germinating inside me too was the nagging doubt that life was passing me by with insufficient purpose and zest. My heart wished to be wilder and freer than my head would allow. The compromise that I had arrived at on this journey was a philosophy of pragmatic recklessness. Be careful, minimise the risk, then go for it! Plan thoroughly, think, and then roll the dice. I wanted what Nietzsche described as *amor fati,* 'the love of your fate.' You must try to believe that everything happens for a reason, and a positive reason at that. Then you will look back later in life at the difficult moments as being the times that shaped who you have become today. You must try to tackle everything with positivity. I liked the theory but struggled with the implementation.

Before I began, I had planned the ride thoroughly and sensibly. Then, just two weeks after I rode out of England, the September 11th terrorist attacks changed everything. That day shook the complacent stability of our post Cold War world and, as war brewed in Afghanistan, I was forced to change my plans and pedal unprepared down the length of Africa instead of through Central Asia to Australia. I would never have been sufficiently impulsive or bold or naïve or thoughtless enough to have left home with the purpose of cycling through Africa and with no plan. But once I had achieved it I was so glad that I had done it.

I wanted to justify the faith that people had shown in me by not giving up, and I wanted to thank those who had supported *Hope and Homes for Children* on the basis of my ride. I knew that if I did not ride all that was possible to ride, I would regret it. In my heart I knew that the risks were small and the potential rewards much greater, but I knew that everybody who mattered to me just wanted me to come home safe. I wanted to be brave and stupid and go for it. I knew how chuffed I would be if I made it through. But I also felt that I should be cautious and sensible, and that to admit to being afraid was the bravest thing of all.

Everybody knows that the press hypes stories, yet still we often take what we see and read at face value. News of violence and horror in the Middle East are daily events, and have been for decades, yet I have rarely felt safer than I did riding through Lebanon and 'axis-of-evil' Syria. Sudan had been at war for many years, but the Sudanese people were the most hospitable I had met. Robert Mugabe had declared that by August 2002 all white people in Zimbabwe would be removed from their land. I rode through Zimbabwe in that month. It was a sad, sad ride, but I never felt endangered despite probably being the whitest white person there. I wondered whether Colombia might also prove different from its reputation.

There were many exiled Colombians in Quito and their message was mixed. Sure, Colombia had its problems. They wouldn't be living in Ecuador if it didn't. But they also said that their country was the most beautiful, exciting, friendly and fun country in South America and it would be a real pity for me to miss it. During the pleasantly gentle diversion that a week's high-income teaching provided, I spoke with more people about what might await. I met a Colombian father whose two young children had seen their mother shot dead in their car in Bogotá. Face to face with that father I mumbled embarrassed platitudes of condolence and felt ridiculous asking him trivial questions about a bicycle trip. I learned more about the Colombian guerrilla group FARC, and the war that had rolled back and forth for so many years that nobody seemed to quite remember any more what they were fighting for. I spoke at the South American Explorers' Club which had beautiful photographs of Colombia and strong advice that I should not try to cycle through. Bus journeys in convoy and the cities were fine, they told me, it was the long, empty roads between the cities that were vulnerable. The long, empty roads that I planned to pedal alone at a meagre 10mph. I took bets from a boisterous class of 16-year-old boys amounting to enormous sums in hypothetical loot, over whether or not I would make it through Colombia alive. Their certainty of my imminent, violent death was touching. I received a pessimistic email from a BBC correspondent in Bogotá who I had met a few years before on a motorbike in Central America. He did not rate my chances. And supervising a maths test one afternoon I was very aware, in the silent, still room, that my shoes stank.

An ex-SAS man I had met ran a defence and security company which specialised in providing security for Embassy and oil workers in Ecuador and Colombia. They analysed the risk of foreign investments and handled kidnap negotiations and rescues. I knew that there, if nowhere else, I would be given hard facts about the feasibility of cycling alone through Colombia. The office walls bore detailed maps of Ecuador and Colombia, and the air hummed with professionalism and purpose. The guys who had agreed to meet me were ex-British and American military and it was a refreshing change when they met me dead on time. It was a small detail, but rare in South America and unheard of in Ecuador. It conveyed competence and respect, and I felt that I could trust these people. I promised myself that I would do whatever they suggested.

For 30 minutes they cut through all the rumour and paranoia about Colombia, briefing me from their maps about the position, numbers and activity of government troops and guerrillas. I asked them about the Darién Gap, and told them that I had decided not to tackle it and hoped instead to find a sailing boat to carry me around it. Had I made the right choice? In reply one of the Americans walked to a map of Darién that was nothing but jungle and rivers. The swift summary he gave me of guerrilla movements and numbers, and a couple of grisly tales of internecine slaughter was enough to convince me that I had made the right decision.

What about the rest of Colombia? What about this exotic, sensual country with its heady concoction of *cumbia* music, cocaine barons and beautiful women and the unknowns that had been lacking on my ride north from Patagonia? Could I cycle through Colombia? Could I cycle to the end of this continent I had almost crossed, or would the ride stop here? I dreaded asking these questions, because I dreaded the answer. And I had promised myself that these men knew what they were talking about, that they were not cowards or drama queens and that I was going to heed their advice. I looked at the four men sitting across me at the conference table.

"Should I cycle through Colombia?"

They looked at each other, and they looked at me.

"No."

Imaginings of fear

Present fears are less than horrible imaginings.
– William Shakespeare

Dondé estan tus amigas, esta tu tierra
(Wherever your friends are, that's your land).
– Poker Beer

Outside my tent I looked at the curves of road dropping away below me, at the patchwork of emerald fields, at the setting sun sharding through the clouds beyond a white-capped volcano. I thought of all the other campsites, all the other passes and full moons on the haul north through the beautiful landscapes of South America. There were only 2,000 more kilometres to the end of the continent and I knew that I really did not want to break that chain now. But I also knew that this would be my final peaceful wild campsite. I would not be sleeping wild and vulnerable in the forests that lay ahead. I had crossed the equator the day before and the stars of the Southern Cross were barely above the horizon any more. A couple days' more travel and they would sink below the horizon for good, replaced by the more familiar constellations of the north.

I had changed my mind a hundred times. I had taken weeks to make a decision.

I went to bed thinking, 'no.'

But in the morning the sun was shining and I packed up my tent and thought, 'bugger it, let's have a go.'

And I rode quickly into Colombia before I had chance to change my mind.

Crossing from safe, stable, touristy Ecuador into Colombia the atmosphere changed instantly. Colombia is a country whose four decades of conflict has left 40% of the country guerrilla controlled, churning out 80% of the world's cocaine and 25% of the world's fake US dollars, where three people are murdered each hour and 3,000 a year are kidnapped. It was early morning and still cool. The border was pleasantly quiet, too early for the con artists and beggars, the moneychangers, whores and dealers of smuggled blue jeans and pirated music who normally buzz around border towns like wasps at a jam jar. I had never crossed a border with such a drastic change in vibe. Normally nations morph slowly away from their neigh-bours into their own identity as you travel further away from the border. Here in the small town of Ipiales, the transformation was sudden, and the change in atmosphere made up my mind: I had made the right decision coming to Colombia. From the ultra-reserved people of Ecuador where coaxing a smile was an achieve-ment, I was among friendly, energetic people telling me how beau-tiful their country was and how well I would be treated. Even the border police assured me that I would be safe and welcomed. The doom and gloom of the last few weeks in pessimistic Ecuador evap-orated. I fell in love with Colombia, a reckless love affair fired by an irresistible brew of beauty and danger and lifelust. After the uncom-plicated pleasures and trials of the moderate, steady people of South America so far, suddenly I was back in a country buzzing with potential. I was alive again! I began to ride north. North towards the beautiful white mansions and churches of Popayan, the verdant cof-fee hills around Manizales, and on towards the Caribbean.

In Pasto I found a tourist office. I was not sure who was more surprised: me, at finding a tourist office open in Colombia, or the friendly, balding man behind the desk, at finding a tourist. He had an excellent map of Colombia and I had not been able to find one in any shop. Unfortunately he had only one copy and it was not for sale, so he locked up the office and we walked round the town together until we found somewhere to photocopy the map. I was beginning to think that everyone in Colombia was friendly. Everyone except for the murdering, kidnapping guerrillas, bandits and drug barons.

I ate lunch in a café with a man my age who had just served three years in jail in Miami for smuggling drugs ("good food, lots of TV, nice uniforms, lots of ping-pong, but it got a bit boring, *un poco abburido*, after three years…"). Diego was a small, cheery man with gelled hair, a wonky smile and a shiny gold chain. He became so good at ping-pong that after his release he often entered, and always won, the regional ping-pong tournaments. As we ate lunch and drank the sweet juice of one of Colombia's many weird and wonderful fruits, Diego talked about how much he had learned to love his country while he was in prison, despite having being delighted to have left when he first went to the States. He told me that he had recently smuggled two bags containing US$500,000 in fake banknotes to the US, but he assured me that he had now given up that career as his mother had been nagging him to get a proper job. I knew how he felt. We finished lunch with cups of chopped mango sprinkled with lemon and salt, and Diego offered me a present of a fake $100 bill he had in his wallet. I declined and paid his lunch bill as thanks for his eye-opening company.

Television news told daily of displaced peoples, kidnaps, murders, captures, organised crime, drugs busts and raids. The roads heaved with soldiers from the contra-guerrilla units, swathed in belts of bullets. They were not slovenly and bored like most soldiers I met in the world. Colombian soldiers patrolled with their weapons held at their shoulders in the alert position, their eyes and ears concentrating fully. Helicopters patrolled slowly overhead and I was stopped and searched daily. One day, soldiers who had been camouflaged in a bush stepped into the road and I swerved with fright. They shook my hand and teased me, laughing that I was scared of the FARC (the largest guerrilla group). Damn right I was scared, with a bicycle as a getaway vehicle. I never camped in Colombia, the only country where I took that precaution, and I was always sure to be off the roads by late afternoon.

One weekend, elections were being held, and the accompanying security operation was massive. The sale of alcohol was forbidden nationwide in the days before and after the election. Vehicles had to travel in convoy, escorted by police cars. The military ordered me onto a bus until I reached a safe town. For once I did not argue at this removal of my freedom. Travel is always a lottery, at any moment some countries are safe, others impassable. On any given day, there are certain places in the world you are better off not to be. A year or two later these situations may well be reversed. I had been in La Paz a few weeks earlier and loved it, but now I had heard that there were riots there and that travel into or out of the city had been prohibited.

Southern Colombia was lush, hot and mountainous. I had not felt much of a buzz from cycling for a while, but I was loving riding again. I was loving the scenery and loving the sensation of riding. Cycling is a popular sport in Colombia and occasional recreational cyclists would zip past me in lycra outfits on shiny, humming racing bikes. They gave me a wave or a cheer as they passed. The road was flanked by green mountains and the road followed rushing rivers through steep canyons. In southern Colombia the traveller Ted Simon was, "prepared to swear that [he] would never see anything more beautiful than these great mountainsides clad in greenery and bursting with flowers and flame trees." Flatter valleys were lush with palm trees and bananas and crops grew tall in the fields. Around Cali, known for the most beautiful women in Colombia, the temperatures really started to soar, climbing to a sweaty 36°C.

The hills were tough work and I made a special effort on one, head down and sprinting, to keep alongside a passing truck so that with a final lunge I could grab at its bumper as it passed and hold on for a free ride. I grabbed, held, and relaxed and at the same moment noticed that two teenagers on bikes had already had the same idea and were happily hanging on to the back. A motorbike roared past us, seemingly having solved the problem of being passed too close by the mad overtakers of Colombia: he had a chainsaw strapped on the side of his bike, switched on with the blade spinning lethally. We chatted as we swept along, and they warned me not to cycle through the USA. It was far too dangerous. The boys saw Colombia simply as 'home.'

I tried to assess how I felt to be approaching the end of the continent. South America had been a beautiful ride, through extravagant landscapes and up the biggest mountains I had ridden in years. The people had been friendly and kind, and I felt safe and accepted, yet there had not been the spontaneous embracing of strangers that had made the Middle East and Africa so rewarding. In Colombia I had recaptured the gleeful sensation of being out of your normal environment but happy to embrace whatever the new place threw at you. I felt I was having an adventure again, connecting with people, challenging myself, learning and having fun again. And to think that I came so close to taking a plane over Colombia.

The towns and villages I stayed in each night, in the cheapest rooms I could find, were bustling places. I enjoyed strolling round the plazas in the evenings, imagining what lay ahead, watching pretty girls on mopeds and kids chasing pigeons. I sat one evening at a street café, swatting mosquitoes and chatting with the café owner and his wife about my journey, my experiences in Colombia and the perception of his country in other places. Three children sat in the shadows of the bright bulb outside the door of the shack and listened, fiddling with their bare toes and leaning against each other. Huge red flowers grew beside my bench. It was late and there were only a handful of customers left drinking. José Maria, the owner, gave me a Poker beer and made me peel off the label and stick it into my diary to remember him by. "*Dondé estan tus amigas, esta tu tierra,*" proclaimed the label "Wherever your friends are, that's your land." Each village that I stayed in "of twenty adobe houses, built on the banks of rivers of clear water that ran along beds of polished stones, which were white and enormous, like prehistoric eggs" felt more and more like Macondo, the village in Gabriel Garcia Marquez's *One Hundred Years of Solitude*. In those humid lowland villages, filled with laughter, I half expected mad gypsies and swirling, magical happenings. Instead I would settle for answering the questions of inquisitive children, relax with happily lazing families and watch the sunset football matches, games of terrible skill, awful pitches, and high passion, even by the worldwide standards of village football.

Day by day, Colombia was becoming a country I wanted to stay and live in. I loved the smiles, the pats on the back, the countryside, the music, the charming villages and villagers, the laughter and the welcoming atmosphere. I bought a red, yellow and blue bracelet, Colombia's colours, from a street child to show my alle-

giance. He told me to wear it for ever, or at least until it fell off.
The day it fell off I must make a wish and he promised me that it
would come true.

Only once, I stayed in a town where I felt uneasy. It reminded me of a rough town in England, plastic shop fronts and budget clothes stores strung along the ugly main street. The kind of
town where you avoid catching anybody's eye. I stayed in a hovel
above a pool hall, a scary saloon with a row of pool tables, a forest of cues in a fog of cigarette smoke, thumping music and clink-
ing beer bottles. I scurried through it, head down, and up to my
room where I jammed my bed and bike against the door to barricade it closed, splatted a few mosquitoes and lay sweating naked
on the saggy bed with a smelly pillow over my head to try to muffle the music.

Along the Cauca valley towards the River Magdalena, picturesque waterfalls tumbled into the river. People had rigged
hosepipes into these waterfalls, diverting some of the flow and the
villages there had spawned a whole carwash industry. The hoses
were 'on' permanently, blasting high into the air whilst young men
waited by the road for business. Occasionally I would call out as I
approached and ask them to cool me down by soaking me with
their hoses. Not surprisingly they seemed to get a great deal of
pleasure drenching the *gringo* and I would bellow a greeting and
punch my fists in the air and cry out, "*gracias, amigos!*" as I escaped
their range, soaked to the skin and cool once more, at least for a
few kilometres.

I timed my arrival in Cartagena to coincide with the Miss
Colombia fiesta, a week-long carnival of beauty parades, street
parties, flour bombs and water pistols. There was music and dancing until dawn. I had been ultra-cautious when I first arrived in
Colombia but had enjoyed it so much that I let my guard down
and celebrated ending the continent in style, with a week of dancing at the fiesta's endless parties. The end of South America was
not nearly so emotional or significant a moment as finishing
Africa, but it was a lot wilder!

Cartagena was a perfect place to celebrate finishing a continent, a World Heritage town full of character on the shores of the

turquoise Caribbean Sea. At school I learned about the heroics of Francis Drake. In Cartagena they call our man a pirate and a privateer. Drake caused havoc with persistent raids, and captured so much gold from the Spaniards, which they in turn had stolen from the native Indians, that mighty defences were built which still encircle the magnificent old town. The streets are narrow and the colonial buildings painted in jaunty colours or whitewashed until they dazzle. Shuttered windows, decorated with boxes of flowers, hid the cool, graceful homes within. People lounged on balconies, idly watching you, watching them. Church bells rang from all directions and an austere white convent stood imposingly dominant as if to remind locals not to have *too* much fun, not to be *too* relaxed about life. Fruit juice sellers served huge glasses of incredible blends of fruits, many of which I had never seen before, and in the early mornings I perched on one of their stools, watching the world, thinking back over the past thousands of miles and wondering what lay ahead as I waited to leave South America.

The mighty swells of the Andes subsided to choppy waves in Ecuador and Colombia, steep and difficult hills but nothing compared with the epic passes of the past months. These hills too had petered down into the flat, hot northern plains with dusty villages of playing children, damp-eyed old folks watching and remembering, and the rhythms of swinging hammocks and music. On and on, hotter and hotter, until one day there was nothing more left ahead of me. Nine months after nervously swirling my fingers in the cold waters of the Beagle Channel, I crested a final rise and saw before me the Caribbean lapping gently at the grand walls of Cartagena, gorgeously blue and the end of South America. I raised my hands from the handlebars and lifted my head to cheer. I freewheeled down the final hill to the end of the road and there was no further left to ride. The end of South America. The end of my road. Another continent was in the bag.

As I cruised down into Cartagena, I planned to buy a plane ticket home to England. Colombia, wonderful Colombia, seemed as good a place as any to call time on this ride that had demanded every minute of my time, every ounce of my stamina and every drop of my determination for the past two-and-a-bit years. I was proud of what I had done. I had experienced the best days of my life. I was ready to go home, and I would go home happy.

Before going to a travel agency, I rode to the yacht club to take my 'end of continent' photograph, wheeling my bike to the end of the furthest jetty, perched out in the warm waters of the Caribbean. Photo done, job done. I turned and walked back down the jetty past the rows of yachts towards town.

A middle-aged American yelled from a yacht as I walked by, "Hey! Are you lookin' for a ride to Panama?"

I said, "Err, well… yes, I suppose I am," completely taken aback.

"Sure, buddy, you can come with us! Do you want a beer?"

It seemed as though I would not be flying home after all. The ride was still on.

Throwing off the bow line

*Years from now you will be more disappointed by the things you did-
n't do than by the ones you did do. So throw off the bow lines. Sail
away from the safe harbour. Catch the trade winds in your sails.
Explore. Dream. Discover.*
— Mark Twain

My new beer-and-yacht-offering American acquaintanc-
es were preparing to return their friend's yacht to her
winter home in Mexico. The owner of *Hannah Rose*
had sailed down to Colombia from Mexico with his friends Dale
and Ed, but had to fly home to work, and so a third body was
needed. My arrival seemed to have worked out well for everyone.
They needed help on board, I needed to get to Panama.

Ed and Dale were very different characters but they shared a
wandering spirit, a love of sailing, and a fondness for booze. Ed
(Rum and Coke) was a portly Californian with a bushy grey
moustache. A handy-man by trade he had married after a hard-
drinking, womanising youth of long hair and folk concerts. They
bought a small boat and sailed away. Sadly the happy times had not
lasted and he now lived on his own in a trailer park in Los
Angeles. Ed was generous, friendly, and cooked great pork chops.
He adored nature, stopping for ages to watch birds or dolphins or
turtles and making a fuss over whatever unloved stray dogs we
encountered on shore.

Dale (Gin and Tonic; red wine) was an expert climber, skier
and sailor, with mad tales of winter ascents of Denali and first
descents of crazy ski routes on Mount Rainier close to his native
Seattle. He had run a psychiatric institution for many years but
had now opted for a freer life as a carpenter, getting out to the

mountains or away on a boat whenever he could. I think Dale saw some of his younger self in me. He was an ardent George Bush hater, a skeptic, a passionate atheist and a terrible cook.

We left Colombia with a tear in the eye, hoisted the sails, and set a course for Panama. It had taken about a week for us to get the boat ready to leave and to clear the paperwork. Bobbing slowly out of Cartagena harbour past the high steel flanks of an American gunship on this classic drug smuggling route, we were a little unnerved that we could not raise the coastguard on the radio for permission to leave Colombian waters. As *Hannah Rose*, our little 37-foot yacht, pulled further and further from shore I sat at the radio repeating over and over our yacht name and our request to speak with the coastguard. No reply, no reply, no reply and we were sailing ever further from shore. Suddenly Dale cried, "f★★★ 'em! Let's have a drink and get out of here!" We were on our way and I waved farewell to South America.

Cartagena had been unpleasantly hot and sweaty for working on the boat so Dale and Ed had decided that it would be preferable to get away as soon as possible and spend a few days finishing our repairs, anchored somewhere calm and clean with a cooling breeze instead. The San Blas Islands are the true tropical cliché of tiny islands. No more than a few palm trees ringed by sand and circled in coral reefs. We found a tranquil, empty cove that was ideal for the maintenance work required, and for me to recover from my usual few days of seasickness. When work became too hot and sweaty we could just jump overboard for a refreshing swim. I spent most of those days holding my breath and diving down to scrape a year's growth of barnacles off the bottom of the boat. It was my first insight that owning a yacht is not as glamorous as it sounds. Something is always broken and yacht owners must feel like pelicans: whichever way they look there is always an enormous bill in front of them.

I was working hard on the yacht and so, after a few days at sea, Dale and Ed asked me if I would like to accompany them all the way to Mexico. I would be a big help to them in negotiating the Spanish-speaking officials along the way as well as a useful spare body and a willing cook. It felt good to be useful, to be wanted, to be part of a team. I had not really helped anybody since I left home yet so many people had helped me.

Their suggestion threw up one of the regular dilemmas for me as to what exactly I wanted out of this expedition. I was on this boat now because there was no road between Colombia and Panama, and I had opted out of coming through the jungle. But there was a perfectly good road between Panama and Mexico. Was I not duty bound to ride it according to the challenge I had set myself?

I asked myself what would be more exciting, interesting and rewarding: two months at sea, or two more months on the bike along a road that I had already ridden? That my answer was not the bike perhaps suggests that I should have been trying to sail round the world rather than cycle it. I knew that road because I had already ridden it during a summer holiday when I was at university. If I had ridden it before, did I really have to make myself ride it again? I felt that two months at sea would be a more novel experience, that I would learn more, and that it would be good fun as well. I often had to remind myself that having fun was actually allowed on this trip. I did not have to always inflict puritanical options on myself. So I thanked Dale and Ed for their invitation, accepted it, and settled in to sail up the Pacific coast of Central America. By bike or by boat, I was edging ever closer to home. I cast an anxious eye at how few books there were on the small shelf above the navigation table. I had already read most of them. I feared that I would end up having to read Ed's cowboy novellas before the end of our journey, '…his eyes were cold flint as the hot lead flew. But only he could save the world now. And maybe, just maybe, the beautiful woman he loved.'

We sailed on to more pristine islands in the San Blas archipelago and spent two days there stripping and re-greasing winches. I tried in vain to tune the shortwave radio to catch the World Cup rugby final. As England were out-playing Australia and Jonny Wilkinson kicked off a joyous English celebration, I was lying in the sunshine on a yacht in a tropical archipelago. Paradise is no place to be at times like that.

After dark I would dive from the bow into the warm black

water and haul myself down the slimy anchor chain to the sandy lagoon bottom then burst back up to the surface, lungs gasping, a handful of wet sand the proof of where I had been. I swam on my back and spooned spirals of glowing phosphorescent water with my hands, the light rising up from under the water into the saucers of moonlight that flitted across the calm surface. The air and water were almost the same temperature. The stars, the moonlight and the phosphorescence all merged with the black sky and sea, cocooning me in a warm feeling of awe at the unblemished beauty, majesty and scale of our surroundings. I daydreamed about Sarah, the girl I left behind. About my chances of getting back together with her when I got home, persuading her to quit her job and heading off to share the magical calm of the world with her. The odds of achieving all three were slim, but if I could achieve just one I would be happy.

The ocean was full of life. Occasional tuna and dorado tinkled the bells on our trailing fishing lines, punctuating the hours and enlivening our diet. We would dash to the stern in excitement when we heard the bells and haul in our catch. As part of my efforts to make myself useful on board I had taken on almost all of the cooking duties. I would prepare *ceviche* or slice fillets from the fish and fry them in butter, lime and a drop of coconut milk. I tossed the scraps and guts overboard to feed the next generation of my dinner.

Birds tried, with admirable perseverance and little common sense, to land atop our wildly swaying mast. Gormless turtles slept on the surface until, waking confused at our approach, they pawed at the surface and tried their best to dive quickly. A seagull perched on a turtle eyed us beadily as the turtle dived and it was forced to fly off in search of a new resting spot. Whales broached occasionally and, best of all, dolphins raced in our bow wave, leaping high out of the water, spinning and flipping spectacularly. One morning I was snatched back into the world I used to know when we pulled into in a small bay to refill our water tanks. We learned that Saddam Hussein had been captured. I often wish that I was back aboard the uncomplicated world of the *Hannah Rose* watching dolphins and the sunrise.

A wrecked yacht on a reef warned of hazards as we prepared to anchor in 30 feet of water in another warm lagoon. Spumes of spray leapt from the encircling reefs and we were on edge as we guided the boat carefully through the hazards. Inside the lagoon all was calm. Cuna Indians in dugout canoes paddled to our yacht from the nearest island to try to sell us crabs, lobsters and coconut.

The cheery Cuna ladies sported pudding bowl haircuts, gold rings in their nose like a bull, rouged cheeks, bead bangles tight all the way up their forearms and calves and bodies wrapped in intricate sarongs, called *mola*. Their children wore old shorts and T-shirts. To my delight, one little boy, Eric, was sporting a Leeds United shirt (fake, circa 1997). He posed for a photo with me, smiling at my obvious pleasure at meeting my first ever fellow Leeds supporter.

The Cuna were friendly and not too pushy as they tried to sell us *mola*, but I still felt uneasy amongst them. For the past couple of years I had tried my best to live similarly to the people I met along the way, living simply, and trying to be accepted as a fellow human rather than as a mobile cash-point or an über-rich European freakshow. One of the appeals of travelling by bicycle is that you do not make an immediate display of vast relative wealth. This means one less barrier to overcome when you meet new people. When you arrive by yacht it is impossible to conceal or deny. Looking down on the Cuna's homemade, primitive canoes from the shining white yacht I was on, I could no longer keep up any pretence to myself about the affluent society I came from. Did my life have anything at all in common with these people? I cringed at what they must think of me, at the jealousy, distaste and resentment that they were bound to feel. Once again, this journey was teaching me lessons. It was apparent, on those sunny days in paradise, sitting on the gunwales of an expensive yacht, sharing questions and answers and insights about our lives with the cheerful Cuna, that being rich or foreign are not in themselves any barrier to interaction.

Being the junior crew member earned me the 'graveyard watch' each night, but I loved the midnight watch. Dale and Ed were sleeping, and I was in sole control of the boat. I enjoyed the quietness, sitting on the cockpit roof in just a pair of shorts, silver waves splashing the hull, sails and halyards flapping occasionally. During the day we all worked, slept and relaxed on an informal basis. But our evening routine was set. After I cooked dinner, Ed and I headed for our bunks while Dale the night owl remained on deck smoking cigarettes and drinking wine. He woke me at midnight and I took over until 4am when I would wake Ed to see in the dawn and I slept once more until breakfast.

Alone on deck I scanned the horizon for ships, checked the charts, plotted our route and adjusted course if necessary. There were frequent tropical lightning storms around the horizon, with sheet lightning lighting up the whole sky. Green phosphorescence streamed behind the boat as I lay on my back comparing my simple star chart with the mighty canopy above me. I taught myself to navigate with the sextant, using the GPS to check my calculations and marvelling that a couple of stars, or the sun and a wristwatch, could reveal to me exactly where on the planet I was. I listened to squeaking, distant voices on the shortwave radio, a host of languages from all over the planet swirling together around the ether, oscillating between loud and clear and faint and distant. Voices bringing news, weather, religion, music and chatter into our boat. One night, hunkered at the navigation table under the glow of the GPS and the radar, a distant voice from a crackling BBC World Service told me that Leeds United had just got a draw at Manchester City and I was glad, feeling a small connection with home despite being so far away. Another night the GPS ticked past 90 degrees West: I was a quarter of the way round the world now.

I sneaked the satellite phone up on to deck. Calls were very expensive so it was only supposed to be used in emergencies. Sitting on deck in the darkness, I was nervous but excited. I wanted to phone Sarah at work in her office to wish her a Happy Birthday. I had not spoken to her since I was in Cape Town almost a year earlier. It seemed weird that she was in a smart, busy air-conditioned office whilst I was sitting with salt-tangled hair on a yacht in the pitch blackness of an ocean. As I dialled the only voice I heard was an automated one with the disappointing news that the phone number I had for Sarah was no longer valid.

The continent-spanning Panama Canal spares ships a journey

of two months and 9,000 miles around the treacherous Cape Horn. The canal is an astonishing construction achievement that effectively formed and defined a nation. Indeed Panama began with a neat palindrome, 'a man, a plan, a canal: Panama!' The man was Ferdinand de Lessops, buoyed by his success in the construction of the Suez Canal. His plan was to repeat the feat at Panama, but after a decade of work only 20 miles of canal had been dug. The company crashed and the venture ended in disaster, defeated by extravagant living and tropical disease. At the same time as the French effort, the USA was working on its own canal across Nicaragua. This project was also doomed and ran out of money. The Americans switched their operation to Panama, and began with an enormous operation to sanitise the canal area from tropical diseases, notably the mosquito-borne Yellow Fever. They launched a massive pesticide-spraying, mosquito-slaughtering campaign. This ground-breaking procedure was one of the prime factors in ensuring the canal's successful completion in 1914. The logistics involved in constructing the canal were phenomenal. The total length of boreholes drilled during the canal's construction could pass right through the centre of the Earth, and the excavation was equivalent to a canal 55 feet wide and 10 feet deep, right the way across the United States.

We docked in Colón at the mouth of the canal and I spent my 27th birthday queuing in sweaty offices to collect the stamps necessary for our passage through the canal. Then we waited several more days until our turn to transit came. After piles more paperwork an experienced pilot joined us on board to guide us through the canal. As we pulled into the Gatun locks behind an enormous cargo ship, I said a final farewell to the Atlantic Ocean as the gates closed behind us. The waters poured into the lock, swirling and curling around the *Hannah Rose*, and we rose slowly above sea level to begin our journey across the isthmus to the Pacific Ocean. At the top of the third lock we eased forwards into a gigantic artificial lake, 85 feet above sea level.

Hundreds of islands, once hill tops, dotted the lake. We followed the channel marked with red and green buoys past the islands, through the sweet smell of vegetation and the shrieks of howler monkeys in the forest. Toucans flew past and enormous ships looked incongruous, appearing from behind forested hills. From the lake we entered the eight-mile Gaillard Cut, a narrow channel leading to the Miraflores locks that lowered us efficiently, dropping down out of sight of the spectators' galleries and into the Pacific Ocean. We had travelled from the Atlantic to the Pacific in eight hours and we sailed under the Bridge of the Americas into Panama City and the North American continent.

By Christmas Eve we were in the Gulf of Tehuantepec, notorious for gales and storms. We hugged the coast tightly, moving like guilty children, sure that trouble is about to catch up with them. We were very close to the shore, to palm trees and palm huts and small, thin fishing boats pulled high up the beach.

Trouble did catch up with us, and the storm hit in the night. The whetted wind shrieked and ropes cracked and we scurried around dropping all the sails. The foredeck lights threw wild shadows from the thrashing American and Mexican flags on the mast as I clawed my way up to the bow to help pack away a sail with the boat heeling and salt spray stinging. I was holding on very tight and feeling very alive. Waves thundered over us and I braced hard, clinging to whatever was to hand as the gale peaked at 56 knots. The grey waves spat cold spray across the marble-streaked waters, crouching and sprinting from the crests, tumbling over in the wind. I knew little enough about sailing to find it all great fun. When I was helming, soaked by the waves that were crashing over us, Dale cursed the saltiness of his spray-filled gin, tonic was not taken in these situations, and I sang the Foo Fighters at the top of my voice, *'it's times like these, you learn to live again!'* It was a spectacular Christmas Eve and certainly preferable to battling crowded shopping streets back home.

On Christmas Day Santa brought us the perfect present: a calm, sunny morning. We set about clearing up the chaos below decks. Food, plates, books and clothes were strewn in puddles everywhere. Later that day we reached the bay of Zihuatanejo where I was going to leave the boat, leave the company of Dale and Ed, get back on my bike and head for the hills. I was excited by the smells and variety of everything on shore, by the variety of shades of the colour green and by the prospect of having a spacious campsite. I looked forward to not having to crouch or brace as I walked around, not having a salt-crusted bed and not having to wedge myself into a damp bunk to counter the rocking of the boat. The prospect of dry, motionless sleep was very appealing.

It was good to be independent again. Good to be on the road, in the tent, wherever I wanted. I was seeing life through fresh eyes again. After so long at sea I appreciated the beauty of hills, the colour of trees, the pain and sweat of climbing, the slowness and absurdity of crossing countries by bicycle, the stimulation of daily interaction with new people. Being unfit again gave me a fresh insight to how physically gruelling my life was, and how much I took that for granted when I was at peak fitness. I looked forward to riding hard again. I looked forward to getting fit again. My love of the road was back.

Closer now

Poor Mexico! So far from God, so close to the United States.
— Porfirio Díaz

After reassembling my salt-crusted, rusted bike which had been lashed to the stern of *Hannah Rose* for two months, I pedalled away from the ocean and towards Mexico City. There my path would cross that of my previous journey and I could ride north once again. After a mountainous few days that were a shock to my body after two seaborne, immobile months, I arrived in the staggering enormity of Mexico City. It took another full day of riding to reach the city centre through a grid-locked chaos of honking green-and-white VW Beetle taxis and irate and perspiring motorists. The first impression of Mexico City is of its utter vastness. Compared to the concrete sprawl of 23 million people, the seething wildebeest migration of the Serengeti resembles a few pals at a quiet game of bridge. One of mankind's largest gatherings is squeezed into a shallow valley with insufficient water, roads or infrastructure to cope. A shroud of smog and an impending water crisis on a colossal scale hang over the city. The city is sinking under the pressure, literally sinking: there is the astonishing sight of large buildings that are sinking slowly but surely into the soft earth, their doors noticeably lower than the pavements. Mexico City is an uncomfortable demonstration of how we are destroying our environment.

With that many people living their lives at Latino volume there is a tremendous energy to the city and inexhaustible variety. So many bars and *barrios*, lifestyles and stories: you could never truly know Mexico City. I spent a couple of weeks trying to grasp a slice of it. The city's enormous central Zócalo plaza is a rare focus point in the out-of-control growth and evolution of the uncontrollable beast. The plaza's hundreds of metres of open space are a welcome respite for your senses. In the centre of the world's second largest square (only Red Square in Moscow is larger), flies an enormous Mexican flag, 25 metres across. The red, white and green stripes undulated slowly in the hazy polluted sky.

On one side of the Zócalo is the National Palace where Diego Rivera's superb larger-than-life murals, made famous to uncultured souls like myself through the film *Frida*, depict the history of Mexico. Rivera's Social Realism is powerful and damning with corrupt politicians, evil looking conquistadors, down-trodden Aztecs, and fornicating, fat Catholic clergy.

On another side of the Zócalo is the cathedral, a mighty edifice crammed with lavish gold and icons of miracles and martyrdom. The whole structure, built on soft land, has visibly subsided several feet below ground level. Walking inside feels like being at sea, as the floor rolls and the horizons are not horizontal. Wonky columns rise at odd angles. The cathedral represents the Catholicism that the Spanish conquistadors imported to Mexico, that is today the religion of all Latin America. The cathedral was built on the very heart of the city of Tenochtitlan, the sacred Aztec city. Tenochtitlan was razed by the Spaniards and Mexico City was built provocatively over the ruins. Now, in a twist of ironic symbolism, as the cathedral sinks slowly into the soggy earth, the ancient pyramids that were buried are rising out of the earth beside it once again.

As I rode into Mexico City, I passed gigantic rubbish dumps on which people were living a grim life as professional scavengers. Their homes were built on the stinking dumps out of rubbish. Their survival depended solely upon what they could salvage from what the rest of society had discarded. A few days later, I found myself at a party in a penthouse suite of an ostentatious extravagance difficult to find even in rich London. The contrast with the families in the rubbish dump was deeply disturbing. The walls of the apartment's library were lined from floor to ceiling with books. They had all been bought brand new and none of them had been read. They served no other purpose than to look impressive.

Music thumped and rich, beautiful people danced and drank and snorted cocaine. I loitered in a corner feeling like an idiot. On a plinth in the hall was a life-sized bronze bust of the girl who lived in the apartment her Daddy had bought for her. She was depicted in a classical pose with her hair flowing in an imaginary breeze and her two silly little dogs clutched to her chest.

To my surprise and embarrassment, the morning that I left my hosts in Mexico City, I burst into tears at the breakfast table. Previously I had always managed to delay my tears until after saying goodbye. I had been treated so kindly by the family of a friend of a friend and had felt so comfortable with them, I had shared long lunches with the whole extended family, laughing and chatting over olives and tequila. I had, for the first time in many months, been stationary and relaxed for long enough to make really good friends. When my friend, Sofia, had to go away for two days she gave me a list of girls' telephone numbers. They had all been briefed to call and entertain me. But, yet again I had to say goodbye.

A television news crew followed me out of the city and cars hooted cheery recognition from an interview I had given. I often did interviews like this, but in Mexico they had generated by far the greatest response, with cars hooting and waving at me for days, and a steady stream of free food at *taco* stands.

I gave a talk about my ride at a halfway house for homeless children in Guadalajara. All of the children had been addicted to drugs and had committed crimes to fund their habit. The home was trying to prepare the children for release and reduce the chances of their re-offending. It was rewarding to talk with children who really needed some dreams and goals. They needed the focus and structure which had been gifted to me in my own upbringing to fight against the hand they had been dealt, against their own mistakes and ultimately try to get their lives back on track. I loved the excitement that those tough children showed when they saw my pictures of elephants and dolphins and Maasai men with spears. They had countless questions at the end and I was interested to hear them ask questions that were virtually identical to those asked earlier in the day, by children at an affluent private school where I had spoken.

The only country in all the Americas I had to go through the rigmarole of obtaining a visa for was the USA. This was because I needed more than the three months allocated on a tourist visa. It appeared that the 'special relationship' was not special enough. After a series of very unhelpful phone calls with the American consulate in Mexico City, charged at an offensive 50p per minute, I headed to the consulate in Guadalajara to apply for my visa there instead.

Outside I found a queue, 200 metres long, of people hoping to get to America. Two women walked up and down the line renting out chairs. Evidently the queue was going to take hours. Feeling a bit cheeky, I strolled nonchalantly to the front of the queue. I justified it as a reward for a year of people shouting, "*gringo*," at me every day. I waved my British passport at the American policeman on the door and, to my surprise, I was shown straight inside.

I jumped a few more queues, answered a few questions put to me in a voice notably friendlier than that used for most other applicants, I handed over $100 and emerged with a visa valid for ten years.

I had been looking forward to seeing the spectacular Copper Canyon in northern Mexico, a canyon system larger and deeper than even the Grand Canyon. However a good friend who I had been planning to visit in Los Angeles emailed me to say that her dates for moving back to the UK had changed. I was faced with a dilemma that neatly summed up much of how I had been feeling recently. Which was more important; superb scenery and new sights, or seeing a friend? A friend who knew me, somebody who shared common memories and experiences was a precious thing, something that I had only come to appreciate fully by giving it up. For two-and-a-half years I had interacted predominantly with strangers. It was a privileged experience, but the prospect of staying with an old friend was more enticing than yet more spectacular scenery. I abandoned the canyon and rode due north on the quick coastal road instead.

I rode quickly. For a few days I simply rode up a toll road, enjoying the safety of the broad hard shoulder and the chance to listen to music and blast through some miles. The road was dull and the only Mexicans I met were toll booth attendants, numbed by the monotony of their job. One toll booth was bypassed by all the traffic as everyone was just turning off the tarmac and rattling their way round the booth on a dirt track before resuming their journey, gratis, on the other side. The attendant looked on with glazed, slack-jawed indifference.

Tiring of this life I returned to the longer, winding country roads with lunatic macho overtaking, but with all that I enjoyed about Mexico as well. I passed sleepy villages, bent old pigtailed women wearing skirts, cardigans and wide hats, carrying piles of firewood, and men who called out to me from garages and fields. There were shaded trees to snooze under and the gloomy stores that sell the same things the world over: dusty packs of pasta, cans of sardines spotted with rust, tins of powdered milk, washing powder, warm fizzy drinks and stale biscuits. In the plazas old men sat in the white sunlight and watched the world go by, their faces carved with shadows beneath wide-brimmed sombreros. Curious old ladies stared at me unblinking. Preconceptions are generally there to be broken but I was delighted to see that, in the best tradition of Speedy Gonzalez, rural Mexican men really did wear very large sombreros and shout, "*andalé! andalé!*"

One evening I sat by my campfire dismantling a pedal that kept locking tight and seizing as I rode. I repacked it with grease but the problem persisted. I had no more ideas about how to fix it so I simply removed all the ball bearings and then put the remains of the pedal back together. It seemed to work perfectly! But surely those ball bearings had some sort of purpose?

After a couple more days the pedal seized up for good. I continued pedalling with one leg, past fields of baseball-capped tomato pickers and on until I reached a town where a mechanic heaved off the seized pedal with an enormous spanner and sold me the pedals from his own bike. Bi-pedalled once more I continued, past the turning to a town called Piggy Back, on a road busy with trundling trucks loaded high with tomatoes. I gathered sufficient fallen tomatoes from the roadside to keep myself well fed. The towns along the road became more dilapidated and irrigated fields became more scarce. Both the land and the towns were becoming more dusty, drab and lifeless. It felt as though the world was fizzling out to nothing as the cacti multiplied and the towns became fewer. What a shock it was going to be to cross the border into America!

The Sonora desert was a hot, scrubby expanse of rocky hillocks and cacti. The hot black road steadily ate up the empty expanse of miles, and seemed to exist solely to get everyone to the American border. Heat shimmered on the horizon and the tarmac reflected pulses of heat up at me. The border was all consuming in my thoughts now. The desert nights were cold and, though I was lugging six books around with me, I had only a few T-shirts to wear. My tent was smeared with a thin veil of ice by morning and I shivered until the fierce sun rose and the sweating began once more. Campsites through the Sonora desert were precious times for me, times to reflect on my ride through Latin America and enjoy the last of this world before the USA hit me. They were peaceful, idyllic campsites, far from the road, hidden behind cacti. The moon, growing larger at every camp, raced relentlessly through patchy clouds.

By the time the moon was new again I would be in America. Sitting beside my fires I watched the horizons melt from orange to purple as the first stars burst out with the brightness typical of cold nights. I was going to miss Latin America. I hoped that I would return to live here one day. Some things were annoying, certainly: the machismo, the lateness for everything, too much talking and insufficient listening, an occasional superficiality. But the tightness and importance of families, the love of life, the culture and landscapes, the beautiful language, soft as music and light as spray, huge meals, parties and the warmth of the people more than compensated.

Ten miles ahead lay the border, one of the most striking border crossings of all the arbitrary lines I had crossed on the journey. It was not just the border between two nations, but between two ways of life. I camped a few miles before Nogales and lit my final campfire in Latin America, well hidden in a wood. Tomorrow night I would have a bed to sleep in, a much-needed shower, and people to talk to in English.

I had never been to America, though in many ways I felt familiar with it: the big HOLLYWOOD sign, the Golden Gate Bridge, fat cops eating doughnuts, Britney Spears. Now I was excited to really see the place, from the 2-Dimensional world of television and popular culture to the 3-D reality of that most unreal world. I was intrigued. Something I enjoyed during my ride was the dissolving of the preconceptions that invariably exist about every country. In every country people cautioned me about their dangerous, thieving neighbours but assured me that their own country was perfectly safe.

More than for any other country, polarised opinions about the USA range between envy and scorn, hatred and imitation. I had been surprised at just how strong the global anti-US feeling was, matched only perhaps by the number of people who asked me how they could get an American visa. I did understand the resentment: is it mere coincidence that the country is called, in big capital letters, "US"? Yet I had always been a fan of the States; of their self earned success, the hard-working mentality and *Baywatch*. So I was looking forward to letting America speak for herself. I was curious about what I would find. I leaned forward to the next crazy 'venture beneath the skies.

I was excited about being back in a rich country again, speaking English, being anonymous and ignored, exploring my preconceptions. But would it be fun or would the Material World be too easy and boring? My gluttonous, slothful, greedy side – three sins out of the seven – was impatient for the next few months; the burgers, the smooth and easy roads, the shiny bike shops. Yet there was nowhere I would have rather been that night than out there dreaming and homeless in the desert, for no luxury home can compare with a small campfire, a jewel-bright Venus welcoming the other stars to the night, and the wistful solitude of the desert at night.

In the morning I wrote in my diary:

It's early and the sun slants sideways though the sky. Nogales,

Mexico. The border with the United States of America. It's cold and ice rattles in my water bottles. Smoke from a thousand wood stoves blankets blue over the town. Stars of sunlight burst from the corrugated iron roofs of the shacks on the hillsides. It's quiet. A few dogs bark and somewhere the inevitable developing world rooster is crowing. Sunday morning. Piles of rubbish spill down slopes, lying where it was dumped. Smoke smoulders from a few half-hearted attempts to burn it. Thin dogs slink over the mess. Layers of hills rise around the town, shadowed dark blue in the east, glowing orange-brown in the west as they reflect the rising sun. My toes are cold but my back is warm and I'm making excuses to linger.

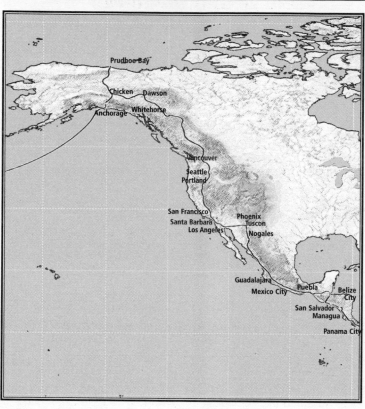

Panama to Anchorage

Large and in charge

Travel is fatal to prejudice, bigotry, and narrow-mindedness.
— Mark Twain

I wiped my hands on my dirty trousers at the border control, trying to clean them for the fingerprint-scanning machine. The customs officer studied my passport, looked up at me, flicked back through the pages of my passport, looked at my bike and said, "Sir, would you mind coming into the office, please?" in a tone that suggested neither 'Sir' nor 'please.'

In his office he sat down at his computer on the other side of his desk with a grunt. He tapped at the keys for a few moments, scrutinising the screen in front of him then asked, "Sir, could you tell me please why you have a visa for Iran in your passport?"

"Well I thought that it sounded like a nice place to bicycle through."

Rattle, rattle, rattle on the keyboard. "And Sudan, Sir? Syria? Lebanon? Pakistan? Colombia?" He didn't seem convinced that they all sounded like nice places to bicycle through. As he grumbled suspiciously I had a brainwave business idea. All of those countries are incredible places with such variety of history and culture, landscapes, food and wonderful inhabitants. There must be a market for '*Axis-of-Evil Holidays* plc.' I had the feeling that the customs guy would not be one of my first clients. He grunted a few more times then handed back my passport. I was on my way.

It was exciting to be at a new beginning once more. America — wanderlust surged through me as I hoped for exciting times in new places. Everything was new, everything filled with potential. I pedalled away from the border in high spirits. "Woohoo!" I whooped to the highway ahead of me. The hot, dry earth had not changed over the past mile but everything else had.

The words 'LARGE AND IN CHARGE' scrolled in bold lights across a billboard close to the border. A fitting slogan as I entered the United States? Perhaps, but it was only an advert for McDonald's. I began reading shop signs and billboards voraciously, drinking in the rarity of completely understanding everything. I could understand everything people said and, talking to people, I would be able to express myself perfectly again.

After the separate worlds of Europe, the Middle East and North Africa, sub-Saharan Africa, and Latin America I was definitely in a New World again now. I found myself converting miles back into kilometres in my head, the opposite of what I did everywhere else in the world, and bemoaning how much longer a mile felt than a kilometre. I pulled into a roadside rest area to refill my water bottles as my odometer ticked over to 40,000 kilometres – or 25,000 miles. Clean smelling toilets, fresh water, no litter and nobody saying hello to me: I was not used to all of this. There were white people all around, they looked so pale and drained in comparison to Latinos. I kept thinking that I recognised people. I didn't actually know any of them, it was just that I was surrounded by people who looked similar to me. I had grown accustomed to being a minority. In the restroom, I looked in a mirror in for the first time in a fortnight. I was shocked at how filthy my face was. It was surprising that I was allowed across the border at all.

In Tucson I went with the first of so many kind American hosts to a supermarket. I gawped at the heaving shelves, the individually wrapped tomatoes, the astonishing variety of breakfast cereal and a whole aisle of pet food flavours. Nobody stared at me (I had washed my face by now). Paul Theroux wrote that, "one of the pleasures of travel is being anonymous." A white person on a bicycle in most parts of the world would disagree with him, but in America I was anonymous at last, and it was a pleasure.

I felt self-conscious talking in English; everybody could overhear us and understand our banal discussion about how much broccoli we would need for supper. But I could also listen in to everybody else's conversations. Where people's daily chat in Arabic or Amharic or Xhosa or Quechuan had sounded exciting and exotic I now realised anew, now that I could understand it again, that most of what people talk about is pretty mundane and unexciting.

While in many ways the US was much like the fortunate life I had been brought up with, where it is normal to have some degree of cash to spend, food to eat, clean water to drink and so on, I kept catching myself thinking like an outsider. I was comfortable now with the frustrations and inconveniences of life in the developing world, and I enjoyed its good sides too. Whilst I knew that I could never belong there, I did feel at ease. Now, as I rode along in America I was mesmerised by what, in contrast to much of what I had seen, was the unimaginable wealth around me. Stepping back from things sometimes alters your perspective. I thought of the man in Africa who asked a friend of mine in disbelief, "is it true that in your country you really give food to birds?"

I had been confused for a long time about why most countries are poor and a few are rich. Was it as simple as environmental and geographical differences and then centuries of positive and negative feedback loops? I had seen an awful lot of poverty since leaving Western Europe. I had not seen many thriving nations. Perhaps America could help shed some light on this depressing conundrum. America is such a young country, yet she has risen so fast from "barbarism to decadence." Perhaps, as Oscar Wilde mused, without the usual intervening period of civilisation. To have caught up, and overtaken, every country on Earth in just two centuries was remarkable. What had gone so right there? What could they teach the world? At the same time I was interested in the different perspectives of hardship and poverty. Do a rural Mexican family saving money for a new tin roof for their shack and a Californian family living ten miles away who are unable to afford a second car experience different feelings of struggle? And if you feel unhappy is there any point in differentiating that feeling along a scale of poverty and misery?

Phoenix was a city where, even after a week, I had absolutely no idea where I was at any time. Wherever I turned were identical malls, gigantic supermarkets, swathes of new housing and brand logos in bright neon lights. Arriving at my destination always came as a surprise. Even poor people's houses looked neat, inviting and affluent. The roads were smooth, traffic lights worked, cars were big and shiny, shops were crammed with goodies. I felt like I was on a film set: everything looked so glossy and seemed oddly familiar to me, the yellow school buses, the mail boxes with little arms on the front lawns, despite me only having seen it all on TV before. Life in America was, in many ways, very similar to life in England, but there were enough slight differences to keep me entertained. A sign outside a hardware store advertised 'Lawns & Garden, Bike Parts, Cooler Supplies, Ammunition,' and I was greatly amused by a signpost beside the road cautioning, 'STATE PRISON. DO NOT STOP FOR HITCH HIKERS.'

Apart from the novelty gawping value of being in the land of plenty, cycling through American towns and villages was actually quite boring. In most places in the world you see people working outside, either in the fields or on the carcasses of old vehicles. People sit outside their homes to peel potatoes and watch the world. Families chat in the street. Roads are busy with farmers and their animals or children walking to school. Street vendors and windscreen-cleaning boys liven up city streets. There is always something to look at, always someone to greet, always children waving at you. But America was an insulated, insular, inside world. Nearly everybody was in a car, and those few not in cars avoided catching my eye in case I then decided to blow them away with a big-ass gun. Everywhere was quiet, so finding my way through towns was difficult as there were few people to ask directions from. Drivers waiting at traffic lights were scared if I approached their vehicle to check my route. Some people refused to look at me, even when I asked a simple question like, "Is this the way to Amarillo?" Some quickly wound up their windows as I approached. One family car even gunned its engine and darted through a red light to get away from me. I sought out a mirror to check whether I had suddenly become more hideous than usual.

Asking for directions I soon learned that, if I could not find friendly Mexican street-sweepers, it was best to stop ten yards away from people and hail loudly in my best English accent. I realised how much I had come to take for granted in countries where people trust you enough to stop and talk, and care enough to try to help you. The irony in America was that once people understood that I was English, and I really did only want directions, they were invariably very friendly, courteous and welcoming. People would say, "enjoy our country," with a pride not found in England.

Riding out of cities felt like being trapped in a hamster's wheel as shopping malls rotated by for mile after mile. Suburbia sprawled forever. Fast food joints were rife and a smell of burgers filled the air, but for four days I ate nothing except a carrier bag of energy bars I had been given at a talk that I gave. One bar was nice, two were OK. But breakfast, lunch and dinner for four days almost broke me.

I realise now, with shame, that a part of me had been looking forward to snorting in derision at the war-hungry, nationalistic, ignorant population of America driving to the supermarket to load up on guns and bullets. Hopes were high of novelty-boobed, excessively blonde airheads, and that was just the men, as I rode north through Malibu and Beverly Hills. I did see a 'God Bless America Barber Shop,' and a billboard shouting, 'DON'T YOU BUY NO UGLY SMALL TRUCK,' and I met a man who said that he would not visit England because, "I only go to countries where I'm allowed guns."

But my real impressions of America were of efficiency, a strong moral conscience, quiet cleanliness, safe streets and very polite people. It was a fantastic place and it felt like an ideal role model to be the dominant nation on earth. Once again I was confronted with the obvious but globally ignored truth, that the preconceptions we hold about other cultures and countries are often misplaced, simplistic or just plain wrong. I met so many Americans who cared about the environment, who worried about their government's foreign policy, and about the image that America portrays to the world through exports such as Jerry Springer, Michael Jackson and George W. Bush.

Nate, a Baptist youth minister, looked after me in Phoenix. We drove together to see the Grand Canyon, that most famous of big holes. I knew that we were on the right road because a huge

McDonald's billboard told us that we were. The road climbed steadily higher until snow was falling in heavy flakes through thick fog. We arrived at the canyon to find that it had played an impressive disappearing act in the fog. I longed to be eight again just to be able to stamp my feet and howl, "But you promised we were going to see the Grand Canyon!" To see nothing at all of this wonder was so disappointing.

Fortunately, after a couple of hours the fog began to open in gasps showing tempting, tantalising glimpses down into a billion years of history. The sheer depth of the canyon and the eternal number of shapes and shades were mesmerising. It was a wonderful sight, and hurling snowballs into the void to watch them fall, fall, fall, fall is perfect behaviour for all closet eight-year-olds.

I swallowed my principles and went onto the *Fox News Breakfast Show* to talk about my trip, promote *Hope and Homes for Children*, and to try to find a sponsor to replace my fast-dying bike. On top of that somebody gave me $100 to wear a T-shirt with the logo of his construction business when I went on the show. I entered the studio to meet the presenters. Slathered in fake tan the man was a classic caricature of the cheesy breakfast show host. Crushing and pumping my hand up and down, and grinning brilliantly he boomed, "Hi, I'm Mike Raffone. But I'm sure you knew that already!"

"Errr…" I replied and was whisked in front of the cameras and spotlights to describe my journey in about 25 seconds before the weather forecast and a commercial break.

My interview failed to interest any bike companies but, thanks to Nate, a group of people from various Mormon and Baptist churches in Phoenix clubbed together and bought me a new bike. It was an extremely kind, generous act, and as I purred down the remaining roads of my world I constantly remembered the friends who had made it possible. I was disappointed to discover however that, even on a very shiny bicycle far smarter than I had ever ridden, 100 miles still hurts. On top of their generosity, hospitality, and friendship, Nate's friends threw a birthday party for me on my final night in Phoenix, a mere three months late, or nine months early. They sent me on my way with a high-calorie birthday cake and a chocolate éclair as big as a brick.

I spent an enjoyable weekend with the climber Tom Whittaker and his family in the hills north of Phoenix. Tom, an ex-pat Welshman, is the first disabled person to have climbed Everest, having lost a foot in a car crash in 1979. Sitting in a sledge with his young daughter on my lap I clutched a rope attached to the back of his car whilst he drove down a snow-covered trail towing us behind. Little Georgia cheered and cried out for more as we hurtled along. Tired, laughing, and miraculously free from broken bones we all retired to a bar. The waiter asked for a credit card deposit from us to prevent us running away without paying. It seemed an unlikely scenario as we were the only people in the bar. Tom appealed to the waiter, "look at me: I only have one foot. Do you really think that I could run away?" The poor waiter did not know what to say, and fled, mortified. Tom chuckled, knowing full well that he could happily outrun the waiter.

I had never met anyone who had climbed Everest and stood on that privileged summit. My over-riding memory from the weekend was of us all lounging on his sofas, Guinness in one hand, whisky in the other, and me thinking, 'this all seems so normal, yet what extraordinary levels of drive and dream-chasing energy he must have to have joined that exclusive merry band of achievers. Everest! Wow!' I felt fortunate to be able to talk to and learn from somebody with so much determination to make the most of his life and his potential. He had also done admirable work with his *Cooperative Wilderness Handicapped Outdoor Group*. And all with one foot, giving him license to tell lame jokes too.

I rode 100 miles a day down the desert highway from Phoenix to Los Angeles, excited by the prospect of staying with an old friend. I didn't even detour to see the old London Bridge, bought by an American and now sunning herself in the Arizona desert. I was too set on racing west to California, towards the rich extravagant sunsets and the land of golden promise, excited and hopeful like the Joad family in *The Grapes of Wrath*. I had been looking forward to my ride through the USA for a long time but I was particularly excited about California. Camping in the desert at night reminded me of Jordan or northern Argentina with white dunes of sand curved around spiky tufts of yellow grass, the heavy white moon above blood-red rocky hills. What set America apart was the nose-to-tail drone of traffic throughout the night on that desert highway and the sky smeared and crossed with the vapour trails of so many planes. This was a country on the move and the torrents of trucks were a symbol of a country busy producing, consuming, buying and selling.

The desert petered out as I crossed eastern California. The grass grew greener, the cars sleeker, the houses larger and the palm trees stood tall and proud. Snow-covered mountains shone. I rode through an amazing valley with 4,000 giant wind turbines, a whole spiky, twirling valleyful of them. I was impressed. Despite this eco-effort, the car still rules in America. Cycling into Los Angeles without riding on a freeway was almost impossible. I tried hard to stay off them, but America was so car-centric that at times there was nothing for it but to brave the seething traffic. Inevitably I got caught by the police. Their siren howled behind me and I stopped to face the music. A very serious officer walked towards me, pistol on hip, looking at me through mirrored shades as though I was somewhere between dangerous and stupid. Dangerously stupid perhaps.

I escaped punishment by combining the plummiest English accent that I could muster with playing the very dumb tourist. "I'm sorry, Sir. I didn't realise that it would be dangerous to cycle in six racing lanes of cell-phone talking, coffee-drinking traffic hell. Terribly sorry!" The police car escorted me, lights flashing, to the next motorway exit. The road that he told me to take was long, hilly and eventually fizzled out. After much frustrated faffing and getting lost, I had little choice but to rejoin the freeway. I pedalled as fast as I could down the terrifying road, hoping that my policeman friend was no longer on duty.

Just when I was verging on a serious sense of humour failure at the velophobic roads I came across a cycle path pointing towards the ocean. Hugely relieved, I enjoyed 30 blissful miles of traffic-free tarmac that whisked me straight through the city to the beach. The freeway and the bike path was a good example of the yin and yang of America. The cycle path was wider and better maintained than many highways of the world. It was a delight. I also got a very immature thrill from overtaking lycra-clad men out for joyrides on their dainty little racing bikes, giving them a cheery "afternoon, chaps!" as I zipped by on my beast of burden towards the Pacific. It was childish showing-off, but it was a fun reward for 25,000 miles of training.

The beachfront was busy with cruising open-topped cars and bicycles, skaters, joggers, power walkers on their cell phones and a blonde woman carrying her tiny dog down her shirt. A homeless man sat on the beach watching handfuls of golden sand slip through his fingers. Riding along the shore towards the house of my friend, Fogie, I stopped to ask three very blonde and very pretty rollerbladers for directions. I knew exactly where I was going but it seemed a good excuse to talk to some beautiful people, and maybe even charm them with my cute English accent. As I slowed to a stop beside them, I forgot that my brand new bike had fancy clip-in pedals. With a cartoon waving of arms I wobbled, then collapsed, bike and all, in a crashing pile at their feet. I am not sure that they were impressed. California, here I am.

It was exciting, knocking on Fogie's door, to know that I would recognise the face that opened it and to be greeted and hugged by an old friend who was as happy to see me as I was to see her. To be completely relaxed and to not have to fill each other in on the history of our lives was so much easier than what I was accustomed to. It was fun to be myself and to measure my character against her, like a child on the kitchen wall, to see if I had changed much since I'd been away. Fogie was working in California as an engineering consultant. She went to America on a three-month project, did well, was asked to stay on, and two years later was still there. But her time in L.A. had come to an end and she was about to return home.

We went to an ice-hockey match, the Los Angeles Kings versus the Phoenix Coyotes. American sports are different to my experiences back home at Fortress Elland, home of Leeds United. We sat on padded, wide seats in a quiet but jolly atmosphere ready to cheer on demand when the organ music and announcer encouraged us. It felt more like a trip to the pantomime than a gladiatorial sport. The game went on for hours, pausing every few seconds for something. I had no idea where the puck was or what was going on, but I enjoyed the fights and the flashing lights and music.

We drove round Hollywood and the plush mansions of Beverley Hills, Bel-Air and Holmby Hills. Were the mansions an illustrious example of what society can achieve, or were they an indecent extravagance in a tragically skewed world? Rodeo Drive is the shopping zenith of Los Angeles' extravagance, wealth and consumerism. As I passed the shop windows of Gucci and Cartier, I wondered how it would feel to be massively rich and able to indulge in every spending whim? I realised that it must feel exactly as I feel, for in most countries people gazed at *me* in fascination, at my unattainable wealth and at my opportunities. In the USA I was riding a heavily-laden bicycle, therefore I was very poor. In most of the world, I was riding a heavily-laden bicycle and therefore I was very rich.

After a few days I had to drop Fogie at the airport for her flight home and then drive her convertible, hairdresser-style car back from the airport across the vast city. I had no insurance and was unaccustomed to travelling faster than my usual 12mph. It was a relief to get back to her house intact. I did not really enjoy the city of Los Angeles as I never got any real feel for the place. It felt like a soulless sprawl, a frogspawn of cities, a lonely place. There seemed to be no centre, no defining area for a tourist to sit and think, 'this is Los Angeles.' It was indecipherable to the fleeting visitor. It felt like the edge of the world and all of Western civilisation. I pedalled onwards quickly.

After the structural and personal anonymity of Southern California, Santa Barbara was a beautiful, refreshing welcome into the very different world that is Northern California. Squeezed between peaks and the sea, Santa Barbara's Spanish colonial architecture with terracotta tiles and the notable absence of giant billboards was delightful. There was a massive outpouring of Irishness to celebrate St. Patrick's Day, which seemed to be a bigger event in America than in Ireland with enormous volumes of Guinness flowing, rivers dyed green and a celebration of heritage. Americans are all very proud of where their ancestors came from. Everybody knew their lineage and everybody's ancestry is a mixture of nationalities. It was common for Americans to tell me they were, 'a quarter English,' or more elaborate cocktails such as 'one-eighth English, an eighth Irish, a quarter Polish and half Italian.' Even MTV celebrated St. Patrick's day, although it did so with a stirring, skirling, nostalgic bagpipe rendition of *Flower of Scotland*.

Northern California reminded me of South Africa. The coastline was very similar to the Wild Coast, there were vineyards and sunshine, and both San Francisco and Cape Town are surrounded by water and countryside. California also felt like a sunnier, quieter, prettier version of home, like England on those too-few precious summer days with the sweet reek of flowers and trees, a dazzlingly fresh blue sky and immaculate green hills, the days so wonderful that millions of people doggedly endure the rest of the British year for them. But in California that feeling was normal. I was on Route 101 and the Pacific Coast Highway, hugging the coast on a winding, hilly, cliff-edge road through glowing fields of flowers. It is the kind of spectacular road that you see in car adverts on TV. Eucalyptus groves offered welcome shade, and throaty roars of weekend motorbikers thundered past with waves and hoots. The infuriating headwind that had riled me on and off since Patagonia continued to blow strong. Grotesque elephant seals lounged territorially on the beaches like German tourists while jagged black rocks guarded the shoreline and heavy green waves smashed white in exaggerated slow motion.

Purring along one of California's superb coastal bike paths I rounded a corner and there in front of me was the Golden Gate Bridge. I let out a cheer. The bridge was an icon of my journey as Hagia Sophia, Petra, the Pyramids, Table Mountain and Machu Picchu had been before. Partly, I confess, it was from a Lonely Planet style tick-sheet mentality, a sort of, "been there, done that, need to wash my T-shirt," attitude. But these emblematic places were a measure of how far I had come, a reminder of how far I still had to go in life and how exciting the journey was. As is the case with human icons and heroes, the bridge seemed much smaller in real life than I had imagined it to be. The next landmark on my list was the Arctic Circle.

So, I arrived in shining white San Francisco. Unoriginal perhaps, but where better to read Jack Kerouac's *On The Road*, that encapsulation of wanderlust and the excitement of movement, the hope for huge times in new places, the potential of new journeys and experiences, the people you meet who define and personalise places and a tremendous excitement for life. Every moment is precious. And, boy, here I was at last! San Francisco – 'San Fran,' or 'Frisco,' as the goddam tourists call it. Little Italy full of Italians, Chinatown full of Chinese, the crazy wild Castro district and riding my darned bike up Hyde Street, that crazy steep street you always see in the car chase movies with the wild old trams and the tram-tracks burning silver-white in the sunshine, and down Lombard Street I went. They say it's the windiest of streets in the whole world, and I do sure believe them. There's eight crazy hairpin turns in just one block for the hills of Frisco are steeper than you can even imagine. I ain't never seen nothin' like 'em. San Fran is sure full of interesting people too, the ones who are mad to live, mad to talk, I felt so ordinary and un-unusual in a way I hadn't for the past couple of years. When everybody's somebody then nobody's anybody and that suited me fine. Homeless guys in Nikes with two shopping carts full of their stuff. Two carts man! California sure must be doin' something right if even these poorest and saddest of guys have gotten more stuff than I do. Old Chinese folks in the parks, doing their Tai-Chi and thinking about the past, mesmeric dreadlocked girls lookin' and smilin' real pretty. Outside a cheap Indian restaurant white men were begging and a waiter hollered, "*Tres* naan bread!" and that's three different languages in just three words, which must be some kinda record, but it sort of tells you what San Fran is like. "Ah, it was a fine night, a warm night, a wine-drinking night, a moony night, and a night to hug your girl and talk and spit and be heaven going."

I wandered the streets of San Francisco for several days, absorbing the atmosphere. The city felt a little like an island. Wherever you looked either water or hills showed at the end of the long, straight streets. Out in the bay, white triangles of sailing boats glided slowly past Alcatraz. I passed an empty barber's shop where the bald proprietor was practising his clarinet in the chair while he waited for customers. Down by the waterfront a beggar leapt out of a rubbish bin, shocking pedestrians and soliciting money. His cardboard sign that leaned against the bin read, "White Trash!"

In this city of surprises I was ambling through the slick, quiet financial district of mighty, gleaming glass towers so high that I had to lean back my head to see the sky, when I bumped into the family I had stayed with back in Guadalajara, Mexico. Who said goodbye is for ever? Dave and Stephanie had come to San Francisco for a short holiday. It was fabulous to see them again, and Carlie, my favourite two-year-old, gave me a good excuse to go and watch the sea-lions on the tacky, touristy Pier 39. Dave and Stephanie were relishing the epic responsibility and life-changing adventure of having children, an adventure that made my trip seem so selfish and trivial.

I often used to wonder how the kind strangers, the friends of friends, that I imposed myself upon reacted when I eventually left their home. Did they cheer with glee and pray to never see me again? I desperately hoped not. So I was relieved that Dave and Stephanie did not flee when they spotted me and actually seemed almost as happy to see me as I was to see them.

I lay in bed looking over San Francisco bay. The beam from the lighthouse on Alcatraz raced rhythmically across the ceiling and seared into my brain, 'You've come so far, you can't quit now. You've come so far, you can't quit now. You've come so far...' I loved San Francisco. The best city in the world? Probably. It was hard to leave.

The best consolation for getting back to work, back on the bike, was to ride a spectacular road. The coast road of California and Oregon was certainly that. It was one of my favourite rides in the world. The Redwood forests of Northern California are spell-binding. They tower to about 80 metres high, weigh 2,000 tonnes and live for a couple of thousand years. As I camped, hidden in the forest, I reflected that campsites like these were one of the reasons I had begun my ride; to be close to the sublime beauty of nature and to experience a timelessness far from the busy familiarity and comfort of home. Over the years on the road, both the journey and I had grown and changed, and I found myself contemplating 'what next?' more and more frequently. I was wrapped in the splendid contentment of dusk in the Californian Redwoods, halfway round the world, but I was daydreaming about future plans. The wilderness I loved so much was no longer sufficient. I wanted to sit there and drink in the majesty, but I also wanted to be tucked up in bed back home. I wanted so many things that I did not know what I wanted. I had so much. The expedition had opened my eyes to the potential and opportunities in the world. My problem now was choosing what to do with them.

The forest was tranquil and mesmerising in the cool air of morning. The first shafts of sunlight painted gold on the trunks as I packed my tent. Only a few birds sang. Two deer stood as statues on the riverbank when they saw me approach for a wake-up swim. A pair of water snakes swirled away across the surface as I slid into the cold water. It was Easter morning and it was extraordinary to think that as Jesus died some of the trees around me were already alive. Thousands of years of stoic, mighty, majestic silence engulfed me. Millions of small, smooth leaves shone bright and fresh and the creased trunks of the trees glowed deep red. Time stood still in this ageless scene. The forest made a powerful impact on me that Easter Sunday, more so than a church I passed that day with a note on the door, 'Sorry – no service this Easter.'

It is a sad fact that only a handful of the irreplaceable Redwood forests remain. How could anyone be so short-sighted as to want to cut down the few remaining trees? How impressively far-sighted the original people had been who thought, when the forests were still relatively widespread, "hey, we need to preserve these before it's too late."

Despite the splendour of the Redwood forests, there was still an American need for kitsch. Horrible RV parks and cheap gift shops clustered around dubious roadside attractions. There were a variety of tree-oriented novelties such as the 'Step-Thru Tree,' 'Drive-on Tree,' 'Immortal Tree' (which has heroically survived both fire and flood), the 'Eternal Tree House,' 'Grandfather Tree' (complete with a random Viking ship), 'The World Famous Tree House,' and 'Confusion Hill,' where all sorts of spooky mysteries are reputed to have occurred. The 'Drive-Thru Tree,' which lured me was fantastic; my most naff tourism since viewing the Pyramids from a Kentucky Fried Chicken store. It is worrying that something as spectacular as a 2,000 year-old, 300 foot-tall tree is not deemed sufficient fascination in itself, so it has had a huge hole chain-sawed through it, and you can drive your car through its trunk. I love such depths of entertainment. It was even a disappointment that they let me ride through the tree for free on my bike when drivers had to pay for the pleasure. For utter satisfaction I would like to have been swizzled out of a few bucks as well for the experience.

There were always logistical challenges to keep me busy on the road. From day to day I needed to think about food, water, what route to ride and where to sleep. Further down the line I worked on venues to give talks at, made arrangements with contacts in cities who had invited me to stay, and calculated when and where and how I could replace broken equipment. I always had a long-term project or two simmering away as well, things that required long-term planning and thought. That Easter I was working on two topics which were intertwined. I was cycling to the north of Alaska. That was clear-cut and uncomplicated. But deciding where to begin Eurasia after that was a difficult decision. There were several starting points and routes that appealed, and they all had pros and cons. I had to begin somewhere on the east coast of Asia and wind my way westwards towards home. The cities that I was considering beginning in were Sydney, Singapore, Shanghai, Tokyo, Magadan and Vladivostok.

Most of what would make the decision for me would be where any boat I could secure a lift on was heading to. I was not very optimistic about finding a yacht across the Pacific as the wind patterns were not favourable, although I did persevere in contacting as many yacht clubs up the West Coast as I could. For the main focus of my search, though, I turned to container ships.

I learned that hitching a lift for free across the Pacific Ocean on an industrial cargo ship is not as easy as it sounds. Red tape and insurance meant that it was far easier for shipping companies to say "no" to my request or, more typically, to not even reply, than to say "yes." Every time I did an interview, every family I met, every lecture I gave, everyone I talked to, I made sure to ask whether anybody knew anybody who knew anybody who owned a ship. The odds did not feel good. It looked like my search was going to be difficult but, by beginning six months early and asking everybody I met, at least I had done all that I could.

I left fabulous California and entered Oregon. I did not know much about Oregon. Now I know more: it has lots of rain and lots of trees. Unfair perhaps, but days spent riding in rain and nights lying in a wet sleeping bag did little to encourage curious-minded travel. My ride through Oregon was travel at its most basic and most pointless. I was simply moving for motion's sake. I put my head down and spun the pedals. I was not looking or seeing or learning or listening. As the rain trickled down my neck I was merely feeling the miles edging beneath my wheels, taking me ever further from home and the beginning, ever closer to home and the end.

All that cold rain and hundreds of miles of introspection left me feeling like a nice hot cup of coffee and sending my mum an email. Fortunate then that, via fun Portland, I arrived, after tedious miles of uniform McSuburbia, in stylish Seattle, home to both Starbucks and Microsoft. It was also home to Dale who I had last seen toasting me with a glass of red wine as I rode away from the yacht in Mexico. It was good to see him again.

I could see why Dale loved Seattle so much. The city is surrounded by Puget Sound, an inlet of the Pacific Ocean, and Lake Washington, busy with ships and sailing boats. To the west and east of Seattle are mountains, rivers and forests. The city's downtown was a rush of high-rise caffeinated energy with enough glimpses of the ocean to keep you sane. Tourists clustered into the Pike Street Market to watch the famous fishmongers hurling enormous fish around, and I wandered, wide-eyed and greedy, through second hand bookstores and outdoor shops full of all the shiny gear a man could want.

Every city I had visited since L. A. seemed to be challenging me, calling me to put down roots and stop. There was so much going on in those American cities, a vibrant energy of people fortunate enough to have both leisure time and money to enjoy it with. I felt as though I was in a fabulous dream world after the grind of riding through so much poverty. After regions where people worked only enough to eat today, and spent the rest of the time sitting in the sunshine and enjoying themselves, I had started to dread the rich world's work-addicted lifestyle of suffering fifty weeks a year for the sake of a two-week vacation. I did not know whether I could settle into that. Willie Loman in *Death of a Salesman* laments the Great American Dream, "My own apartment, a car, and plenty of women, and still, goddamit, I'm lonely." Yet in America I was beginning to think that, with a job I enjoyed, one that was worthwhile, I could maybe find my niche in the career world after all.

Dale and I decided to climb Mount Rainier, a snow-covered volcano that was imposing even from the sparkling waterfront of downtown Seattle. At 10,000 feet, the weather started to close in and we conceded defeat and turned around. I was secretly happy as I had been carrying Dale's heavy ski boots all the way up the mountain for him. He had his skis over his shoulder. Unfortunately Dale only had one set of skis so I was due to slide back down the mountain on my arse while he skied down. I handed Dale his boots, he clipped on his skis and rocketed back down the mountain like a mad thing. Much later, numb-bummed, tired and soggy, I too completed the descent.

With a new friend, Chris, I climbed the South Early Winter Spire in the Cascade mountains. Somehow she assumed that, because I was used to cycling a long way through remote parts of the world, I would also enjoy wading through waist-deep snow (I did enjoy that), donning crampons and an avalanche alarm (quite exciting), climbing bloomin' high up a very narrow, very steep channel of snow (errr...) to a summit which required pulling myself up a few foot of vertical rock. This last bit would have been fine at ground level but, with a stomach churning drop of what looked like a couple of thousand feet below me, I absolutely froze. As Chris nonchalantly tucked into her packed lunch at the top I lay on my face gripped with terror. But I was hungry enough to pull myself up to the waiting lunch and the thrill of an eagle's view over the snowy mountains. I gazed northwards, always north, the way my road had taken me for so long. Canada lay just over those mountains, just a couple more days' ride away.

I find it difficult to summarise America neatly. I saw only a sliver of the country. My experience of the west coast tells me almost nothing about life in Texas or New York or Kentucky. However with the language being, for the most part, more understandable to me than Swahili or Arabic, I learned more than in many other countries. The United States is so diverse, so confused and so confusing that no two conversations or people are the same. I encountered creationists and evolutionists, Democrats and Republicans, conservatives and liberals, racists and mixed-race families, idealists and defeatists, atheists and Christians, gay marriage supporters and spittle-flying homophobes, Bush voters and Bush haters, anti-abortion and pro-electric chair, pro-choice and anti-electric chair, enormous wind-farms and enormous RV's, triathletes and couch potatoes, pristine National Parks and massive cities, drive-thru cash machines and epic trans-continental bike routes, anything-goes liberalism and old-fashioned bigotism, intrepid world travellers and folks who had barely left their state. I met millionaires and passed an Indian reservation as poor as the developing world. I rarely felt comfortable enough to knock on strangers' doors to ask for a place to camp, but one family let me stay in their house alone for a week while they were out of town. America was the most overtly religious country I had been in since the Islamic world, yet arguments raged about the appropriateness of the word 'God' being on the dollar bills. It was the most patriotic country I had been to, with the 'stars'n'bars' flying everywhere, yet many people were despondent about the state of the Union. Bumper stickers told many tales, from American flags and slogans like 'United we Stand: the Power of Pride' and 'These Colors Don't Run' to 'No War for Oil', 'If you can read this you're not the President' and 'I'm pink therefore I'm Spam.' I rode through a tree and the enormity of LA. I watched a lot of television, especially the shopping channels. I spoke English and Spanish. I consumed enormous amounts of food and drank bucketfuls of coffee, but even I could not manage the extraordinary two litre cups of fizzy drinks that petrol stations sold. It was little wonder that I needed the first dental filling of my life. I ate Indian, Mexican, Korean, Ethiopian, Chinese, Thai, Italian, Japanese and Israeli food.

America is wealthy, hard-working, beautiful and welcoming. It also displays the things that anger people around the globe: consumerism gone crazy – the size of the supermarkets has to be seen to be believed – a disregard for the environment, most noticeable in the massive vehicles everybody drives, and a lack of interest in the affairs of the rest of the world. America has certainly made mistakes recently, but then the man who makes no mistakes does not usually make anything.

I had entered America unhappy at the direction their President was leading our world and at what I perceived to be his government's arrogant, ignorant, ill-judged behaviour with the British government trotting embarrassingly along behind. After a brief few months in America my feelings changed. They did not change towards the government and its foreign policy, but they certainly changed towards the American people. As a reflection of this, as I pedalled on to Canada, I hoped to return to America one day. Not only for a holiday, but to live there for a couple of years.

Coming alive

Just once in his life,
A man has his time,
And my time is now,
And I'm comin' alive.
– 'St Elmo's Fire,' John Parr

I f the criteria for qualifying as a 'great' city include, as I believe they should, mountains, ocean, parks, ethnic and cultural diversity and cricket pitches, then Vancouver is up there with the best of them. Shannon had hosted me back in Tanzania, and had since returned home to Vancouver, where her apartment once again became festooned with my tatty belongings and greasy bike parts. I said a second grateful farewell as I left Vancouver.

I followed my friend Dave, pedalling slowly through the traffic of downtown Vancouver. Dave and I had previously ridden in Central America together, and he took three months leave from his management consultancy job to join me, cycling from Vancouver to the Arctic Ocean. After we cycled through Central America together Dave vowed that if ever he was seen on a bike again, I had his permission to shoot him, but the shackles of a city desk and the rose-tinted glasses of time had eventually persuaded him that maybe it wasn't so bad after all.

We rode out of the city, past the polished clean and quiet of the downtown skyscrapers, past the green gem of Stanley Park and the peaceful bays with sea-planes, cruise ships and yachts, past empty beaches and green forests and across the Lions' Gate Bridge. We cast a final fond look back at the Vancouver skyline then pointed our noses towards Alaska and the emptiness of the

North. The end of the Americas was creeping ever closer.

It was good to see Dave again. We had been friends at school and university, where we planned expeditions and looked forward to getting done with studying and starting the rest of our lives. Dave had spent the last few years in a variety of jobs, interspersed with lots of travelling and increasingly ambitious mountain climbing. He was very successful at all he tried but was easily bored and never stuck at anything for long. He was looking hard but had yet to find exactly what he was looking for. I hoped that a big ride may help him mull over some ideas.

We left town looking grizzly with fake tattoos on our biceps – me: rose-entwined dagger; Dave: busty mermaid – and we began a beard-growing contest. We were looking forward to the enticing North. Dave settled into life on the road, as we cycled every day for three tough weeks, from Vancouver to Whitehorse, colossal landscapes of lakes, rivers and trees. The sheer enormity and emptiness of Canada was thrilling. The lure of the North, the, "great, big, broad land 'way up yonder', [is] the forests where silence has lease, it's the beauty that fills me with wonder, it's the stillness that fills me with peace."

The Sea-to-Sky Highway climbs from the shadows of towering walls of rock in Squamish, through gloomy forests and up above blue lakes. Snowy mountains and the island-strewn bay below us enhanced the view as we climbed up towards the descriptively named 70 Mile House, 100 Mile House and 150 Mile House. Dave found it amusing to ask people how far it was between each of these settlements. The Fraser River surged strong and brown, and bounced with loose logs and broken tree stumps. I saw the corpse of a deer in the river with its leg still trapped in a wire fence. It bucked and thrashed in the river, struggling frantically, even in death. In the long light evenings, red-headed woodpeckers rattled the silence. We saw moose, deer, beavers, bald eagles, foxes and coyotes, and one evening, our first black bear.

A mother and her two cubs grazed amongst dandelion clocks and we stood transfixed and delighted. Adventure Dave, tourist extraordinaire, decided he would stalk them with his video camera. He had not got very far when he stood on a twig that snapped, and the bears fled. For such big beasts they seemed rather timid and not very scary. Three months later, after many black bears and grizzly bears and countless horror stories from locals, I became very scared of them. One night we heard rustling sounds right outside the tent and we tensed in fear, our eyes wide with fright. When I could not take the tension any longer, I carefully eased up the zip on the tent door and came face to face with our fate. The beast was right outside. There, right in front of me, not two yards from my face, the source of our stomach-clenching anxiety: a tiny little bird was hopping around in the leaves.

That summer was one of the hottest ever, temperatures climbed to 37°C. This was not how we had imagined the great frozen North to be. Dave cursed because he was carrying a heavy winter sleeping bag and a down jacket that he was never going to need. They were just dead weight in his panniers. He was particularly annoyed because it had been my recommendation to bring them along. We pedalled, parched from one river to the next, cooling ourselves and calming our thumping heads by jumping blissfully in all our clothes into numbing meltwater streams, shining in the sun and bubbling and chortling. Under the cold water I felt the tensions melting away. To leap into those rivers and come up laughing hard and throw back your head in howls of shocked delight at the burning cold was to feel like you would be young and alive for ever. Back on the bikes, the horrible sweating would soon start again, as we pushed hard on the pedals, creeping through the long miles.

The summer sun set late and slowly at those latitudes and in the tent at night, we lay stewing in the setting sunshine. Both of us sweating and uncomfortable, it was hard to tolerate each other's radiating heat and stench so nearby, but we were confined in our tent by the worst mosquitoes I had ever encountered. They covered the outside of the tent like a patient army, dotted over the canvas and waiting for us to emerge, when their screaming attack would launch. When we stopped riding in the evening, evil clouds would close round our heads, humming like dentist drills, teasing and torturing, sharp as sailors' knives, until we managed to throw the tent up and hurl ourselves inside, itching and irate.

Whoever's turn it was to cook would sit outside, concealed in their waterproof jackets and trousers, gloves, hat and mosquito head net slapping themselves until the food was ready. The other would lie in boxer shorts, sweating inside the tent. Dave had been reading about Buddhism, and he managed an impressive two days without splatting one mosquito before his karmic resolve crumbled. I, on the other hand, was reading a biography of Margaret Thatcher so was in ruthless mood, mosquito-slapping without compunction.

Riding along, we discussed techniques for charming women. It was June and there was more daylight than we knew what to do with. We talked a lot of rubbish. We woke late in the mornings, cycled all day with plenty of rests, swims and unsuccessful fishing attempts, and were left with a few spare hours of sunshine each evening. As night rose in the forest it first faded the trees to blackness while the sky darkened much more slowly. Then, at last, a blessed cool calmness settled. The sweating of a hot, hard day was over, we were away from the mosquitoes and sleep was sweet. As a result of our woman-scheming Dave began a daily regime of sit-ups and press-ups, having concluded that big muscles was the way to a female's heart. I chose a different strategy, and took up writing poetry. We looked to forward to testing the relative merits of our approaches, should we ever bump into any unsuspecting females to practice on.

I always woke a couple of hours before Dave. If a breeze kept the mosquitoes away, I would climb out of the tent and sit on the pale pine needles, my back against a tree, and prepare my morning coffee. My legs and back would be stiff from the long, hard days riding. Although I greatly enjoyed Dave's company, I also savoured this quiet time alone when I could swim, drink coffee, and read my book. Or, under the new regime, write poetry. I relished the long weeks, trekking through fabulous Canadian countryside. Life felt simple and good and I felt sure that I could rattle off a couple of cracking poems before Dave awoke to do his sit-ups. How hard could it be?

I will spare you the embarrassment of my efforts, which turned out to be no more than painful prose, chopped into lines. When Dave eventually awoke, he couldn't be bothered with his sit-ups. It seemed as though the women of the Yukon may be able to resist our approaches after all.

The hills rolled steeply through the trees. Broad as buffalo we barrelled downhill on our heavy bikes. Laden like sherpas we crept up the other side, hurting, gasping and cursing as mosquitoes feasted on us. The sweet, swift reward at each summit was the racing acceleration and smoothness as the road blurred and the wind cheered in your ears and cooled the sticky sweat. Kilometres purred past and the day felt good once again. At day's end, with the distance done, the best was yet to come. Lily pads of sunshine puddled the forest floor and, barefoot, we felt our bodies unwinding. The simple food was eagerly inhaled, brief notes were jotted in the diary, and then it was time for welcome sleep once again.

A serious issue for us that summer was to find televisions to watch England's matches in the European Football Championships. To watch the England-France game, we resorted to spending a night in a cheap motel in Williams Lake, a drab town of ugly people with bad haircuts, sallow skin and beat-up pickups. It was also the home town of Rick Hansen, a heroic paraplegic who travelled 40,000 kilometres round the world in a wheelchair. His ride took two years, crossing four continents and 34 countries. The 80s song, *St. Elmo's Fire (Man in Motion)*, was written about his journey. I had been trying for months to get in touch with Rick but my emails never received a reply.

After a characteristically inept performance from England, we headed out to find a bar. The night took a huge turn for the better when we stumbled across a classic frontier town bar. As we opened the door our first instinct was to flee. Muscular lumberjacks with big moustaches were in town, along with large numbers of inebriated Indians, politely called First Nations people in North America. We didn't rate our chances of finding anywhere else open on a Saturday night, so we pushed through the crowd to an empty table in a dark corner. The bar reeked of beer and smoke, drunks were slumped at the bar, insults flew over the pool table and country music was blasting. We grinned and ordered beer. The next morning I was surprised to find a late-night scrawl in my diary, some of which was legible and hinted of an entertaining night.

We succeeded in finding a television to watch each of England's matches. The last match, against Portugal, we watched in Jade City. Jade City is, by any stretch of the imagination, hardly a city. With a population of twelve, it boasts two jade stores, a gift shop, of course, and, thankfully, a nice family who cooked macaroni cheese for us and let us watch the match in their sitting room. England lost. We rode on.

The road turned west, towards the sunset and home, then north, towards Alaska. We followed the Cassiar Highway for 900 kilometres to where it joined the Alaska Highway. One evening we camped by a river, determined to finally catch ourselves a bloody fish. We had persevered with our fishing, despite not having hooked any of the shining bars of silver that filled the cold green rivers. And, sure enough, we ate noodles again for dinner that night rather than salmon. A couple of local fishermen walked by our campsite on the river bank. We chatted, quizzing them as to why our fishing technique was not working. When they left they gave us $20 and a couple of beers from their bulging bag which I had assumed was heavy with salmon. Perhaps they had not been the best people to be getting advice from after all.

Since leaving Vancouver we had heard talk of two other cyclists riding the same direction as us. They left Vancouver about a week before we did. Like us, they were heavily laden, but clearly on a higher level of expedition as they had food dumps stashed at communities along their route north. Their stashes of sponsored goodies were huge, and at each one they had left behind all the surplus that they could not carry. When shopkeepers told us of the other two riders, they would often hand us piles of left over chocolate, nuts and energy bars. We learned that the cyclists were Colin Angus and Tim Harvey, two Canadian adventurers travelling from Vancouver to Moscow to promote emission-free travel and a healthy lifestyle. They planned to cycle up Canada, paddle down the Yukon River, cross to Russia, then ride on to Moscow. We were slowly catching them up.

"They're a week ahead of you," people told us.

"They passed through here 'bout four days ago."

"They're only a day or two in front now."

Then one morning we saw two ridiculously heavy bikes leaning outside a café. It had to be Colin and Tim so we went inside
to meet them. We introduced ourselves and asked whether they
fancied riding with us to Whitehorse. Colin and Tim were well
into their second cup of coffee, eating Danish pastries and looking contented. Danish pastries. That is how cycling expeditions
should be. I always liked meeting fellow cyclists and chatting about
our respective projects. We enjoyed riding together, sharing advice
and plans as we rolled along taking it in turns to lead the line of
bikes into the headwind. We made it to Whitehorse that evening,
where all of us had previously arranged places to stay. We all had a
burger together and headed our separate ways. Dave and I wished
them good luck with their adventure and left the burger joint
before them. We could not resist slipping a large rock into each of
their panniers to slow them down a little bit. We were very pleased
with our juvenile prank and chuckled as we pedalled away, eager
now for a rest and a shower after three weeks' riding.

Whitehorse is a low, peaceful town on the banks of the Yukon
River and the largest town in the Canadian north. Whitehorse has
less than 25,000 residents, but as this is more than 75% of the
Yukon's population, it is an important hub for the region. I was
looking forward to a well-anticipated rest and a less welcome date
with a dentist's drill after a few months gorging on North
America's ubiquitous free Coca-Cola refills.

Before 1896, only First Nations peoples and the hardiest of fur
traders, prospectors, missionaries and Mounted Police officers
ventured into the Yukon Territory. In two short years, the people,
the history and even the landforms of the Yukon were changed
forever by one word: Gold!

The modern history of the Yukon began when gold was discovered on the Klondike River in 1896. Skookum Jim Mason,
Kate Carmack, and her husband George discovered enormous
gold deposits in Bonanza Creek near the site of modern day
Dawson City. Word filtered down to the United States and a stampede began. Small numbers of indigenous people had lived sus-
tainably in the area for millennia, but so many white men arrived
suddenly in the gold rush stampede, scrabbling and mucking with
dreams of booty, that by the next year there were serious fears of

a famine in the region. From a pre-gold rush figure of under 5,000 people, the population of the Yukon soared to over 30,000 in 1898. After the gold rush, the population dropped again sharply. Today the territory, twice as large as Great Britain, is home once again to around 30,000 people.

The drive and determination of the early prospectors to even make it as far as the panning rivers is a testament to the power of gold fever. There were no roads, maps or shops. You had to make your own way cross-country, carrying everything you needed, and you had to be able to survive once you arrived. The crowds travelled north as far as Skagway, by ship from west coast cities. Then the struggle began. The first obstacle was the gruelling Chilkoot Pass. Old photographs show the pass crowded like an ant trail with people struggling up through the snow and over the top to Lake Bennett. Because of near-starvation in the first couple of years of the rush, a police checkpoint was established at Lake Bennett to check that each man carried a year's supply of food and supplies. Lakeshore activity was frantic as everybody built rafts to carry them down 500 miles of Yukon River to the fast-expanding Dawson City. The land was stripped of trees by the motley armada of homemade craft. In winter the river and lake froze fast. After the sudden spring thaw, known as 'break-up,' competition was fierce to reach Dawson. The earlier you got there the better your chances of securing a stake with good prospects. As the ice-floes on Lake Bennett cracked, strained and burst with the force of spring melt-water, scores of craft were launched eagerly at the river, and the race was on. Many drowned, sank or capsized. The Yukon River claimed many dreams and lives.

Those who finally reached Dawson found that the best claims had all been staked the year before. Many would-be prospectors simply gave up and headed home sad and ruined. Others stayed and found wealth in different enterprises. It is said that more fortunes were made in Dawson by entrepreneurs selling goods and services to the miners than in the goldfields themselves. There were only a few big winners in that gold rush, but they were such spectacular winners that, when word got out about another massive gold strike in 1899, the race was immediately back on, and this time to even more remote parts. Hopes and dreams of glory and gold burst back to life and once again thousands of people raced madly down the Yukon River, this time to Nome, on the shores of the Bering Strait, on the western tip of Alaska.

I found it exciting to be in an area where the history was so fresh and tangible. I envied the bold and reckless men and women who arrived in that vast, tough landscape and learned to thrive. I was enjoying my own tame little adventure on the same stage as I pushed on ever northwards, the edge of the continent now only a couple of months away. Had those men and women of the gold rush been footloose, courageous adventurers, or were they just naïve and ruled by greed? Both, perhaps, but as I read their tales from the comfy armchairs of a Whitehorse coffee shop with chill-out music and people tapping at laptops, I was envious of them.

By paddle and track

With saddle and pack, by paddle and track,
Let's go to the Land of Beyond!
– Robert Service

Smoke tickled my nostrils and haze hung in the sky. Our progress was in jeopardy. Forest fires raged to the north and west of us. An area the size of Wales, over two million hectares of forest was burning, and beyond the power of humans to extinguish. It was one of the worst fire seasons in history, and smoke hung over the Yukon like a pall. All that the fire services could do was try to manage the blaze. They had closed the only road to Dawson City, the road that Dave and I had hoped to ride. The police did not know when it was likely to re-open.

In that part of the world roads are new things, new-fangled intruders. Long before any road reached the North, the routes had been the rivers. Inspired by the optimism and heroics of the gold rush boys, Dave and I started to wonder whether we could take to the water ourselves to continue our journey. Perhaps we could canoe down the river to Dawson City, and get back onto the bikes there. We became excited as we studied our maps and the idea took shape and grew in our minds. We chattered about catching salmon, running rapids and whether we could fit two bicycles into one canoe. Canoeing down the Yukon? That did sound like an adventure.

Fortunately the Yukon is an easy place to get hold of things like 16-foot canoes. Its population also likes to tell dramatic stories to outsiders, known as *cheechakos*, about how tough the North is and how soft little Englishmen had no chance of surviving a long canoe journey. We noticed that Canadians, *en masse*, worried about things more than Dave and I did. We were given many pessimistic, gloomy prognoses about our plans. The ease of getting a canoe, and everyone's conviction that the journey was too much for the Brits sealed our determination. Neither of us knew anything about canoeing so we asked the locals. Like locals all over the world, they were not short of opinions.

"The river's too high…"

"The river's too cold…"

"You don't have a map…"

"You'll sink if you load your bikes onto a canoe…"

"The smoke is too dangerous…"

"Five Finger rapids will get you…"

"The bears will get you…"

"The fires will get you…"

The moniker for a long-term resident of the Yukon is a 'sourdough.' It is a term used with respect. We, clearly, were not sourdoughs. We were a pair of hopeless Englishmen and we had no chance. The verdict was a red rag to a bull and we began the search for a canoe. As Mallory said, "The greatest danger in life is not to take the adventure."

Sara, a cross-country skier and sourdough extraordinaire, was hosting us in Whitehorse. There's a song in those parts called, '*I Gotta Find a Woman with a Chainsaw.*' It goes, '*I don't care if she's skinny, I don't care if she's plump, I don't care if she's pretty or ugly as sin, If she's got a chainsaw she can move right in.*' I have no doubt Sara could wield a chainsaw with confidence, and she was certainly neither plump nor ugly. She gave Dave and me a beginners' canoeing course and lots of frightening bear-avoidance advice over a two-day training run on the nearby Takhini River. We felt ready for anything. Sara's young brother Erik helped Dave and I to load up the canoe on the riverbank at the bottom of their garden. Dave asked him, breezily, "Do you think we'll make it?" Young Erik said, "I don't think so."

Fuelled with a manly farewell breakfast of bison burgers and bear sausages we felt ready for anything. A new adventure began. As well as two bikes and all our camping gear we stocked the canoe with food for ten days, crackers, peanut butter, mashed potato powder, spaghetti, garlic sausage and Werther's Originals.

We had no map, but neither did any of the brave early explorers. At least *we* knew that somewhere down the river we would eventually reach a town and food. We had it easy. This was a good chance to put into action my travel philosophy of pragmatic recklessness. We had sought advice about the river, its difficulty and strategies for coping for it, we had done all we could to make the trip safe and successful, now we just had to launch into it and hope for the best. Tied on top of our huge load of luggage was a moose skull we had found. We hoped it would be our lucky totem. We squeezed ourselves into the laden canoe and waved Sara and her family goodbye.

Our spirits were sky high and we set to paddling with gusto. We were off, warnings about our fate at the Five Finger Rapids and the cold and the current and the forest fires and the grizzlies still ringing in our ears as we wobbled precariously out into the current of the river.

For the next ten days we would be far from road or rescue with no phone to call for help. It felt very liberating.

After a short while our arms grew tired and we had to stop and take a little rest. Our arm muscles were completely unaccustomed to any form of strain. Fortunately we were around the first bend and out of sight of Sara's family, so they had not seen how quickly we had tired. That was the moment when we *really* began to enjoy our new means of transport. We appreciated then that in a canoe, unlike cycling, you can lie back and relax and, with absolutely no effort, cruise towards your destination. Huck Finn was dead right when he celebrated life on the river as, "kind of lazy and jolly, laying off comfortable all day, smoking and fishing, and no books nor study." We set to lying back and cruising with gusto. Yukon Ho!

Sometime on that first afternoon the current slowed, and then stopped. We had entered Lake Laberge, and it was time to start paddling again. By evening our arms and shoulders were complaining and we paddled over to a sandy beach to pitch camp. We were extremely satisfied with our progress. We had not capsized, and we had begun to find some rhythm to our paddling. Best of all, we were completely away from roads and houses and people, away from anything created by humans. This is something that can never really be achieved on a bike journey. The campsite was idyllic and safe, a curved bay of smooth grey pebbles and bone-white driftwood. We camped on a ledge above the water, a breeze kept the mosquitoes at bay, the water burbled the shore and stars of sunlight danced on the water. We had unlimited drinking water and could even rinse off with a swim before getting into our sleeping bags. Life was good and cycling suddenly seeming like an unnecessarily arduous means of transport.

Paddling the length of Lake Laberge proved hard work and Dave retracted his earlier claim, expressed with enthusiasm on the first morning, that he wanted to paddle round all of the Great Lakes. Canoeing on flat water is hard work, especially paddling into a headwind. The wind grew stronger and the water turned choppy and chalk green. We were surrounded by low, forested hills, dotted with snow even now in mid-summer. Ahead of us was a denuded hillside of bare rocks like a pile of pale intestines.

We continued to paddle hard, yet futilely, into the wind. Barbed arrows of resentment lurked at my lips as tiredness mounted, pinging round my head and desperate to be released.

"Paddle harder, Dave!"

"Why not this way?"

"I think we should turn this way."

A calmer voice knew that I was just tired. Dave was trying hard, and he was probably thinking exactly the same sort of things about me. I had doubts about Dave's levels of effort later, though, when he re-launched his evening campaign of sit-ups and press-ups. The wind rose and as the waves grew and threatened to swamp us, we turned the canoe and fled for the shore. We hauled the canoe high up the beach, put up our tent and settled back to wait for calm. Surrender is, at times, the better part of valour.

By evening the wind had dropped, the sky cleared and we skimmed stones across the mirror-smooth lake, kicking up silver crowns along the golden road of late sunlight. The sun sinks slowly at the top of the world, noticeably slower than at the equator where darkness falls swiftly. We fancied that we could almost see the end of the lake not impossibly far ahead and we went to bed hoping for a calm morning.

The next day, a few more hours paddling brought us to the end of the lake, and we celebrated as we felt the current taking hold of our boat once more, gripping the hull beneath us and carrying us back into the flowing Yukon River.

After the lake we enjoyed the changing faces of the river all the more, especially as we could sit back and relax. At times, the river was jade green and steady, with strange boils of water rising and slowly swirling the surface, at times a sliding mirror. Sometimes it was shallow and jolly, you could look down and watch pebbles rush past as though they were dashing upstream, colourful time capsules, orange, grey, white and black, each one colossally old. We slipped silently over smooth blue water and silt fizzed the bottom of the boat. The river was our road, we were content on our own and confident in the wild. It was a good feeling to travel through that silence with a good friend. The only sounds were the dipping of our paddles and our aimless chat about favourite foods, favourite films and plans for future expeditions.

Moose with only their heads above water swam the river ahead of us, goofy and striving with huge ears pinned back. They scrambled up the slick bank and disappeared into the undergrowth. Sometimes we saw them grazing on the banks and they paused to watch curiously as we passed. A beaver, his big head stretched out, swam for his jumbled lodge of pale branches and mud. Disturbed by our approach, he slapped the water loudly with his tail and disappeared in a dive. Shaggy bears trotted the hillsides. Bald eagles surveyed their domain and watched us from the treetops with utter indifference. From time to time we heard them screech their haunting cry into the silent sky, then soar and plummet downwards with an audible whoosh of air. Squirrels chattered displeasure at the disturbance. Woodpeckers sounded as though they were banging their heads against a brick wall. Above the water, colourful dragonflies hovered and whirred at the surface, and vanished. Beneath us the muscular salmon were racing, but they resisted all temptations onto our trailing hooks with lures of shiny chewing gum paper, coloured bits of plastic bags, and canapés of garlic sausage. They leaped and splashed in mockery.

At night we camped on islands in the middle of the river.

Islands were more likely to be safe from bears and they were more fun than sleeping on the shore. Camping on an island feels like an adventure. We were revelling in our own *Huckleberry Finn* or *Swallows and Amazons* escapade. At day's end we would look for an island suitable for landing and camping on. We would point ourselves towards an island and paddle hard. Sometimes we were foiled by the strength of the current as we paddled madly, only to be whisked right on past before we reached the island's bank. There was no chance of paddling back upstream against the current so we would have to just give up and keep on floating downstream until another island came into view.

Eventually bumping into an island, we heaved the canoe up the bank, set up camp, swam, fished and then cooked on a campfire. The unusually hot, dry summer had led to record numbers of wildfires in the Yukon, and we lit fires only when we were camped on small islands in the river. We knew that, even if one did get out of control, it could not spread far. We were sick of our canoeing fare; reconstituted mashed potato and coffee for breakfast, crackers and peanut butter for lunch, peanuts and Werther's Originals as snacks, and pasta with cheap but repulsive garlic sausage for dinner. We learned, too late, that a canoeist can carry much more than a cyclist. Weight does not make much difference to a canoe, so we could have carried a far wider range of foods. Apart from the food, those campsites were superb. As Huck Finn said, rafting down the Mississippi, "It's lovely to live on a raft. We had the sky up there, all speckled with stars, and we used to lay on our backs and look up at them, and discuss about whether they was made or only just happened... We said there warn't no home like a raft, after all. Other places do seem so cramped up and smothery, but a raft don't. You feel mighty free and easy and comfortable on a raft." We felt the same with our green plastic canoe and island campsites.

We woke to a sky thick with smoke. Ash had fallen like snow on our tent in the night. We could not see the riverbank and our noses tickled with the smoke. We were approaching the main areas of the forest fires. The breeze changed direction in the night and blown the smoke our way, and the thickness of the smoke gave us an idea of how huge the fires were. The endless cycle of lightning strikes, forest fires and re-growth are what the respected eco-botanist Sir Elton John refers to as *The Circle of Life*. All the land is at different stages of growth. Annual forest fires leave blackened, burned hillsides stripped to bare trunks like porcupine quills. Then comes a bright blush of the pink Fireweed flower. Always the first plant to grow after the flames, it is a sign of hope, like when you first notice that a bad haircut is beginning to grow out. We passed great swathes of gaudy Fireweed, the official flower of the Yukon. Next in the cycle comes small bushes thriving on the lack of competition, then poplar trees grow. And then, at last, the spruce trees begin to return. Summer lightning strikes start new fires and the circle revolves once again. The seasons revolve, the waters roll on and on, and the fires bring new life to feed future flames.

Away from the road, away from the crowd, there is no need for a clock, no need to chat. The silence stood sentinel to time, a tangible presence over the endless river that ridiculed my thoughts of distance or time. The river and the silent emptiness are wed together for ever and each smooth worn, coloured pebble will outlast us all.

Quiet traders and trappers lived along the river for year upon year, until gold was found and the river flowed with men. Now, after scores of years and shattered dreams, and a handful of winners, now I was following on. There were still hints of the past. The history still breathes, the stories live on, but the river runs on and on and on. I felt optimistic for the world in a place that made man's impact feel so small.

We occasionally passed deserted log cabins, relics of the fur trappers and gold panners. It must have been a lonely life, requiring real competence and self-confidence in every skill required for life. This river was the road long before there were roads; by canoe in summer and ski in winter. The history of the region was so tied to its rivers. Paddle boats plied the Yukon River right up to the 1950s when a road to Dawson was finally built. Fort Selkirk was a small trading post on the river, with a log church, a graveyard, a little school and the oldest building in all of the Yukon, dating from the 1890s. Walking through the old, abandoned settlement, peering into log cabins, I tried to imagine a life so remote that the river was the only connection to the outside world.

A First Nations man, 66-year-old Wilfred, came in his motor-boat from the village of Carmacks with his puppy, Toto, and his wife, to check his fishing nets. Canadians of First Nations origin have different hunting and fishing rules to Canadians of European origin, and are allowed to catch far more salmon. He saw our camp on the bank and pulled over for a chat. We asked him if we could accompany him in his boat as he checked his nets. We had a lot to learn about catching salmon. He was happy for the help, so we clambered aboard and motored back upstream. Wilfred was very jolly, very knowledgeable about the land and looked like Nelson Mandela. We asked him many questions about the Yukon as we found the whole area fascinating. His wife was white, and a real misery, making everything sound far worse than it was. She spoke a lot about the rights of First Nations people and the crimes committed against them by the Europeans. She seemed to feel that, married to Wilfred, the white man's sins were no longer her own. I understood the sentiment for First Nations privileges, they were treated terribly by the early European colonists, but I wonder how long the reparations should last. For how long should today's Canadians be punished or rewarded for their ancestors' acts? Do these systems aid integration, forgiveness and tolerance, or do they prevent the wounds from healing?

Wilfred was more concerned about siting his salmon nets.

The rash of civilisation, and the road between Whitehorse and Dawson all cross the river at the village of Carmacks. Carmacks was just a couple of quiet streets of homes, a shop or two, a church, community centre and a school. Growing up in the Yorkshire Dales I had thought that I lived in the most remote place on Earth. There wasn't a McDonald's for 20 miles.

As usual, climbing from the canoe, Dave made a beeline for the burger stand. We asked the bored teenage girl where we could buy groceries. She had the Canadian knack for drama, and launched into a worried monologue when she heard where we were going,

"Huge fires ahead… Nobody will rescue you… Thick black smoke… Very dangerous… (blah blah)…"

"OK, thanks, but where is the grocery store?"

"You have to stop here… Impossible ahead… Too dangerous

for English boys… (blah blah)…"

We decided to look for the grocery ourselves and edged away from the girl. She is probably still wittering and fretting about us now. We bought some food and got back out onto the river before anyone else tried to stop us. There were no more settlements until Dawson City so as long as we got away from Carmacks, nobody could try to obstruct us. The fires were not far ahead of us now, but we were still not worried by the warnings of our impending death. Perhaps we really were naïve, but being in the middle of a very wide river seemed like good fire protection. Anyway, we would find out soon enough.

The sky darkened and rain hurtled down as the wind rose and blew strong in our faces. We had a comical debate, as lightning slashed around us, about whether we were safe or actually very un-safe in a plastic boat on a river in a thunder storm. We duly survived un-zapped and, as evening approached, a roaring sound grew louder ahead. Four great chunks of rock divide the river into five rushing channels and we paddled quickly to the shore. We had reached the Five Finger Rapids. One writer described them as, "chains of reared-up and crashing waves… a vortex that swirled like a black hole in the river."

The endless pessimists had told us that our only option was to portage our canoe and gear round the rapids, or the Five Finger Rapids would be our nemesis. Two novice canoeists, especially English ones, should not run the rapids. Of course, with advice like that, only one option was available to us. We made sure that everything was tightly lashed down, decided that a recce would only scare us, and paddled out to the centre of the river. We were going for it. The likely outcomes were:

1. Death. In which case we would feel very foolish.
2. Capsize and boat sinkage. Better than #1, but much more likely. I would lose everything I owned in the world, plus we would have a very long swim to Dawson.
3. Capsize but boat doesn't sink. Not the end of the world.
4. Survive intact and disprove the doubters. Doubtful.

We alternated seats in the canoe each day for variety, and that day I was in the stern and responsible for steering. We had agreed on the route we wanted to take through the rapids. We paddled swiftly into position and headed towards the right hand channel, as we had been advised back in Whitehorse. I was nervous but excited as the noise of the rapids increased. We paddled hard and smooth and everything was running well. The river picked up speed and we were long past the point of no return. We were committed. There was no more hesitancy, no chance to draw back. We hit the rapids and I shouted, "paddle hard!" Dave pulled hard as I paddled to keep the canoe straight. We hit exactly the route I wanted, head on to the waves. We were bouncing madly. Dave heaved away at his paddle, pulling with all his strength. I even found time for a whoop of excitement. I felt so alert, and was utterly focused on keeping us on line. But each wave we bounced over sloshed into our already over-loaded canoe. We were taking on a lot of water and began to sink lower and lower until, with almost a little sigh of apology, the boat slowly tipped us in and flipped. We had almost made it through. Almost, but not quite.

The canoe was upside down but it did not seem to be sinking. Dave grinned as we grabbed hold of the trailing ropes at the front and back of the canoe. 'Almost made it!' he seemed to be thinking. We swooped downstream hanging on to our massively heavy canoe, talking quickly and planning. We tried to push the inverted canoe towards shore, swimming against it, but the river was fast and the canoe incredibly heavy. If she shipped much more water she could sink. We raced on downstream. Nobody on the planet knew where we were. We swam hard and pushed the inert canoe, trying to move towards the bank, but it was too heavy to make any impact. We floated at high speed down the middle of the river. We tried to jam the canoe against a half-sunken log to slow our progress but the smooth, fast current just hauled us quickly past, and I gashed my shin on the log for my troubles.

The water was cold and we saw a long sweeping bend ahead, about a kilometre long. The outside river bank was a sheer hillside. We would never be able to get ashore there. We had to make one massive effort to get us, and the canoe, onto the near shore before that bend. We had to get out of the cold water as soon as possible or things could turn really serious. We shouted to each other and set our sights on a bluff on the right hand bank. It seemed as though the river may be shallow enough for us to get our feet on the bottom and make some purchase to manhandle the boat into slower waters. Time for one extra effort. It was only a couple of hundred metres away. We pulled with all our strength but the was river dragging us on and on. The long, sheer bend was rushing towards us. We were becoming cold and tired. We knew that we had to get control of this situation quickly. We just missed the bluff but behind it was a gentle eddy where the current dropped sharply. We hauled ourselves into the eddy and heaved the capsized boat to the shore. We managed to stumble ashore. As soon as we were out of the water we knew that we were safe, the adrenaline subsided and the cold really kicked in. We were panting, aching, soaking wet and cold, alone on a river bank far from home. My feet were cut and bruised from hauling over the rocky bottom. But the boat hadn't sunk, we had got it to shore, we were still alive – and we had made it through the Five Fingers!

We shivered uncontrollably. My knees and jaws chattered and my skin was bright red, over a pale blue undercoat. We quickly pulled gear out of the canoe, aware that we needed to get warm before hypothermia kicked in. Some of our dry bags turned out to have been useless. Our camping and cooking gear and most of our food was soaking wet. Our bikes had been scraped along the rocks and our lucky moose skull had its teeth knocked out. Fortunately the contents of my Ark dry-bags, all the way from South Africa, were still dry, and we quickly shared out and put on all the dry clothes we had. I pulled on a horrible fluorescent green fleece that had been given to me by a commune of activists in Portland who had lived in trees to prevent them from being cut down. The fleece had belonged to somebody who had gone to Colorado to inseminate a lesbian couple he had never met. I also had a purple woolly hat given to me by an old lady in a Mormons' knitting team in Arizona. "We knit stuff for poor folks," she told me. "Here, have this."

I quickly got the stove going to make some hot drinks while Dave set about hanging all our wet things to dry. As the sugar-loaded hot chocolate seeped down our throats and warmed our bellies, we looked at each other, still shivering frantically, and we began to giggle with delight. There was a beautiful sunset and skeins of ducks swooshed up the river past our little beach. We were hunched over with laughter, our hands still shivering wildly, spilling hot chocolate, and our stomachs ached from laughing so loud. There was relief that we had escaped from what was almost a very serious, self-inflicted situation, jubilation that we had been reckless enough to take on the challenge just for the hell of it, and a delight that, once again, the pessimists of the world had been overcome. We paraphrased words I once heard from Lance Armstrong, "50% of it was for the adventure, 25% of it was for ourselves, and 25% was for those who never believed." Roll on Dawson City and a celebratory beer.

We passed through an area of forest that was still ablaze. It was an apocalyptic vision of destruction. We felt safe though, as we paddled down the middle of the river, by now about 200 metres wide and scattered with islands. The sun dimmed to a peach-coloured disc as the sky was grey with smoke. The river was grey too, as it merged with the silt-filled White River. Visibility was almost zero. The whole world was grey. Smoke stung our eyes and noses and caught in our throats. There was no horizon and at times even the outline of the sun disappeared. It was very disorientating. With no visibility, the stream slow and silent, and my nose and mouth tangy with smoke, most of my senses had been nullified. We had no idea where we were or where we were going, other than downstream. At times we had to sit still and drift, spinning gently, and allow the river to take us downstream amongst the maze of tiny islands and tangles of driftwood. Without the current we would have been lost in all the channels, but the fires were no real barrier to our progress. We wondered whether perhaps the pessimists had been all smoke and no fire.

With no map of the river, we had little idea where we were or how far remained to Dawson. It was a happy moment then one smoky afternoon as we rounded a bend and saw the small town of Dawson City hugging the right bank of the river. We paddled across, pulled alongside the bank and climbed from the canoe for the last time. We were stiff, tired and bored with our soggy food and the mouldering garlic sausage. Yet we were thrilled to have made it, delighted to have succeeded. When people tell you that something is not possible, it is always satisfying to turn that into a positive challenge to attack with enthusiasm and optimism. We often focus on the reasons not to do something, the excuses to take the easy option. It is easier to do nothing than to do something. It had been an honour and a delight to briefly sample the exciting history of Dawson City, the gold rush and the magnificent Yukon River.

Bath Spa University

Title: Thunder and sunshine
ID: 00263088
Due: 5/11/2012,23:59

Total items: 1
15/10/2012 12:13

Thank you for using the
3M SelfCheck™ System.

A little while longer

Allons! We must not stop here,
However sweet these laid-up shores,
However convenient this dwelling we cannot remain here,
However shelter'd this port and however calm these waters
We must not anchor heré,
However welcome the hospitality that surrounds us
We are permitted to receive it but a little while.
— Walt Whitman

We headed off from Dawson, sweating on the bikes once more. The muddy Top of the World Highway wound along a ridge, above folds of hills and endless untouched trees, towards Alaska.

Alaska. The end of the Americas at long last. The pretty, hilly road took us through the town of Chicken, population 25, so-called apparently because the original miners could not spell "Ptarmigan." The ceiling of Chicken's bar is covered with baseball caps and the shredded underwear of female drinkers who allowed their knickers to be blasted from a cannon and pinned to the ceiling. Bitten by gold fever, we panned for gold ourselves in a river beside an abandoned gold dredge. We squatted beside the river with our pan and plastic bowl filled with gravel. I dipped the pan into the creek to scoop up some water then shook it from side to side. The theory is that the gold will sink and as you tilt the pan and let the useless gravel and dirt wash away you will be left with only gleaming gold. We had no success. We decided that the dredge had been abandoned for a reason and rode on.

Ahead I could see the control post of the Alaskan border and I waited for Dave so that we could cross together. Alaska is the most Northern, Western and Eastern state of the United States. For a year and a half I had been telling people that I was riding to Alaska. At long, long last nobody could doubt my claim, not even myself. It was downhill all the way. It was mid-afternoon when we arrived at the border and the wind blew skirls of mist and sprays of rain across the moor. This time when I entered the USA, the border guards welcomed us with hot cups of tea, a rather more pleasant welcome than my arrival from Mexico.

I was bleary-eyed as we rode out of Fairbanks. I had settled on Eastern Russia to begin the Asian leg of my journey, and I spent three virtually sleepless days and nights on the internet trying to sort out my Russian bureaucracy, find a ship to cross the Pacific, and learn how many woolly jumpers a man needed at -40°C. My time in the Yukon had reassured me about the feasibility of cycling through Siberia in the winter. Everybody I met and talked with managed to function quite normally in the winter and I began to hope that I may be able to do so as well. I had spent time chatting with local dog mushers and outdoor-type people discussing the equipment I would need in Russia. Debate bounced back and forth about the merits of various kinds of winter footwear and the need for wind-proof willy warmers. I had even been given a fur hat and I felt excited about the adventure of the coming winter. I posted my passport back to Britain to apply for the Russian visa, and hoped that it would make its way back to me in Alaska before I had a run-in with the law and needed it. We loaded up with ten days supply of food for the ride up to the Arctic Ocean at Prudhoe Bay and the end of the road.

The summer heat wave was relentless. I had never imagined that I would be sweltering in Alaska. Our bikes were heavy with noodles, crackers and yet more lightweight dehydrated mashed potato powder. Fortunately we did not need to carry much water as there would be plenty of clean, cold creeks along the way. In Fairbanks we had stayed with Craig and his family. Craig worked for a haulage company and on our ride north, his wife and daughters kept us supplied with home-baked cookies, delivered to us by the drivers of 18-wheeler trucks on their way to the Alaskan oilfields. The massive lorries passed us then shuddered to a halt, dust billowing, and a big Alaskan trucker would climb down from the cab with our little tin-foil package. When they returned south a day or two later, the drivers greeted us with deafening blasts on their horns.

The Dalton Highway runs 400 miles up to the oilfields on the Arctic Ocean in Prudhoe Bay. It is a gravel access and service road for the controversial Alaska oil pipeline built in the 1970s, that runs 800 miles across the state. The highway is one of the most isolated roads in the United States. There are no towns on the route, only a few truck stops, and the emptiness was beautiful. I loved the ride along that long road, remembering each dusty day how long it had taken me to get there from Patagonia. I thought of all the people who had helped me, reflecting on the times when it had seemed too much, too hard and too far. I thought of all the people who had written to me or spoken with me or given me a thumbs-up sign in their rear view mirror as they passed. Together they had all given me the will to persevere.

The road climbed Finger Mountain Pass and we looked down over the trees and the enormous boggy plains of moss and lichen that are home to great herds of wandering caribou. After No Name Creek we crossed the Arctic Circle, the line north of which the sun does not set on the summer solstice. We were rewarded with a brief, unexpected, chunk of paved road. I was becoming melancholy and reluctant to rush. The end was so close. For 18 months, ever since I left Ushuaia, Prudhoe Bay had been my goal. Over the last few months it had become increasingly exciting to think of Prudhoe Bay because it had at last become realistically attainable. 'Not far now!' I often thought. 'Alaska! The end is actually in sight!' But once I reached Prudhoe Bay it would no longer be a goal; it would only be a milepost behind me. I would immediately be back at a new beginning with another ocean to cross and another long ride ahead of me. I would be closer to the start of that ride than to the end of it for a very long time. Exciting though it would be, it would entail so much work, effort, commitment and time.

Nightly swims became colder as we crept northwards. The hills were steep and I had to stand on the pedals and grind hard even in first gear. Sweat flowed and dust caked over the sweat. The descents on slippery gravel were skiddy and frightening. I wished that my back brake worked and that my tyres were not so bald. I needed to find time to get my bike overhauled before I left for Asia. It was in a terrible state. The road was challenging but I would not have wanted the Americas to end without a fight. They were ending as they had begun, on a dusty, hilly road with an isolated tin shack settlement at its end. The end of the road, the end of another continent.

Just a few days from the end, we met a Japanese chap who was attempting to cycle all the way from Prudhoe Bay down to Ushuaia. As we chatted about what lay ahead I could barely believe that I had ridden all that way, that I had kept riding for so long. Places that for him were still just names on a map, roads that were just lines on a page: all these were now memories for me. I felt overwhelming relief that I was near the end of the continent and not just beginning my ride like the smiling, clean, eager Japanese guy on his shiny new, functioning bike. We wished each other well and rode off down roads that were already in each other's memories, making our own memories as we went along.

Approaching the Atigun Pass, the final pass on this final road, we passed the final tree. There was nothing north of here but tundra. Straight ahead you would not see another tree until you were over the North Pole and down the other side into Scandinavia. The 1,400 metre high Atigun pass is the only road pass over the Brooks mountain range. Big, dizzy mountains closed in, craggy majesty all around us.

We tackled the pass late in the evening in warm sunlight. This was the last climb in the Americas. I thought back to the rhythmic grind of the mighty Andean climbs. I remembered the sheer, tropically sweaty hills of Colombia and the steepest roads of all in San Francisco. I had overcome doubt about my capability to persevere. I no longer worried what others may think of me failing but only about what I would think of my own failings. I had faced my fears about Colombia, I had learned another language, made many friends, and almost made it along the span of the planet's longest landmass. I was happy and more confident than I had ever been. I thought back to the last hill in Africa. I had attacked that with every bit of power, anger and fight that I could muster. I had sprinted it, blown myself out and arrived at the top roaring and defiant. The last hill in the Americas was very different, the ride had been so different. I rode the Atigun Pass slowly. The Americas had been good to me and I had enjoyed so much of it that there was no way I could just attack this last mountain as though I wanted to put it behind me. I had to savour it and be grateful for it. I stood on the pedals as I had done so often before, left-right, left-right, grinding away and the gravel crept past my wheels, stone by stone, surge by surge by surge with each stroke of the pedals. I got a puncture halfway up but I didn't care. I sat on the deserted gravel road and slowly repaired it. I almost did not want the pass to end because I was happy there. Right there, right then was exactly where I wanted to be. If the end of Africa was an unexpected and exultant victory over a fierce opponent, the end of the Americas was becoming a sad drawn-out goodbye to a friend. At the top Dave and I shook hands. The hardest days were behind us. It was all downhill to the end now.

Outside the Deadhorse Post Office, in Prudoe Bay at the end our ride, the end of the road and just 1,200 miles from the North Pole, we felt sadness, but also a gentle satisfaction. The oilfield's Post Office had a pin board of Polaroid photographs of the beaming faces and battered bikes of men and women who had cycled or motorcycled the road from Ushuaia to Prudhoe Bay, and the shiny bikes of those about to start. After a quick dip in the Arctic Ocean, I posed proudly for my photograph, but could not muster the joy and excitement I saw on the faces of all the other people, who had just finished their journeys. I could not escape the thought that this endpoint was also a new beginning, with a hemisphere of the world and all of Asia still between me and my home.

Prudhoe Bay is not a town, not even a village. It is an oilfield and it is inhabited mostly by male oil workers. The Post Office sells pornography in multipacks, as well as knife and gun magazines, patriotic 9/11 merchandise and lumberjack shirts. For the few women who worked in Prudhoe, finding a man wouldn't be difficult, 'the odds are good, but the goods are odd.' The men, meanwhile, consoled themselves that there was, 'a woman behind every tree.' There was not a tree in several hundred miles.

Alcohol is forbidden in Prudhoe Bay, and only one café was

open to the public, and it was too expensive for us. There was little potential for celebrating. Instead we hitchhiked back to Fairbanks. From there we would cycle down to Anchorage, Dave would fly home, and I hoped to sail away across the Pacific Ocean. A 13-hour drive brought us back to Craig Hughes' house. The 'Hughes Zoo' welcomed us with brownies and ice-cream and barrels of good humour. The two young daughters were endlessly amused by our weird English accent, and their dog was endlessly amused by the four of us chasing it round and round the lawn. I wanted to sleep, relax, celebrate, reflect and stay in America, but I had a ship to find.

The ride towards the peaks of Anchorage was superb. We passed Denali, the highest mountain in North America, which Dave had summited on a previous expedition. We rode into autumn and an unexpected jumble of colours and light after so long among uniform green dark forests. One evening a lady from Iowa stopped her car and gave us half a pizza. It was still warm and one of the best gifts I ever received from a passing driver. Streams splashed with salmon, frantic as if they knew that they were late. These were the last of the run, the losers, heaving themselves up the shallows. But the game was up. It was a desperate effort but it was too late and they were too weak. Many lay dead in the water, mouths open in final submission and exhaustion. They had given their all, but they had still failed. At night the stars returned in the sky after a long summer of light nights. The North Star shone high above us. I lay with my head out of the tent, eye-level with the dandelions, looking up and enjoying my first ever Northern Lights display. Bolts of light and folds of pale and ebbing colour grew and flowed above me, feeling very close yet maybe very far.

In Anchorage I had just time to hide a substantial boulder in Dave's bag before he flew home, lugging it through passport control and having to charm his way out of an excess baggage fine. He returned to his high-flying, big-earning city job, but his heart was no longer in it. A few months later he quit to join the HALO Trust. He now travels around the world, clearing landmines in wild and exciting corners, then exaggerates wildly to girls on intermittent visits to England.

I spent only a few days in Anchorage. I was nearly at the end of normality, anonymity, safety, ease of conversation, luxury, easy living, fair prices, blonde girls, maps, road signs, logic, order, comfort and familiarity. It was the end of all that I had been eager to leave behind three years ago in Yorkshire. Now I was reluctant to leave it behind, it was all ending with such a mad rush. Through a friend of somebody in Arizona who came to one of my slideshows, I had found passage on a ship and dashed madly around Anchorage buying equipment for Siberia. I was still hoping that my passport would arrive before the ship sailed, as the 187-metre *Canmar Dynasty* and her Indian crew would not wait. I was back to work, I supposed.

My passport arrived, with a three-month Russian visa. Alaska was an ideal place to learn about and buy the kind of surival gear needed at -40°C. I had to trust the judgement and expertise of local Alaskans, who knew much more than I did about what I was going to face. I thought about how cold the Andes had been. The -20°C temperatures there were the lowest I had ever known. They had been shockingly, brutally, frighteningly cold.

Waiting in a café to give a newspaper interview, I enjoyed a rare moment of calm and reflected on what lay ahead. I thought about the excitement of escapades on a new continent. Making quick, strong friendships with kind people who cared that I get through intact, and all the unknowns that lay in wait. I had been away from home for three years now, but right then I could have kept on riding for ever. Perhaps it was all just brave talk from the sunny sanctuary of Starbucks.

I sat back in the sunshine and closed my eyes. I breathed deeply and tried to clear my mind. I tried to blank the whole ride just for a few peaceful moments. But I could not do it. The journey was everything to me. It was literally my life. I resolved to treat myself to yet another layer of thermal underwear, and settled back to appreciate the late summer sunshine. There wouldn't be much of that where I was going. I was ready to feel the real world, raw and struggling, beneath my wheels once more. Six months in civilisation is enough for any man. I anticipated that Siberia would be grim, but it was exactly that which appealed and excited. It was time to go. I had a ship to catch.

Part 2

'Blue Mountains'

ASIA

Siberia to England

We are the Pilgrims, Master
We shall go always a little further,
It may be beyond the last blue mountain barred with snow,
Across that angry or that glimmering sea.
  – James Elroy Flecker

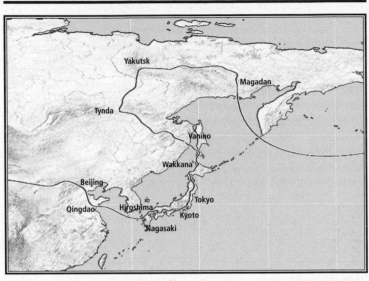

Magadan to Beijing

A road in the forest

I raise my glass to a road in the forest,
To those who fall on their way,
To those who cannot drag themselves farther,
But are forced to drag on.
— Varlam Shalamov

Russia is vast. Twice the size of Canada. A great swathe of green on my map, above the red deserts and purple-white mountains of China and the Himalayas. It stretches across eleven time zones from the Bering Straits to the Baltic. In contrast to Europe's spaghetti of roads and rash of towns and cities, the yawning emptiness of Russia is stark. My eyes, heading east from Moscow across the map hurdled the thin grey stripe of the Urals from Europe into Asia, and there was still a quarter of the globe to go. On, on, on across millions of square miles of soggy forest, *taiga*, permafrost and rivers. Yet, dotted in this nothingness, my map showed a few towns. People actually lived out there. What were people doing at this minute in Nadym, Pyl'karamo, Noginsky, Ekonda, Zhigansk, Lazo, Zyryanka, Chimchemenel? What was life like for the people who lived, worked, loved and died in such isolation?

Striking among the colossal blankness on my map was a solitary red thread, a road on the eastern edge of Russia. A road through the thousands of empty miles. I followed it with my finger, tracing it north from the Trans-Siberian railway, through Skovorodino and Tynda to Yakutsk where it bent southeast through Khandgya and Susuman, eventually reaching the Sea of Okhotsk at Magadan. That was how I learned of Magadan. The town at the end of the road, at the end of the world.

Magadan is a place that most have never heard of, yet it is a word that should generate the same feelings in us as 'Auschwitz.' Outlasting the Nazi Holocaust by decades and out-slaughtering it vastly, the great Soviet Communist experiment was begun by Lenin and championed by Stalin. It continued for decades after his death. The era was marked by suspicion, bureaucratic chaos and a complete disregard for humanity. Death, war, famine and imprisonment were seen on a scale unrivalled in the history of our planet. Stalin alone is credited with the deaths of somewhere between ten and sixty million people. He makes Hitler look like a novice. Few people grasp the scale on which the Soviet machine destroyed its own citizens. Even today, much of the former Soviet Union remains in denial about the whole era. I encountered little moral outrage or sorrow, and a great deal of shoulder-shrugging, from individuals who had forgotten the past and were reluctant to face their country's history. Many remembered Stalin with fondness, for at least back then there was a degree of employment and order. In Stalin's hometown (the aptly named Gori, in Georgia) I was staggered to see a statue of him still standing. It is impossible to imagine Braunau in Austria celebrating their own famous despot like this.

Accelerating rapidly from the 1930s was the terrifying waves of arrests, the mass deportations and the Great Purge, together with the desire for cheap economic productivity. This led to the massive network of prisons known collectively as 'the Gulag.' Millions of people were interred. The economy of the Soviet Union depended on the output of the camps yet they were callously inefficient. People could be imprisoned for the most trivial of offences. In the *Gulag Archipelago*, Alexander Solzhenitsyn described a Communist Party event where a standing ovation for Stalin continued for 10, 20, 30, 40 minutes because nobody dared to be the first man to stop clapping. Eventually, exhausted, one man stopped his reverence and everyone else, greatly relieved, stopped also and sat down. The next day that man was arrested and sent to Siberia.

Harshest of all the Gulag were the forced-labour camps of Siberia. Criminals, political prisoners, unlucky souls deemed enemies of the state, people rash enough to crack a joke about Stalin in the presence of an informer; all were herded east by rail in cramped cattle carts. After the rail journey many were then packed into the holds of ships in the port of Vanino to sail for Magadan. Prisoners built the harbour at Magadan, then the town and then the road to connect the town with the mines. Then they worked the gold and uranium mines and they died in their multitudes from cold, disease, starvation, murder or simple despair.

I was trying to do the journey in reverse, from Magadan back to Vanino. It was a journey that millions of victims never made. I would ride the road they had built with their lives, the infamous Road of Bones that linked Magadan with the mining city of Yakutsk and the navigable Lena River 1,400 miles away. It was said that a life was lost for every metre of progress as the road was built, and the workers bodies were simply ploughed into the road itself as work continued.

Even today the waste, cruelty and de-humanising of the Soviet system is an endless presence in Russia. Vodka, stifling stupid bureaucracy and despondency pervade everything. That, and awful cold, were the backdrop for which the next phase of my journey was set. Kindness, exhaustion, robbery, death and doubt would make a powerful supporting cast.

I would not be alone through the emptiness that promised to be the harshest leg of the ride so far. I had been mostly alone for three years now; an experience that had ranged from sublime to desperate. I learned a lot about myself, not least that I was not as interesting company as I had thought before I left home.

Ever since we were at school, Rob had dreamed of cycling from Shanghai to London. Like most glorious dreams it was destined to remain a dream as life rolled on busily. That was until I began a devious email campaign, politely pointing out to him that his life was dull and that he was wasting his years. If he didn't do it now, he never would. I quoted one of history's great thinkers, Eminem, "Look: if you had one shot, one opportunity, to seize everything you ever wanted – one moment – would you capture it or just let it slip?"

Rob had already joined me to ride in Ethiopia and South America. He had been teaching in Oxford for the last couple of years and it did not take much to persuade him to escape. He loaded bags full of winter gear onto his bicycle and flew, round almost half the globe, in less than a day. We estimated that it would take us a year and a half to reverse the process by bicycle.

We met in Magadan, Rob grinning broadly in the biggest fur hat I had ever seen. I had been boasting to him of the heroic fur hat that I had been given in the Yukon. On arrival in Russia, Rob rushed to the market to find one to out-do mine. His hat looked more suitable for guarding Buckingham Palace than for riding a bicycle, but he was very proud of it.

Magadan was like all the Soviet towns I saw, from the Pacific to the Black Sea. Peeling paint blistered on rows of dreary, identical apartment blocks, five or six storeys high. Tears of rust streaked the walls. Metal security doors, their locks broken, slammed and clanged hollow through unlit, unswept passages. Fading murals on the sides of buildings showed sturdy men straining hearty muscles, grafting nobly for the shared benefit of the mighty, indestructible Motherland before it all fell apart. Battered cars, imported cheap from Japan, crashed through puddles, and rubbish lay in piles on street corners. Each block of flats had its own little shop on the ground floor smelling of dust and sausage, the fullest shelf being the one with cheap vodka and strong beer. Parks lined with trees featured a statue of Lenin in his overcoat, his cap in his hand, gazing thoughtfully towards his brave new dawn. Across the dismantled USSR, statues of the atheist father of Communism, (was it not Lenin who sang, "imagine there's no heaven, it's easy if you try"?), are being removed or, as in Magadan, relegated from prime position in the main square to a less prestigious location.

Also prominent in Magadan were massive, unfriendly-looking administrative buildings, and a memorial to the Great Patriotic War of 1941-45, as World War II is known. Ladas and little buses swerved round the potholes and kiosks sold cigarettes and trashy newspapers. Translating the headline, 'George Bush – Bisexual!' cheered me immensely, for the outrageous headline itself and for my improving facility with the Russian alphabet to have read it. Department stores tried to hide the dearth of stock by spacing items carefully across the shelves. In the markets *babushkas,* old women wrapped in layers of cardigans, sat stoic and quiet, stout legs splayed from calf-length floral skirts. They sat with their meagre piles of home-grown produce on the pavement before them, small heaps of vegetables on upturned wooden crates, buckets of berries, jars of jam, a few eggs. There was not much money to be made. There was no hope of a relaxing old age for them.

Middle-aged women looked prematurely defeated and far from their brief glory days. With dyed hair and bright lipstick, they scared me and were terrifyingly grumpy. Younger women were beautiful, many in outrageous mini-skirts whatever the weather, but their flourish is brief before the harsh life, climate and cigarettes take their toll. Men in tracksuits, knitted jumpers and leather or denim jackets had sprouting hairdos and pale, spider-veined faces. They were tough and gruff, yet generous and courteous once they opened up to you. Honour and respect were important words to them and you had to earn your friendships. They smoked a lot and drank too much.

A doctor I met earned just £100 per month, and spent summer weekends tending an allotment to stockpile food for the long winter. Her small, tatty apartment had dodgy plumbing, lumpy beds and a burst sofa. She had a black and white portrait of her grandparents, a couple of religious images and a small TV for comfort, but she was indomitable. Her spirit and generosity were typically Russian. I came to greatly admire, respect and like the Russians, who were nothing if not resolute.

Life in Magadan appeared tough, but children still played and laughed as they do everywhere in the world. And, as the days passed, we came across some bright spots of hope and regeneration, like new blades of green grass growing through the ruins, fragile and tentative, but hopeful. The growing middle class was still too poor to leave, though some families had photos albums to recall a cherished foreign holiday. Some nice apartments hid inside the grubbiness of the uniform tower blocks. They boasted Western electronics and full bookshelves. There were also a few shops in Magadan different from the basic market stalls or the old-style Soviet department stores that sold everything but stocked nothing. There were fishing and hunting shops with pictures of fun summertime fishing trips on the walls, and a new Nike and Adidas shop with glossy posters and bright-lit shoes that seemed utterly out of place in the town.

Rob and I had no idea what we were getting ourselves into. The last leaves of autumn still lingered when we arrived but we knew that it was going to be extremely cold in a couple of weeks' time. We had no experience of true cold and we had no idea about cycling on snow and ice. Would our bikes cope? Would the oil and grease freeze solid? Did we have enough clothes? Would we cope? We were going to be learning on the job. Only one thing was clear, the local people were convinced that our plan was not possible. With a vocal, though well-meaning determination they rubbished our ideas and tried to persuade us to abandon the ride. I looked to the poster of a roaring David Beckham outside the Adidas shop and the bold slogan in Russian that declared, 'Impossible is Nothing.'

We stayed at Magadan's Catholic church which is twinned with one in Anchorage. It was home to two humble and inspiring American monks, Father Dave and Father Mike. Father Mike had moved to Magadan in 1994 to help former victims of the Gulags. He had fought with determination against the hostile local mafia and authorities and, together with Father Dave, raised money to build a lovely new church. Their devotion and faith was inspiring. It was a real help for Rob and me to have a base where we could organise ourselves, spread everything out and check our equipment. Before arriving in Russia we had researched equipment for temperatures that we anticipated would drop to -40°C. I had been aghast at -20°C in the Andes, and Rob's personal benchmark of cold until then was a chilly campsite in Northumberland.

As temperatures fell, we realised that much of the equipment I bought for us in Alaska was perilously inadequate. Fortunately we were able to buy extra things locally. Into our already full panniers we squeezed sheep fleece gloves, more layers of clothing and an extra foam sleeping mat that we bought from a hunting and fishing shop to supplement the two each we already had.

Best of all our purchases was some new footwear, *valenkis,* which looked like welly boots made from cheap carpet tiles and are perfect for snow and ice. They gradually mould to fit your feet like slippers. They served us brilliantly, despite costing only £9.

Our feet still became numb with cold, and we would often have to get off the bikes and run to revive them, but at least we avoided frostbite. One of the perennial problems of winter travel is the build-up of frozen condensation. Sweating and breathing gives off moisture and, as this freezes, sleeping bags and clothes become rimmed with ice. At night our boots froze solid, each morning we had to force our feet into them by melting the ice with the warmth of our feet. It was a deeply unpleasant start to each day. The ice in our boots thickened day by day as the cycle of sweat-freeze-melt continued, and it was our first priority whenever we found a warm place to struggle out of our boots and dry them. Unfortunately the boots shrunk a little bit each time they dried. By the end of Russia we both had to slash great slices across the heels and toes of the *valenkis* to squeeze our feet into them. We both lost all feeling in our toes for many months after leaving winter behind.

Another difficulty of equipping ourselves for the conditions was the limited amount of equipment that we could carry on the bikes. Weight was crucial. We needed to ride as fast as possible to minimise the number of freezing hours we were on the road each day, but I was carrying more than ever before. In addition to my usual load of four panniers and a large dry-bag strapped onto the back rack, I also now had another big dry-bag on the front rack to carry extra winter gear. We needed a larger tent now that Rob had joined me, and a company had kindly given us one. I could not afford to buy a tent suitable for a Siberian winter. The new one did not really seem up to the job, but at least it was free. We were carrying two complete stoves as we could not risk being without the means of making fire. We also had several fuel bottles, masses of clothes, spare parts and tools, up to ten days' worth of heavy, high-calorie food supplies and a heroic-looking axe that we loved, despite its weight. On top of all that, debatable as to whether they were worth their weight yet utterly indispensable to us, were enough books to see us through to the next bookshop 3,000 miles away in Japan. Our bikes were horribly heavy.

Pointless, inflexible bureaucracy still dominates life in Russia. Our first encounter with the system, apart from the hassles of securing visas, was when we had to register our arrival in Russia.

Registration is dealt with by a government department called the Office of Visas and Registration. They hide in an unmarked office, unadvertised on a random street. The office opens late, seldom, and closes ten minutes before it opens, except on weekdays and days beginning with 'S' when it does not open at all. You might have thought that OVIR would know about visas and registration, but it took Rob ten trips to the staggeringly grumpy and unhelpful woman to finally get our visas registered. His trips were interspersed by marathon queuing sessions at the rarely-open bank to pay associated fees and charges. After all that we were registered to be in Russia for just ten days. We were told to re-register in every town we passed through. We promised we would, and decided to do nothing of the sort. We made every effort to avoid officialdom until it was time to leave the country.

There was another reason why we did not want to draw attention to our visas. A Russian tourist visa is valid only for 30 days, an impossibly short time to ride 3,000 winter miles. So we had concocted a fictitious company, snazzy letterheads and all, and acquired 90-day business visas. Officially then, we were in the country to "promote working relations between Russia and Britain" for our Travel Publishing company named EWW Ltd (the English Wildmen's Wafflings). We were the proud President and vice-President of EWW Ltd, and we did not want any officials questioning us about our visas.

We were introduced to one of Magadan's only cyclists. Sergei worked at the Institute of Permafrost in Magadan and would have liked nothing more than the opportunity that Rob and I had, to have time and money and an easy passport to travel on. He invited us to his flat for dinner. Sergei was in his 40s, he wore dark glasses and a handlebar moustache and was a keen sportsman. He enjoyed travelling vicariously with us and helped us as much as he could, although he too doubted our chances of making it through Russia intact. Sergei translated my 'Magic Letter' (see page 353) into Russian for us. This letter, a basic summary of my trip, had been fine-tuned and translated into dozens of languages over the last years and was always my first line of defence to explain myself to inquisitive people, grumpy officials, and people I felt were about to rip me off.

We enjoyed roast chicken and potatoes together and Sergei showed us the only detailed map we had ever seen of the region we were trying to ride through. The best map we had found was a wall map of the entire Russian Federation. There was only one road through the region but navigation would not be as simple as it sounded. The dirt road involved river crossings, swamps and mountain passes. At times it faded to nothing more than a cross-country ride. Some stretches of the road were open only in winter, others only in summer. Even Sergei, who was far more intrepid than any other person we met in Russia, had not travelled very far down the road. After the difficult northwestern leg from Magadan to Yakutsk we would point our noses due south until we reached the Trans-Siberian railway line at Skovorodino. Then we would turn east and follow the famous railway line to the Pacific.

On a hill above Magadan stands a memorial to the millions of people from 27 nations who died in the prison camps of the Kolyma region. Sergei took us to visit it. The 17-metre monument, in the shape of a crying face, is called the Mask of Sorrow. I thought of the memorials I had already visited, the World War cemeteries in France, the Monument to Peace in Beirut, Spion Kop in South Africa, the Falkland Islands' war memorials in Patagonia, the Holocaust memorial in San Francisco. Now this. And soon Hiroshima… Lord, what fools these mortals be. Behind the Mask of Sorrow a statue of a kneeling girl covers her face in tears or grief or denial or prayer, or perhaps she was just another faceless victim.

The Mask of Sorrow is a monument, but it also described the tangible atmosphere of Magadan that I felt when I first arrived. I have never been to a place that felt so devoid of life, where the people seemed so like shells, like objects on a conveyor belt merely going through the motions of life that a system had completely sucked dry.

Beneath the confusion I felt in coming face-to-face with this awful history I was churning with excitement at the challenges that awaited. But was excitement not appropriate here? What would all those victims think of me as I prepared to ride down the road they had built at such cost; riding for fun through their hell, their exile, their prison and their graveyards? They had been prisoners; I was a young man, with more freedom than I could cope with at times. Was I making all that I could of my fortunate life or was I frittering precious time away? Preparing to try to take on a Russian winter gave plenty of scope for soul-searching.

We stood there, Rob and I, in front of that hilltop memorial on a cold grey damp afternoon. We were numbed, shocked and silent. Sergei turned away from the statue and from us and, looking over the city, the autumnal hills and the two quiet bays, he said, "I love my Magadan."

The pessimists had succeeded in persuading Rob that he had jumped in right at the deep and very cold end, and he became terse and nervous. I felt that I was the only person left for thousands of miles with any unthinking puppy-dog optimism left. It was hard trying to generate enough optimism for two. I tried to balance respect for the hazards with enthusiasm and confidence, believing that once we were actually on the move things would begin to look more feasible. We would learn and adapt and overcome. Plus, with Rob being a geography teacher I was comfortable that at least we would not get lost. This was important for my peace of mind. But, as we loaded up our bikes, about to ride away into the wild, Rob turned to me and asked, "does the sun always set in the west?"

Sergei rode out of Magadan with us for a couple of hours, filming us on his old video camera. It was a magnificent autumn day, crisp but sunny, the sky a gorgeous blue, the trees a fabulous riot of colour. It was a perfect day to ride. All of Eurasia lay ahead of us and, once again, it seemed absurdly ambitious and presumptuous to dare to take the first pedal stroke. What little impact that push on the pedals made on the distance between me and my home. How many millions more awaited? We had been told that winter would hit hard within a week, so I made sure to enjoy those final few days of autumn. We waved Sergei a very fond farewell; yet another new friend I did not expect to see again.

Our feelings were mixed as we began. We were excited to be riding but our enthusiasm had been severely damaged by the endless negativity we had been subject to in Magadan. Rob had now come up with these insane odds for our chances, "25% we get through fine, 25% we just scrape through, 25% we have to quit, 25% we die." I didn't know whether to think he was completely nuts to be having a crack anyway if that is what he believed the odds to be, or to think him very brave.

That night we camped in a forest. Neither of our brand new stoves worked. We axed down a tree but the wood was too damp to burn. We ate chocolate for dinner and for the first time I felt a splinter of real fear at what we were attempting. When the world is frozen solid you simply cannot survive unless you can melt ice and snow to drink. Siberia does not treat fools lightly. Eventually we fixed one stove, made a note to buy some fire-lighters and kept going. The temperature free-fell daily. In gloves and hat and cold feet I stomped into a small shop where the radio was playing the song *Sand in my Shoes* by Dido. It set me dreaming of sunshine and summer holidays and Sarah and laughter, "I've still got sand in my shoes, and I can't shake the thought of you." Outside it was bloody cold, and we had barely even begun.

In sub-zero sunshine we rode through a small town that seemed dumped at random in the middle of nowhere. The collection of crumbling, ugly tower blocks, streaked with rust, spiked with improvised television aerials was coloured only by lines of washing hung out of windows to dry. As we progressed deeper into the Kolyma region, the condition of these occasional towns deteriorated. We began to pass shells of towns, abandoned victims of the collapsed artificial economies of the Soviet Union. Towns that could not survive when they were no longer propped up by subsidies from the State. In the last decade people had left these small towns in droves and gone west to the big cities, to Irkutsk, Moscow and the Baltic searching for work.

Now the towns were ghost towns, smashed and empty, inhabited only by the wind and old memories. It was eery and sad to wander through people's silent front rooms, crushed hopes and torn friendships. I had the same song running through my head as I picked my way through the open wall of some family's kitchen. "Try to remind myself that I was happy here, before I knew that I could get on a plane and fly away…" Two ravens rolled in the sky, their coarse cries the only movement among these empty towns and dreams, where a system failed its people.

We rode under a blue sky as autumn colours burned joyfully, a blazing celebration of brief defiance before bone-white winter arrived to strangle the land. We relished the fresh, golden days until one night winter slid its appallingly cold pale hand over autumn's soft flank and the first snow fell. The pine needles shivered down leaving bony skeletons of trees bracing for the freezing onslaught that was rushing over us fast, squeezing, squeezing the life out of all it touched. Siberia is a beautiful, pure but daunting land. We skidded and slid and fell and bruised as we struggled in that first freeze to learn how to cycle on snow. We were on a very steep learning curve. Some days the skies were grey and pregnant with more snow, others were bright like a new razor. Shining, slicing. Snow settled deep into the land. Winter had arrived.

One night I plucked up the nerve to rip off my clothes and run naked through the snow into a river crusted with ice. This was a response to Rob, leaping like a lunatic from his sleeping bag at dawn and dashing into a pond to seize a lead in our Great Siberian Swimming Contest. Now I had dragged the score back to 2-2. We were about to turn off the main road and embark on 750 miles of almost deserted track to Yakutsk. We had loaded up with high-calorie food to get us as far as the next, village, Tomtor, known as the 'Pole of Cold.' Tomtor has the dubious record of being the coldest village on Earth with a world record low temperature of -71°C. We crammed our bags with 60 Snickers bars, 9kg of pasta, 3kg of oats, 3kg of sugar, 4 huge sausages, 1kg of cheese, 11 cans of meat and 5 litres of petrol. Unfortunately we forgot to buy toilet paper.

Just as we were about to depart on this long, isolated stretch my rear freewheel body broke. This collapse of my bike's gears was a problem I had not known before, and one that I was not prepared for. I was unable to repair it, and unable to continue. We were still only 24 hours of drunkard-filled buses away from Magadan, a mere stone's throw in Siberia. We beat an embarrassing retreat back to Magadan to sit and wait for a FedEx replacement. When we left a fortnight earlier, Father Mike cautioned us, "There are old pilots and there are bold pilots, but there are no old, bold pilots." He was amused to see us back so soon.

We waited an agonising ten days while FedEx messed around. The days crawled and the mercury crept down. I fretted and paced. The snow fell deeper and deeper as vital days were lost from our visa. Eventually we gave up on FedEx and Sergei came to the rescue. He stripped my hub down, custom made a metal tool and, miraculously, got my wheel spinning again. Saved by Sergei we were ready to ride again. He shrugged and smiled at our grateful admiration. "In Russia we just have to fix things," he said. We took the bus back to the small village where we had left the bikes in the workers' hostel. With this maddening delay, 'furious winter's rages,' grew more fierce each day, and our visas were running out. Having now had a taste of real cold, Russia's Far East, and the wonderful hardy people who lived there, I was more eager than ever to get back onto one of the hardest and most exciting stretches of the road so far.

Heaven and hell

This could be heaven or this could be hell.
– 'Hotel California,' The Eagles

We had two options to choose from, the 'summer road' or the 'winter road.' Each one was only passable during the appropriate season. Weeks of hearsay and guesswork had washed us back and forth over the sharp rocks of indecision. Now a decision was called for. The 'summer road' was passable only in summer because it crossed high mountains. The 'winter road', across a swamp and severed by rivers, was only passable when frozen solid. We were there at the worst possible time of year, not yet mid-winter, no longer summer. Too cold for high mountains, too warm to walk on water.

All advice about what road to take was contradictory, except for the unanimous verdict that whatever we attempted would be impossible and foolhardy. The junction was only a day away now, a decision was needed and so a decision had been taken. We chose the summer road. We felt better knowing our fate. That evening though we spoke with the boss of a village power station and he was adamant that the winter road via Ust-Nera *would* be passable by bicycle even before the imminent big freeze. We changed our minds again and settled on the winter road.

The winter road, flatter but hundreds of kilometres longer, was the route used by heavy trucks driving to Magadan in winter time. As far as we could ascertain, some of it was a proper dirt road and some of it was pure cross-country. It sounded tough but if we had a crisis we could count on help coming along the winter road eventually. Nobody would travel along the summer road for at least six months. We were told that the winter road became passable only after at least a week of temperatures of -30°C. The temperature was dropping steadily, a degree or two per day, and we anxiously watched our thermometer and hoped that it would continue to fall until we reached the river crossings. Were it not for the ominous tick-ticking of our visas and the 3,000 miles that lay ahead of us we could have sat around and waited for the rivers to freeze. We pushed blindly on and hoped for the best.

We escaped the horrors of the tent one night by sleeping in the kitchen of a coal mine. A skin of ice-crusted nylon provided little shelter from the astonishing cold, and nights in the tent were becoming awful. The thought of avoiding sleeping in the tent always cheered us and we rode on with renewed zest if we saw lights in the distance at evening time. It also made us feel less alone. I wondered whether our occasional chance of respite and escape made life easier or harder than for people on polar expeditions. In Antarctica you simply know that there will be no warm beds or showers until your expedition is over. Did our occasional escapes make life easier, or did they make the nights in the tent all the more miserable?

We trudged through the snow towards the building. We banged on the wooden door with our thick gloves. Night-time visitors were presumably rare at that remote mine so as the door opened, all faces turned towards the ice-clad Englishmen on bicycles. Our hesitant hellos and attempts at explanation were waved away by hands motioning that we should come quickly inside so that they could shut the door. Then introductions, handshakes and a re-shuffling of seating positions to get Rob and I closest to the log stove. Off with the boots, gloves, balaclavas, hats. A cup of hot tea appeared. The ice began to melt and drop from our beards, the smiles returned to our faces and we could begin to answer the questions from the curious Russians. We asked permission to put our tent up somewhere outside and were instead told that we would sleep inside, which is what we had really hoped for! My life had distilled to a stark simplicity: warmth, electric lights, hot water. Deep, warm, soft sleep – this was all I needed. The miners dragged out a couple of filthy, lumpy mattresses and we grinned happily.

No sympathetic miners rescued us after that. At the end of a long, hard day skidding and crashing on the icy road, the temperature was dropping faster than the tent was going up. It was -30°C and the elastic in our cheap tent poles lost its elasticity in the cold. It took about 30 minutes to fix this, and the same time was required on the same task at every campsite in Russia. My fingers suffered even in gloves as I worked to tie and untie fiddly knots and thread elastic through the narrow tent poles. I had to wear the gloves, otherwise my bare fingers stuck to metal. As soon as we stopped in the evening we donned several layers of fleece clothing, fat Feathered Friends down jackets and enormous fur hats. Before we could do that we had to strip to the waist to remove the Camelbak drinking packs we wore against our skin to prevent them from freezing, and get dressed again as fast as possible.

The plastic window of our tent cracked and broke open, leaving a half-metre gaping hole in our flysheet. It allowed in rather an excess of Siberian fresh air. I made a mental note not to take on a Siberian winter again with a £50 tent.

In the tent the pumps on our stoves were not working once again. We were hungry and desperate for warmth and food. Rob, still feeling the cold, was not thinking straight. He lubricated the stove parts with saliva as we had often done over the years in campsites together on four continents. But in Russia the saliva froze solid in seconds. I put the whole lot down my pants to thaw and headed outside to collect a great mound of snow to melt for cooking. It is amazing how much snow is required to create a pitiful puddle of lukewarm water, and how long bitterly cold ice took to melt, warm and eventually, boil. When the water did boil, the rising steam froze to a skin of ice throughout the tent, and over all our clothes and sleeping bags.

I lubricated the stoves with my lip salve, reassembled them and was very relieved when the reassuring roaring blue flames settled into their rhythm. Rob was shivering deep inside his sleeping bag and doubtless wondering, as I was, what the hell we were doing. He emerged to gratefully slurp the hot noodles with energy-rich pig fat studded with garlic that the miners gave us. The hot calories did wonders for morale and we chuckled together at how much we had to learn. As we drank hot chocolate heaped with sugar, Rob commented on the importance to the local people of fur, fat and fuel. Callously I said that most seemed to need little but cigarettes and alcohol.

Far too soon, the beeping alarm hauled us from the brief escape of dreams into a bitter new day. I cooked more noodles and hot chocolate for breakfast, packed the stove and all my gear, took down the tent, loaded my bike, then waited half an hour for Rob who was still just packing his own bags. We were both out of our depth and we really had to work together in order to survive, but Rob was not coping with the cold. He had only just joined me on the road therefore his drills and riding pace were much slower than my own. I was having to do everything myself. That was fine, indeed it was what I was used to, but I was not used to becoming seriously cold whilst waiting around. Everything we did was taking far too long, stealing vital time away from the only two activities that really mattered in our life in the next few months: covering miles and getting sleep. I waited for Rob and I worried for our prospects. We were not yet working together.

A significant consolation for each new milestone of deeper cold was the better chances of the rivers freezing and our being able to get through the winter road to Yakutsk. In each settlement we were still told that the route was impossible, but it was too late, we had made our choice, we were committed and we had to make it possible.

We rode on and on through a frigid emptiness of low hills white with snow and black, leafless woods. The white road ahead over dark wooded hillsides stood out like a photo negative. The horizon's high mountains looked enticing and I felt happy to be here, to be at the ends of the earth on my bicycle. "I'm out here a thousand miles from my home, walking a road other men have gone down. I'm seeing a world of people and things," sang Dylan in my headphones. It was good to be sharing all this with Rob. Despite the mounting petty tensions between us that are typical of extreme situations I knew that our friendship was strong and I anticipated rose-tinted fireside nostalgia together with bored grandchildren and fluffy slippers in years to come.

One night we had just pitched our tent in roadside trees when a lorry stopped and the driver told us of an empty *dacha*, a cottage nearby, where we could sleep. It would be far warmer than the tent. After we cooked and ate, we broke the camp we had just pitched, packed up our gear and crunched 20 minutes through the black, frozen forest to the riverbank. Sure enough we came across the small, empty wooden *dacha* in a clearing on the riverbank. The door was not locked. We went inside, lit a candle and made ourselves comfortable. We put our axe to use restocking the woodpile, got a blazing fire going in the stove and toasted our good fortune with a cup of tea.

Those wood-stoves were my altars of the North. Head bowed, palms spread, I accepted with grateful adoration the warmth that refilled my veins. Sleeping outside beneath a Siberian night was like a death: fascinating and terrifying. With no beliefs beyond what I experience first-hand, I had to feel that cold to believe it, but I snatched too eagerly at any chance of escape. Escaping fear does not overcome it. But it did feel good to be warm.

We made the most of it by taking off our socks to examine our feet. We had both already lost all feeling in our toes. We got the hut so hot that I fell asleep bare-chested on the bed. Waking chilled later on I poked the ebbing fire back to life and heaped it high with logs before snuggling back into my sleeping bag. By morning the water in the room had still frozen solid. We wrote a thank you note for the unknowing owner of the hut and left it propped on the table. Goldilocks would have approved.

Studying our map and measuring the route with string we calculated that we still needed to do 52 miles per day for the next 50 days, with one day off in Yakutsk, if we were to make it out of Russia before our visas expired. Judging by our current progress this was not possible. We had only managed 50 miles on one day so far. The temperature fell and the days became shorter as winter closed in. It was only going to get harder, and we would only accomplish our goal if we ourselves became harder. The pressure was really on now. It was time now for some simple hardness, for gritting of teeth and getting on with it, for aggressive self-competition and a blunt refusal to quit. Plus a few private tears and prayers perhaps.

Small rivers were frozen solid now, but in larger rivers the stream was still flowing in narrow swift channels through the encroaching ice, steaming in the frigid air. Fortunately the bridges in that area were still standing. Gradually the channels were filling with clear ice jelly and slush was steadily piling up. But the dark blue-green water would continue to lurk unseen beneath the ice crust for a while yet before it froze to solid grey-white ice. How long would they take to freeze? How do you know when a river is safe to cross? Who is the first and last person to make the crossing each year? It certainly would not be me! Does everyone just wait for a vodka-fuelled fool to take his chance and see how he gets on?

After a few more particularly cold days we reached the town of Ust-Nera as the low sun flamed the highest row of hills at sunset. Ust-Nera was the biggest settlement along the winter road. It was made up of a cluster of concrete apartment blocks, a few shops, a telephone exchange, a small clinic and a school. The small town was a typically brave Soviet attempt to impose order on the Siberian landscape. The grubby tower blocks in Ust-Nera were perched on concrete stilts because foundations could not be dug in the permafrost. Heating pipes ran to each building from a central heating factory, its tall chimney belching black coal clouds. Residents had no control over their heating and complained that it was switched on too early in October and turned off too early in May. It was not unusual to see windows thrown wide open in mid-winter to bring some fresh air into the oppressively over-heated flats. Much of the insulating cladding had fallen from the heating pipes and they steamed and sprayed scalding water through rusting hairline cracks. Fat icicles hung from the leaking joints. When the broad pipes reached a road they arched up and over it. They sliced through vegetable plots and over pavements with no thought of aesthetics or common sense. Homemade stepladders straddled the pipes when they ran along pavements or in front of doorways.

Rob went into the school in Ust-Nera to look for an English-speaking teacher who might be able to suggest a place for us to sleep. I guarded the bikes outside and fended off the questions of muffled school children wrapped up in hats and scarves who clearly thought me mad to not speak Russian, to not *be* Russian and to have arrived in their town on a bicycle! In winter! Ha-Ha! This was hilarious! 'Quick, lads! Come here! You'll never believe what's just arrived!'

Rob emerged, smiling English teacher in tow. Aigul was one of my fondest memories of many in Russia, an example of so much that was good and decent among the difficulties of life there. Dressed in a full length fur coat and massive fur hat she spoke excellent English. Some of the English teachers I met round the world could barely speak the language, so it was always pleasant to find an intelligent person with whom I could communicate. Aigul invited us to her home, apologising profusely in advance for its shabbiness. In her standard-issue two room Soviet apartment we expressed our sincere gratitude for her hospitality.

Aigul was about 30 years old, with blue eyes and winter-flushed cheeks. She apologised in superb English about her bad English as we all sipped coffee. She had no opportunity to practice and her students had little interest in learning something that had no relevance in their lives. She asked us to come into her school the next day to talk to her classes, hoping that it may spark some interest in them. Although we could ill afford to lose another day, we readily agreed. All three of us were thrilled by the enthusiasm in the school the next day when, after we had shown photographs from our ride and answered questions, Rob and I spent hours signing autographs for excited children who thought that we were famous.

Returning from work, Aigul's lorry driver husband, Gena, was surprised to find his wife sitting on his bed with two men. Luckily he found it amusing and exciting that all our lives had somehow come to cross paths. That night Aigul and Gena tried to make Rob and me sleep in their bed and they would sleep on the floor in the other room. The hospitality of Russians never ceased to amaze me and we had to be very insistent that there was no way that we would agree to them sleeping on the floor in their own home. We won in the end and slept on the floor with gratitude.

Aigul's father-in-law, also a lorry driver, was a big help to us, talking over our onward route with the confidence of somebody who really knew the land and was not exaggerating his knowledge as so many Russian men did. He told us which settlements had been abandoned on the route and where we could get food, which rivers were bridged and which ones had to be crossed on the ice. He was very worried about us, as was everybody who knew about Siberian winters but had never camped outside in one.

On the morning that Rob and I left, we sat quietly together with all of Aigul's family for a minute or two before departing. This is a lovely Russian tradition; a moment to pause and reflect on the journey ahead, all that awaits and the friends that are left behind. Our panniers were stuffed with donations of food, including a whole roasted chicken. As we said our goodbyes I wished that one day I could return the hospitality for this big-hearted family back home in England. We all made the right noises but all of us knew that, so long as Russia's people were shackled by the corruption, inefficiency and suspicion of their leaders, this family would not be able to leave.

One night, confused by exhaustion, I dreamed that my alarm had gone off and that it was time to wake up. I sat up and began lighting the stove to prepare breakfast. Ice showered down from the roof whenever I moved against the tent. Rob, gruffly, from the depths of his sleeping bag growled in annoyance, "What are you doing?"

I snapped back something curt about how I was cooking Rob his breakfast. Rob ended the debate by pointing out, "It is 1.30, you weirdo: go back to sleep!"

Most nights I lost precious sleep, jolted awake by awful cramp in my hamstrings from cold, hunger and fatigue. I fought to straighten the knotted muscles, stretching my legs inside the sleeping bag as I tried to muffle my moaning sobs. Losing vital sleep to cook phantom breakfasts was irritating.

Fortunately, outside my own private worries and mounting pessimism, Rob was optimistic that we could make it all the way by bike and would not have to resort to taking the Trans-Siberian train to get out of Russia before our visas expired. The riding was good, hard and cold over high snowy passes. Diamond crusted trees sparkled and the sky was unblemished blue. Nothing moved and tiny particles of snow glittered in the air. Descending the mountains we had to wear even our thick duvet jackets to protect us from the flaying wind-chill. No skin was exposed to the air at all. Even our eyes were shielded, Rob's behind ski goggles, mine behind ridiculously inappropriate lawn mowing safety glasses that I had picked up for free in Alaska.

A notable day was the first day that Rob rode faster than me. Rob was slowly getting into the mental and physical shape needed to cope. His mind and body were toughening to the task. Although Rob's increased speed was essential if we were to have the slightest chance of making it through Russia in time, I was still vexed that he was faster than me. My knee was sore and my bike's gears were jumping. Having a companion was definitely a good thing for me after three blissfully selfish years, but I was behaving like a selfish two-year old who still feels that the universe revolves around him.

Life was grim and monotonous. We were riding as hard as we could but the roads were covered in ice and snow so progress was slow. Our bikes were heavy and we were hampered by our bulky clothes. Every task took time. Eating a frozen chocolate bar, drinking from the hydration packs in our jackets, slurping the tepid sludge of noodles and sausages in our thermoses, or even taking a pee, all became complex tasks with so many layers of clothing and three sets of gloves to negotiate. We could not even ride fast downhill because of the ice and often walked down hills to avoid crashes. It was a weary trudge.

Everything becomes difficult in the cold. Mending a puncture is a good example. Getting a puncture is tiresome wherever in the world you and your bicycle are. But in Russia we had to do this every time: Stop riding, shout to the other person to alert them, put on a couple of warm jackets and an extra hat or two. Remove the wheel, take out the tools, set up the stove and light it. Hold wheel in flame to warm it enough for rim and tyre to thaw apart. Do not overdo this stage! Howl at freezing hands and wave them like windmills to thaw. Crouch down to fight the frozen tube valve out through the wheel rim. (Every time I bent over during this entire process I got an icy blast down my Builder's Bum and cursed my too-short thermals.) Bend the new tube into shape. Warm up hands. Get pump. Plastic on pump snaps in extreme cold. Swear. Get second pump. Plastic on second pump snaps. Swear and rage and jump around. Get out superglue and fix pump. Hands really hurting by now, whole body shivering. Put pump into pants (being careful of where the superglue is!) to warm up before using it so that it won't break again. Pump up tyre. Replace wheel and tools. Strip off extra clothes. Get riding fast to begin to warm up your body again.

An hour later the whole saga may be repeated and there was no alternative but to get on with it. Despite the time these repairs took, the stress and the cold, I thrived upon these initiative and patience tests and felt satisfied when I succeeded. I appreciated the importance of a positive attitude. The Finnish have a word for the combination of willpower, determination and calm thought; *sisu*. Similar concepts are common amongst other peoples who live in unforgiving, cold lands. There is a long sliding scale between 'surviving' and 'thriving' in conditions like those and my state of mind made all the difference as to where I was on any day. *Sisu* was what would get us through.

We had worried that no traffic would pass along that track of frozen mud, but our fear was allayed when a tank drove past one day. Noisy and unstoppable on its wide caterpillar tracks, the tank was being used by a road construction crew to survey the track ahead. Tiring of the rutted, frozen marshland the tank decided on a shortcut through a forest. And so it powered, quite literally, *through* the forest, battering over swathes of young trees in its path. We were happy to follow, as an alternative to dragging the bikes over the frozen, gouged waves of mud made in the summer by heavy vehicles battling through the swamp.

On a morning that our thermometer bottomed out at -40°C, I had a massive morale boost when Rob cooked breakfast. Anyone who knows Rob must wonder how having breakfast cooked by him could be a good thing, but it meant that he was taking a grip on the situation at last rather than merely reacting to events. He was working fast enough for us to be able to begin working as a team. I had cooked breakfast, instant noodles and coffee, every day so far because my drills were so much slicker than Rob's, having been doing them daily for three years. For Rob to be now fast enough with his campcraft to share the cooking duties boded well for our relationship, and for our odds of getting through Russia in time. He had become lean and extremely fit, but that is easy to do. He had started to master the details of our life that came only with practice. Now he just needed to become harder. I could draw hope from knowing that he certainly had the will to succeed. "If you want a good polar traveller," one of Captain Scott's companions wrote, "get a man without too much muscle, with good physical tone, and let his mind be on wires – of steel. And if you can't get both, sacrifice physique and bank on will." I was impressed, as I had so often been, travelling with Rob. He had worked really hard and now he had caught me up. His perseverance and quiet determination was a constant inspiration.

One night we passed a weather station and took our chance to knock on the door and plead ourselves a night out of the cold. Can you imagine a merrier scene than two meteorologists and two Englishmen discussing the state of the weather over hot cups of tea beside a roaring fire? I had become, if not comfortable with, then at least tolerant of the extreme cold that we were living in, but when I nipped outside from the warm kitchen to take a pee, the brutal impact of -40°C air was mortifying. This was no place for humans to be living. From his experience as a prisoner in the Gulag, Solzhenitsyn said, "man is a creature who can get used to anything." I felt more able to cope with temperatures now than a few weeks earlier, when the temperature had first dropped sharply to -8°C, and Rob and I settled for an honourable draw in our Great Siberian River Swimming Contest.

The full moon was bright on the white landscape outside. The hills stood out black against the pale moonlight-washed sky. The snow crunched roughly beneath my thick felt boots. And then, with all the magical rush and Pavlovian excitement of Christmas, I heard sleigh bells in the distance. The smooth hiss of sleigh runners and the ragged puffing of animals and then I saw them, racing towards me through the darkness and slowing in a skid to stop beside me. Reindeer! Huddled deep into his furs, the native Yakut driver jumped down from the sleigh, shook my hand and hurried into the station with a package under his arm. Moments later he emerged carrying a box, loaded it onto the sleigh, shouted at the steaming reindeer, waved at me and then they were gone, sliding away into the night towards his own warm stove. I returned inside and found Boris and Andrei dropping into the soup pot some of the hunks of Rudolph and Dancer that my Santa Claus had just delivered in exchange for a few bottles of vodka.

There was one spare bed in the station and Rob slept in that. One of the weathermen offered me his bed. I assumed that he was working the nightshift so I accepted gratefully. Imagine then my surprise (and Rob's hilarity) when I awoke at dawn to find the weatherman snuggled up completely naked beside me! It certainly was a good way of helping me wake up and get out of bed fast. With Rob still sniggering I hastily said our goodbyes and we rode on down the valley.

Sometimes, when Rob was very far ahead, or a long distance behind me, I stopped and watched him ride. It unsettled me to see that small figure creeping tiny over the vast landscape, making no impression on the huge scene; inconsequential, disconnected to the environment, a foreign body unknown to all it encountered. Un-bonded and free, perhaps, yet nobody knew it or awaited its arrival. Nobody cared about it or looked forward to its arrival. When I saw him looking so alone it made me see the last three years of my life in a new light. I could understand now why people marvelled at my vulnerability and loneliness. I looked on with bewilderment that I had managed it for so long. I looked now at that little lone figure with melancholy, thinking of the private struggles, of the solitary triumphs and obstacles that I would never be able to share properly with anyone. Rob had been suggesting in the last few days that we should do a scenic detour to Australia (see www.cyclinghomefromsiberia.com) on our way home to England, but reflecting like this made me want to finish it all as soon as possible. I often wondered how long I should ride for. I could ride for ever and not see all that I wanted to see, but the law of diminishing returns suggested that every day on the road I learned less and experienced fewer new things than the day before. But when should I stop? Certainly at times I was tempted to just keep riding, enjoying the world and the monastic simplicity of the road forever. But, looking back down a long road at Rob, it seemed to me that I should stop soon. I wanted to get out while the party was still fun. Life is so short and I wanted to experience new views and perspectives.

I also thought, from seeing that solitary rider, that the decision to ask Rob to ride with me was the right one, above and beyond the simple pleasure of having a good friend to share it all with. I was finding having company wearing: having to discuss minutiae and trivial arrangements drove me crazy. I had become accustomed to taking and executing decisions myself. I was not used to discussing everything with middle management. Stuff too unimportant to waste breath or time on, things that I had just been doing without thinking for years. And yet a joint expedition had to be a joint expedition. I felt that, at least in those early stages together, we needed to be sharing all decisions. The foibles of another person infuriated me after such a long period of selfish self-indulgence. So it was really good for me to be doing this with Rob. It was helping me to reintegrate into the world.

Khandyga is a large town, close to the Aldan River. A friendly woman, Marina invited Rob and I to stay with her, and her annoyingly drunk husband. I was increasingly saddened and repulsed by the grip that alcohol had on so much of Russia. Nowhere else have I seen such a proportion of men drunk at all hours of the day. The wasted hordes of useless, glassy-eyed men of Russia showed what a dangerous, dirty drug alcohol can be.

All over the world I valued women for honesty, safety and compassion. In Russia they were essential to protect us from the unwanted, enthusiastic attentions of drunk men desperate for us to join them drinking. Marina was quiet and kind and made her drunken husband and hyperactive four year old son let us go to sleep at about midnight. Her husband was a different man in the morning: placid and smiling through his hangover as he brought us coffee and welcomed us anew to his house. How sad I felt though, drinking my breakfast coffee, that he was already drinking a tumbler of vodka. In Russia the gesture for "would you like a drink" is to flick your throat a couple of times with a leering demonic grin on your face in anticipation of the impending oblivion. It looked horribly like a junky slapping his arm to raise a vein. The pressure put on us by people to drink was high. We resisted fiercely, accepting always only one toast of vodka before absolutely refusing more. It was very difficult not to yield.

Despite being made optimistic by the local saying that "no

barrier bars a Russian's path," we were relieved upon reaching the Aldan River to find that the crossing was not going to be a problem. The river had frozen. This was the make-or-break river crossing for our entire ride. There were no alternatives at this time of year as the summer ferry had stopped for the winter. The village on the south bank of the river communally invited us for lunch in their administration office. Afterwards the councillors posed for photographs in their gigantic fur hats before waving us off across a snow-covered field towards the river.

We walked along the riverbank for a couple of hours, the ice crunching beneath our boots. At the point where we had been advised to cross we came across a frozen mound of skinned carcasses of cows. Three men were crouched beside a fire, barbecuing hunks of beef fat and slugging from a vodka bottle. The men were waiting for a lorry to come and carry their beef to Khandyga. They had shuttled it by skidoo from their village across the river and so Rob and I were convinced at long last about the solidity of the ice. They even let us test drive their skidoo!

I enjoyed crossing that broad frozen river. I had imagined it would be smooth like an ice rink but it was a chaos of broken, upheaved frozen grey chunks. The tangled frustration of a fevered person's bed sheets, dusted with thorny thistles of pretty frost. From here we knew that the route was clear to the end of Russia. Now it was simply a foot race between us and time. The excuses had to stop if we were not to surrender the prize of hard-earned success. We needed to start riding longer and faster. As Lance Armstrong said, it was "time to ride like we'd stolen something."

We rode through Yakutia, an area of indigenous people that felt separate from the rest of Russia. Facially the Yakut resembled Mongolians. Linguistically their language, Yakut, sounded like an old cassette being rewound and I barely managed to learn a single word. I was told that the Yakut language was related only to Turkish: a slender thread reminding of some ancient epic migration. The two weeks we spent in Yakutia were the most hospitable of my entire journey, eclipsing even the generosity of the Middle East and America.

Outside the Yakut's well-built wooden bungalows were stacks

of ice blocks the size of paving stones. This was the winter's water supply for the home sawed from the river with long vertical saws. Neat lines of chopped firewood were stacked alongside in the snow. The villages had no plumbing as the logistical hurdles of permafrost and Arctic temperatures meant it was not worthwhile. Toilets were simply longdrops at the end of the garden. It was too cold for the toilets to be smelly, but they were horribly cold. I do not think many Yakut people do their crossword on the loo. Too cold in winter, too many mosquitoes in summer.

Instead of taps, a barrel of water stood inside each home by the wood stove, replenished with the blocks of ice from outside. The log homes had no refrigerators or freezers either: a hatch in the kitchen floor gave access to a cellar in the permafrost, stocked for the winter with jars of pickled vegetables, cannonballs of cheese, jams of autumn berries, bricks of high calorie fat stuffed with garlic, and haunches of beef all diligently stockpiled in the previous months. The storage was cool year round but never too cold. In barns insulated with summer hay cows provided fresh milk through the winter. Stamping in snowy paddocks outside were small ponies, tough enough to survive outside all winter and much prized for their meat.

We had not washed our clothes in a month, but nobody seemed to care. We were not noticeably smelly when we were in all our clothes, but as soon as we removed layers the stench would seep out. We were like onions: the more you peeled the stronger we smelled. Sitting in hot kitchens with our boots thawing by the stove, the icicles steadily falling from our beards and a steadily growing heap of clothes at our feet as we warmed up, stripped off and sipped tea, I enjoyed the company of the Yakut people as much as any in the world. To knock on a stranger's door and to be welcomed naturally and amicably into their home spoke of a quality of life, trust and a perspective on life's priorities that was almost absent in my own culture. I would love to return to Yakutia. To spend a year learning to live in that land where temperatures range across a staggering 100°C, to experience the fierce summer and the hay-making, the gathering of autumn berries, learning to preserve food, driving a skidoo, ice fishing, sitting with pots of tea around hot fires and celebrating the first flower of springtime.

We managed to avoid sleeping in the tent a lot in Yakutia. We were eagerly, even competitively, invited into people's cosy homes each night. We loved the experience, not to mention the warm sleeps and the clotted cream pancake breakfasts, and the families enjoyed feting us and fetching all their neighbours round to have a look at us. People who took us in would write notes introducing us to a friend or relative in a town along the road, and so the daisy chain linked on.

Tension grew between Rob and I over the rivers that we either crossed or detoured round. Rob was not convinced they were all frozen solid enough to cross. I was desperate to stop wasting time and get on with some miles. Rob thought I was being a fool to jump up and down on the ice. I thought that if I was jumping up and down on the ice then it was strong enough to cross. We shouted angrily at each other for the first time in years of adventuring together. Siberia was getting to us.

It was not just rivers, frozen or otherwise, that were slowing us down: we were still being undisciplined and weak and stopping early in the evening if there was the option of avoiding sleeping in the dreadful tent. A few miles lost in the evening out of 3,000 miles is nothing. But if you lose a few miles every day then the odds slowly begin to slide away.

We were also differing in our riding speeds by about 3mph, or potentially 20 miles each day. It was frustrating us both. Our shouting match about river crossings was about more than just river crossings. I apologised to Rob for being so grumpy. He apologised for being slow, though this was not his fault. It was good for us to clear the air. I knew that Rob was riding as hard as he could, I knew he wanted to succeed as much as I did and I knew that I was being unfairly grouchy and resentful. Tolerance, flexibility and understanding were essential. Unfortunately they are traits rarely compatible with being tired, cold and hungry.

We arrived in a village where a lovely Yakut family invited us to their home. The father of the family, a PE teacher, was amused by my complaints of how cold my bum became when riding on my leather saddle (Rob had a gel seat and his bum was fine). He made a reindeer fur cover that we lashed onto my saddle. I enjoyed a toasty behind for the rest of the winter.

With renewed resolve to get as far as we could before the visas expired we had a huge kit explosion that evening in their home, emptying out everything from our bags onto the floor. We threw away all that we could possibly risk doing without to save some weight. To everyone's amusement I discovered a pair of beach flip-flops at the bottom of one of my panniers. We transferred as much communal gear as possible to my bike. Now I could not lift my bike even an inch off the ground, but with my bike heavier and Rob's now lighter we would hopefully achieve similar riding speeds. We recalculated our mileage requirements too: we now had to make 65 miles every day to succeed. So far we had achieved that distance on just one day.

The next day Rob was ill, exhausted, drained and empty. It was a horrible ride. It snowed hard, the road was treacherous and the temperature rose to -15°C. Thankfully the river crossings were behind us now. I preferred -35°C and blue skies to a faceful of fat, wet snowflakes. The white sky hid the horizon and blurred the ruts and ice patches on the road.

Sometime that day a car pulled up beside us. I had no idea of the time or distance we had covered by then. It was probably not very far. All day my head was down, my eyes closed to slits and my mind as far from that godforsaken place as I could imagine it to be. Unbeknownst to us, last night's village had phoned ahead and now the Headman of the next village along the road had driven out to find us and to welcome us with coffee and cakes. He was accompanied by a very pretty teacher who had come to interpret. I chattered away merrily with her in the back seat, gorging on coffee and cakes, whilst Rob sat glazed-eyed and sick in the front, no doubt wishing he was in bed at home. The teacher, Anastasia, wanted to check that we were happy. Aided by her ancient Soviet dictionary she asked, "Are you both very gay?"

"Just good friends," I replied.

Sadly it was too early for us to end the day in the village of the cake-bearing Headman and pretty Anastasia so we said our farewells and pedalled on through the deepening snow. Some time later we were stopped by yet another rusty Lada that had come out from yet another village to greet us. By now Rob was feeling too exhausted to continue so they took us to a café in their village and fussed over Rob. Thawing out with a mug of hot, sweet tea while Rob rested his head down on his arms, I felt so touched by the kind thoughtfulness of these strangers. They bustled off to find us a place to stay and wanted to drive Rob to hospital. He insisted that all he wanted to do was sleep, so they left us in a spare room at the workers' hostel. Rob slept right through until morning, and we spent the next day resting until he felt fresh enough to continue.

After three days of our new, strict, absolutely unbreakable 65 miles per day routine we were 115 miles behind schedule. I was devastated by how meekly we were capitulating under pressure. I was very conscious of how unfairly I was treating Rob in my mind, blaming him for everything and absolving myself of everything. I had been reading that lazy day about pride; love of self and the deadliest of sins. I determined to try to garner some grace and humility under pressure instead. I resolved to establish a happier frame of mind. Rob and I had done so much together and this situation was exactly what we did well. The race, the wilderness, the absurdity, the cold: surely together we could still do it.

In the next days and weeks we worked hard to get back on schedule. They were deeply unpleasant days followed by long rides into the night beneath arcing columns of ghostly northern lights. We had so far to ride that I refused to allow myself to call an end to a day's ride, pushing it mercilessly on and on until we were exhausted and frozen and could no longer hold our eyes open. Through the grisly night rides, riding blind through the slippery darkness, I longed mile after mile for Rob to quit, to say that he had had enough for the day, just so that I could then agree and we could escape into the dubious sanctuary of the tent. Spending 15 hours riding each day, skidding and crashing throughout, and then pitching camp in deep snowdrifts, scooping out a flat sleeping platform in the snow and thawing ice to cook left us barely five hours of sleep each night until the next day began in pitch darkness at 5am. We still had 2,000 miles of Siberia and the Far East to get through, but we were catching up at last.

For another month we raced on, fighting the cold, exhaustion and the desire to throttle one another. At Skovorodino we finished the southward leg, turned left, away from home, and rode east back towards the Pacific once more. We talked endlessly about mileage and the number of days left on our visas, and continually re-calculated our odds of making it. They were long, flat miles spent riding side-by-side on the empty road through repetitive birch forest. We talked of sleep and food, beaches and football and God, and the miles moved by. We moved parallel to the Trans-Siberian railway, hearing ghost-like rumbles of trains through the unchanging birch forest. Occasionally we saw the enormous 100-wagon freight trains. Then we would wave and the drivers would blast their powerful horns in greeting. They trundled slowly past, grinding out the miles on their own colossal journey of 5,700 miles between Moscow and Vladivostok.

Two horrible incidents pierced the following weeks. First, three drunk men stopped their car late one night and demanded money. We pretended not to understand. They shouted louder. We smiled and apologised for not understanding and tried to leave. Losing patience, they pulled a pistol on us.

"Ah, *money*! Now we understand! Why didn't you say so earlier? Of course you can have our wallet."

It was the only time on my journey that I was robbed. Apart from the unpleasantness of a drunkard pointing a gun at you on a dark night thousands of miles from home, I was most upset that this had happened in Russia. I had preconceptions about the criminality of Russia, typified by the Siberian saying, 'God is high up and the Tzar is far off,' but I had come to love the country and trust the simple decency of the people. The robbery felt like an affront to all the good Russians we had met. The only redeeming feature of the robbery was that, after taking our communal wallet – I lost £20, Rob a little more – the thieves gave us directions to the next town. It seemed the quintessential Russian experience: vodka and menace, but with a good streak somewhere at the core.

Much as I tried to reassure myself that the robbery had just been a freak event, it took me a few days to regain my trust in people. Could I continue to love this massive country of kindness, or would that splinter of crime dominate my thoughts? The sweaty reek of ruining vodka to numb the numbness. Three faces, nondescript and wasted. Only the clean black outline of their gun impresses on me now. How outraged, how indignant at those ugly shadows would be all the solid dignity we had met. How unfair it would be for me to forget that. I forced myself to relax and to trust again.

Another night, we were sleeping in a small hut beside a roadside café. Outside, the night was cold and white: snow and silver birch trees gleamed under the full moon. It was a beautiful night and we were thankful to be inside and warm. Normally we slept on the café floors, but there was a hut at the back of this one that the owners offered for us to sleep in.

We had accepted the invitation of Lena, the café owner, to share supper with her and her husband Alexei. We were the only customers so we all sat around one table together, sharing a beer and eating stew. Eating with us also was a quiet little man from Uzbekistan who worked at the café as a general helper. The couple's café was only a month old and they were excited by their new venture. Their baby daughter was staying with Lena's mother for a few weeks whilst the couple worked hard at their new enterprise. Alexei was so enthused by our ride that he asked us to autograph our names on the newly-painted wall. We declined as it seemed a pity to deface the clean paintwork. It was a fun evening when, amongst other things, I learned the Russian for, "To be or not to be," *"bate ily nye bat,"* and Lena weighed our copy of *War and Peace* on her kitchen scales, concluding that it was a ludicrously big book to be carrying on the road. I liked the quiet, humble Uzbek man, but I do not know what prompted me to write a couple of pages about him in my diary when Rob and I headed out to the little hut to sleep,

…after all have spoken and he has listened he now speaks quietly to me. His face, half in shadow, half glowing from the stove, is kind and wrinkled with about 50 years. He talks of home, of the magical sounding 'Samarkand' and 'Bukhara' and the steppe of Kazakhstan and the Pamir Mountains and Afghanistan. He has roved half a continent without vanity or glory probably in search of work, or following a girl, or posted by the army or exiled by the government. And here he is now, a little man talking of the giant places of my ego with the gentle familiarity of a local. He has lived these places, they have been normal for him – home – as he

worked hard to keep afloat, tossed in the currents of Communism but at the same time floating in the vast normality of all our lives. They are too often unnoticed by me, but Russia is full of these scattered 'little men' so far from their homeland. What tales they could tell me if only I bother to listen! There is no such thing as an 'ordinary person', least of all here in Russia.

I don't know why he captivated me, but as I went to bed I realised that I should respect everybody and then their attributes will shine through, rather than only respecting those who are more immediately impressive.

A few hours later I was standing bewildered at my helplessness. We woke in our hut around midnight to see that the café was enveloped in galloping flames, a sky-high manic laughter of unstoppable fire, crashing and thumping and roaring angrily at the black sky. Everything I had done in the last few years had been with a brusque, "of course it is possible, you just have to try harder," mentality. "You can do anything if you just want it enough." But now, whilst I knew that I could not do nothing, I knew also that I could not do anything. Yet never had I wanted something more. The café was enveloped in an inferno, caused presumably by a fault in the wood stove that heated the café. Lena and her husband managed to get out, burned and screaming, and we helped them quickly out of the cold and into our little hut and cared for them. But the little Uzbek was still inside, dying an appalling death. Lena was screaming at me not to go in, but how could I not make an effort? I was right on the cusp of being very foolish and charging inside when, with a hard punch of heat, the kitchen gas tanks exploded and the roof collapsed. The little Uzbek was dead and I stood still, alive under a luminous moon.

No neighbours. No phones. No 999. One man was dead and one badly burned. The café was razed to the ground. Rob and I took it in turns to stand helplessly in the cold on the dark, empty road, waiting impatiently for a vehicle to pass. Eventually we flagged down a passing van and the driver promised to raise the alarm at the next town. Hours later, an old ambulance came and took Alexei away. A car arrived and took Lena, Rob and me to her village, to her mother's house. We cried and we drank coffee. What more could we do? Night paled towards dawn. We were questioned by the police. We tried to tell Lena how we felt but what could we say, even if we had the vocabulary to say it? Awkwardly we slipped her an envelope full of dollars (for her livelihood had been destroyed), said goodbye and cycled away. What more could we do? We could do nothing.

I dislike birthdays more with each year that passes. I grow grumpy at how carelessly I have frittered my time and fret at how little time is left. But as the sun rose that next morning, on my fourth birthday on the road, my frozen tears had stopped and I was smiling and thinking of the little Uzbek. I had cried until dawn at the loss of his life and at my inability to prevent it. But the Uzbek had left a legacy that helped me to smile on my birthday: he reminded me that I was alive. I remembered the grave of actor Brandon Lee, alongside his father, Bruce's, in Seattle. The inscription read, "Because we don't know when we will die, we get to think of life as an inexhaustible well. Yet everything happens a certain number of times, and a very small number, really... How many times will you watch the full moon rise? Perhaps twenty. And yet it all seems limitless." As we rode, numb and sad, away from the smoking ruins, I gulped down gasps of ice cold air, freezing on my lips and billowing out in great white clouds as I panted. My nose freezing in the wind, my legs spinning, gravel and snow crunching, a magpie bouncing on the verge, the constant vibrations transmitting through my bike from the road to my body, shadows from rushes trembling on the snow, the sun so bright it left blinking little green circles on my retina. Every day, every moment is precious. I would try to ride my golden road to his Samarkand with a smile on my face.

On and on and on went Russia. One night we slept on a bench in a warm night-watchman's hut in a little town whose name I never knew. We had been sitting in a café trying to decide where to sleep when two men approached us to say that we could stay at their machinery storage yard. We accepted the offer, gathered up our maps and diaries and followed them down the road. The night-watchman was a woman, about 50 years old, with a coarse woollen dress, felt boots and short mussy hair. She was just arriving at work when we turned up and Rob and I winced when the two men began yelling at her for something and she cowered like a street dog. All three of us were relieved when the men walked away into the night, Rob and I smiled reassuringly at her. She was happy that we were out of the cold and busied herself making the bench as comfortable as possible for us to sleep on. We lay down and the lady made herself comfortable on her chair beneath a small table lamp to sit through her nightshift. I woke in the night to the sound of her crying. Propped on the table in front of her was a letter and a photograph of a young smiling couple hugging in a kitchen. I presumed that it was her child and spouse, with a letter of bad news or simply the ache of separation. My Russian was inadequate, her grief seemed so private and I was too tired and embarrassed to know what to say, so I feigned sleep and lay still, listening to her stifled sobs.

The region became more populated, a relative term in Siberia, but it meant that every couple of days we would reach a roadside café. These regular oases of warmth were fantastic except for the outdoor loos where pyramids of frozen poo piled up out of the too-full pits like a hideous ice-lolly. New holes could not be dug until the summer thaw when, presumably, the stench would be awful. In the cafés we would treat ourselves to a bowl of soup, *borscht*, and a mountain of cheap bread, secretly topping up our soup bowl with hot water from our thermos to eke it out further. We spent some nights sleeping on the floor of 24 hour cafés, grateful for the warmth and the portions of filling food that we were often given, but less keen on the drunks who would stumble in at all hours, shaking us awake and annoying us with demands to share vodka with them. We would smile and say "no thanks" and fight the urge to thump them. Eventually the waitress would shout at them and they would leave and drive drunkenly away and we would grab a little more desperate sleep. One day a lorry driver invited us to join him for lunch, and then decided to buy us a meal in the next three cafés we passed, over a distance of several days. At those cafés we were greeted with cheers from the staff and, as promised, a sponsored slap-up feast.

Rob was fitter and faster now and had finally been gripped by a sense of urgency. We were riding further and we were doing it faster. In *War and Peace* I read that, "a man in motion always devises an aim for that motion. To be able to go 1,000 *versts* (1,000 kilometres) he must imagine that something good awaits him at the end of those 1,000 *versts*. One must have the prospect of a promised land to have the strength to move." We talked daily about our promised land, our dreams of hot showers and warm beds and sweet, sweet sleep. It began to seem possible that we were going to make it. Rob's lunatic optimism was beginning to infect me too. In the towns we passed we began buying cheap ice-cream cones to snack on whenever we paused to drink coffee from our thermos. It was so cold that we could keep the ice-cream in our panniers for a couple of days. Coffee and ice-cream: could a cyclist wish for more?

As we descended towards the coast the mountains ebbed and temperatures rose to a balmy -20°C. The snow was patchy and crappy sun-starved brown grass poked through. It dazzled our eyes with its colour. Icicles, in shivers of breeze, fell ringing from the trees. We rode alongside a river that was a sliding skin of ice. Later, chunks of ice were dancing down the black stream. The world was alive and in motion once more, wonderful musical movement after so long frozen in motionless silence. The days felt warm and cosy, the hundreds of kilometres ahead of us felt a mere fragment. The end was in sight.

Finally, at long long last, we received good news, a break from the constant kicking of the last months. News that made us laugh and jump and celebrate together, to bond us back together again and remind us that we were old friends and would always be friends and that we were going to make it through together. We found out that there was a shortcut, a small road that was not on our map. An undisputed, rumour-free, actually existing, guaranteed shortcut. A shortcut that would save us three whole days of slog. This meant that we would now be at Vanino, the end of the road, in just three more days. It renewed our resolve to pedal hard, fighting a final heavy snowfall that made riding treacherous. We were guided by a shining moon as we woke to begin riding at 4am. The pre-dawn starts were almost over.

And then, below us, beyond the snowy shoreline and the deep-cut anchorage of Vanino, was the bright blue expanse of the Pacific Ocean. We cheered and shouted and laughed with delight. We had made it from Magadan to Vanino, the opposite of the desperate journey of millions of prisoners, and we had won our race against time. After 3,000 miles, this was a landmark that really felt sweet. "Sleep after toil, port after stormy seas, does greatly please."

Against the odds, we had reached the end of Russia just before our visa expired. We took the ferry to the island of Sakhalin, from where we would hop over to the north of Japan on another ferry with a whole day to spare on our visas. We had another reason to visit Sakhalin: a friend of ours, Alexis, had been living on that isolated, frozen outpost for 18 months working for Shell. Unsurprisingly he had not had a single visitor in all that time, so we planned to drop in for tea. It was time for a party.

The records of
a travel-worn satchel

If we don't offer ourselves to the unknown our senses dull.
Our world becomes small and we lose our sense of wonder.
– Kent Nerbur

W e slept the sweet sleep of the truly exhausted as the
ferry crossed the narrow strait between Sakhalin and
Hokkaido, the northernmost of Japan's main four
islands. From one remote, bleak, snow-shrouded island to another.
It was still cold but Hokkaido was not daunting in the way that
Russia had been.

As we stepped out of the terminal to take our first steps in
Japan we found three tiny nuns waiting patiently for us. We had
not thought that anyone even knew of our arrival in Wakkanai, let
alone that we would have a welcoming party. Two of the nuns
were Japanese, one was French and after a little confusion we settled on using French to communicate. It turned out that the father
of a friend of Rob's had a friend who knew the nuns in the northernmost village of Japan. They were very happy to welcome us to
Japan and asked if we would like to spend a couple of nights at
their house, or whether we would pedal straight out of town.
Given that the plan we had come up with so far was to just set up
our tent somewhere in the hills and sleep for a couple of days, we
were very happy to accept their invitation. We pedalled behind
their car, which they drove at about 5mph peering over the steering wheel with the hazard lights flashing. I was not sure whether
they were driving slowly to allow us to follow them or whether
that was how they normally drove.

The elderly nuns cooed and giggled as they ushered us into their home. Once we had put down our bags they sent us immediately off to an *onsen*, a public hot bath, with a male friend of theirs. Perhaps this was a polite response to how badly we must have smelled. Just an hour or so after arriving in Japan Rob and I found ourselves wallowing blissfully in a hot deep bath with a warm *futon* awaiting us back at the nuns' house. We were both incredibly happy, tired and relieved to be out of Russia.

It was Rob's birthday and the nuns made a cake. I gave Rob a copy of *The Worst Journey in the World* that I had arranged to be sent to our friend Alexis in Sakhalin. I thought that it would help put our own slog into perspective. I had read the book before but with a new appreciation of their struggles in Antarctica, I was even more in awe. Although we had spent almost every minute of the last three months together, and were sick of the sight of each other, I was really proud of Rob and glad that we would have those memories to share.

After a lie-in and a huge breakfast – "more toast for you boys? I know your appetites by now!" – a lazy day washing our clothes, sleeping and enjoying some warmth, we left Wakkanai. At 3 o'clock we stopped riding out of sheer idleness. The pressure was off now. We lounged in a heated railway waiting room drinking coffee and reading. The nuns had tipped us off that we could sleep in railway stations throughout Japan. It was fantastic not to have to sleep in the tent, to be out of the cold, to have electric lights and to have chairs to sit on. We enjoyed a long, long sleep, snug in our sleeping bags on the waiting room floor, until the morning commuters arrived.

The transfer from Russia to Japan was the biggest culture shock of my ride. Japan was clean and quiet and cramped. People bowed and were super-polite. There were more traffic lights in little Wakkanai than in the last 3,000 miles of Russia. Food was delicate, tiny, neatly packaged and massively expensive. The quiet Japanese were so different to the Russians who were very forward, loud and tactile. But the Japanese, like the Russians, were also very kind and strangers kept stopping us and giving us food and money despite the language barrier.

Before we arrived, I knew nothing about Japan except for the clichés: Mount Fuji, kimonos, Bullet Trains, neon lights, old temples, sumo and cherry trees. Google wearily reports a million sites describing 'Japan, land of contrasts.' But I know now why writers use them. It is hard to find any one thing to summarise the 'real' Japan.

Japan has thrived partly due to an accepted separation of one's personal views and life, *honne*, from the opinions demanded by your position within the group or society, *tatemae*. This helps the massive machine that is 'Japan Inc' run smoothly. I think of the kimonos and Mount Fuji as the *tatemae*, the official face of Japan, but I never got close to figuring out the *honne*. I am not sure that I got any further than a headful of observations. It was such a fascinating country.

Japan is really not very expensive, unless you want to buy anything. By eating nothing but instant noodles and drinking instant coffee we kept our costs low. By the time I reached Tokyo, my blood pressure was sky high. At least I was slowly regaining the 7 kilos I had lost in Russia. We also learned that we could sleep wherever we wanted to in Japan, that we would be safe and nobody would mind, or at least that nobody would complain. One night we slept at a roadside service station, locking ourselves and our bikes into the enormous, spotless disabled toilet for the night. I am not sure that there is anywhere else in the world where I would consider sleeping on the floor of a public toilet, but I have stayed in many hotels much worse than that Japanese toilet. It was clean, warm, secure and well-lit, with piped music and running water. And, of course, it was en suite.

Travel, in its crudest essence, can become little more than a dash from one toilet near-crisis to the next. What a pleasure then was Japan. Clean water and luxury toilets galore. After Siberian toilets, the heated seats in Japan were heaven. Sometimes there were machines that imitated flushing sounds and concealed any embarrassing noises you may make. There were also control panels of buttons with mysterious Japanese writing to play with, allowing you to entertain and surprise yourself with unexpected sprays of warm water and blasts of hot air.

The fields were smooth with deep snow and in towns the

pavements were piled with snow cleared from the road. Riding was easy as tunnels were drilled through all the hills. But blizzards soaked us and chilled us and our life revolved around petrol station coffee breaks and railway station loafing. Rob had printed, in tiny font, a few Shakespeare plays from the internet. To entertain ourselves in the evenings we performed these in the empty waiting rooms of the village stations. We dared each other to continue our monologues and soliloquies when trains arrived and brief waves of passengers passed through. We put a hat on the ground to collect donations, but never made a single *yen* from our performances. I felt that this was because Rob made a gruesome Juliet but he blamed my poor Portia.

The Japanese word for snow is *yuki* which pretty much summed up the ride down Hokkaido. Our eyes had lost their fire, we were weary of each other's company and we were really in need of a proper break. The Japanese towns and villages were ugly and homogeneous with small, prefabricated homes with corrugated roofs. We passed repeating cycles of petrol stations, small convenience stores, car showrooms filled with ugly little cars, the flashing lights of gambling *pachinko* parlours, mobile phone shops, traffic lights and perhaps a Buddhist temple or Shinto shrine. I saw a statue of Buddha looking very un-Zen-like and quite grumpy with a huge dollop of snow on his head. I knew how he felt.

On Honshu, Japan's main island, the New Year snows and icy roads turned into heavy rainstorms. The roads raced with water, bursting from full drains and the melting winter snows. We were soaked but at least the roads were no longer slippery. Rob wanted to visit a friend on the West of the island, and I wanted to visit someone on the East. It was time for us to split. Rob also decided that he wanted to ride down to Australia after Japan, while I was keen to chase the sunsets homeward, in a straight line across Asia. We had planned to split at the end of Japan, and were both happy to bring the date forward, and to ride off on our own. We planned to meet up further down Japan, but were both ready for the freedom of solitary riding.

I had failed in my plan to travel for a long stretch with somebody else. I had been too selfish and too focused on the ride. I showed too much pride and too little grace and humility. I am afraid that I was something of a grumpy bugger for too much of our time together in Russia. For Rob to have come straight from teaching to ride across Siberia in winter was impressive, although those who have taught in England may consider his the easy option, and I had not given him enough credit. I knew that we would become better friends having been through those difficult times together. I knew we would travel together again. Most important, I knew that, in the unlikely event that I ever rode through Siberia in winter again, I would want to ride it with Rob.

Spring arrived the day I rode into Tokyo. I rode out of winter's monstrous anger and away from four months of snow and ice. As I rode south towards the city the fields turned *green*; a lush feast for my eyes after so much whiteness. There was blue sky and the sun was warm on my face as I sat on a pavement eating a pan of instant noodles and looking at the perfect cone of Mount Fuji. I enjoyed the moment, knowing that winter was behind me at last.

I arrived in Tokyo to stay with a school friend, Michitaka. Mitch left our school when he was 14 to return to Japan. I had not seen him since. One of the first questions he asked was, "Why are you cycling round the world?" That was a normal enough question, but usually it is asked like this,

"*Why* are you cycling round the world?"

But Mitch asked, "Why are *you* cycling round the world?"

The last time he had seen me I was, apparently, "a skinny, brainy version of Ron Weasley," the annoying one from the *Harry Potter* stories. Hence his surprise at my undertaking. Japan had seemed so full of polite people that it was nice to meet a rude one at last!

I stayed with Mitch's parents-in-law. His own flat was barely big enough for bonsai, let alone cat swinging or having guests to stay. I was welcomed by Miyako and Katsumi, and their daughter Keiko. Mitch translated for us all. Japanese people cannot pronounce the letter 'L' so my name, 'Al', was problematic. I therefore became known as Aru-*san*, '*san*' being the polite suffix added to all names. The family was supremely polite, hospitable and welcoming. Miyako, Mitch's mother-in-law, was nervous about me stay-ing but curious about having a foreigner in her home and eager for me to be happy. There was some concern amongst the family over whether I would be able to kneel on the floor for dinner, Japanese-style. Feeling like a clumsy giant, I assured everyone that I would be fine. I knelt at the table and resolved to focus on the food rather than the numbing discomfort that pre-empted the onset of searing agony in my knees. Later, as the meal progressed, I would turn my focus to the pain in my legs to try and forget about the cold jellyfish tentacles I was eating. Miyako had cooked a fabulous meal for me which must have taken ages to prepare. I was touched by her kindness and enthusiastic curiosity. But, after the rustic, simple fare of Russia I found the cold squid, hot horse-radish, cold sticky rice balls and cold runny egg sensations to be very hard work. My knees were screaming with pain, my stomach yearned for a plate of boiled potatoes and my face was fixed in the politest smile I could muster.

Eventually Mitch had to go back to his flat. I think that my Japanese-speaking hosts and English-speaking me were both thinking, "please don't leave me alone here!" It would be my first night alone with a Japanese family that did not speak English. I had grown very comfortable with this situation all round the world but I found the Japanese formality unnerving.

I decided to do us all a favour and pleaded tiredness. I thanked the family profusely, brushed my teeth, did a couple of bows then closed the door on my first night in Tokyo. As I switched off the light I heard the family in the kitchen burst out into laughter and excited chatter. I smiled and lay down on the futon. I would have loved to know what they were saying about me, "I can't believe he actually ate those jellyfish tentacles we fed him! Come on, let's have a burger."

At breakfast I was presented with a fried-egg and a pair of chopsticks. Even a Japanese family were not polite enough to be able to restrain their laughter at the ensuing disaster. I laughed too and the ice was broken. Miyako dug out an electronic dictionary and a special pair of chopsticks that young children use when learning to eat, and from then on we all had a great time together. Miyako was endlessly curious about my life in England. We answered each other's questions with the dictionary and had a lot of laughs together. Miyako took me on her shopping expeditions to parade me to her neighbours and local shopkeepers. She took a mischievous delight in bringing home Japan's most outlandish food products for me to try.

For Miyako it was an opportunity to think anew about her normality and to share the things that she liked and was proud of. I grew very fond of that family which was full of laughter and far more relaxed than I had imagined it would be.

Before saying more about Japanese food; I do not really like fish. But, by the end of my time in Japan, I was enjoying most things that I ate, rarely gagging, and loving some things. I look back now on Japanese food as being some of the most interesting in the world. However, for the first few weeks I came perilously close to vomiting at the table on several occasions. I was served rotten beans, raw squid in squid liver sauce, sea urchin's gonads and chicken neck cartilage. 'Cold and chewy' featured regularly as a texture of choice. Things that I thought would be hot and sweet turned out to be cold and fishy. Savoury-looking things would be stuffed with sweet, cloying bean paste. The unexpected textures were the single biggest difficulty I had in adapting my palette.

In the evenings, Katsumi enjoyed having somebody to drink beer and watch baseball on TV with. I went with him and Mitch to a batting cage, where a mechanical arm hurled baseballs for us to wallop. Katsumi enjoyed showing the Englishman how it should be done.

Keiko, the youngest daughter, was causing a bit of a stir at home. She had revealed that her boyfriend wore white jeans. Katsumi was not sure he sounded like the sort of chap his daughter should be mixing with. The custom in Japan is that the parents would not meet Keiko's boyfriend unless the couple decided to marry. Keiko also told her mother that she was beginning tango lessons. Miyako was shocked. She much preferred that her daughters study the art of the Tea Ceremony, a more traditional and suitable pastime for young Japanese women.

The Tea Ceremony is influenced by Zen Buddhism and, because a practitioner must study not only the preparation of the tea but also kimono, calligraphy, flower arranging, ceramics, incense and a range of other disciplines, mastery is a lifelong study. Yoshiko, Mitch's wife, and Keiko invited Mitch and me to their Saturday morning class. Mitch had never been before and I got the feeling that he would rather have been playing football. The sisters tottered in kimonos and high wooden sandals onto the Metro, with Mitch and me following behind. The calm atmosphere of the ceremony helped my mind unwind, although an uncultured person may describe it as, "a lot of time kneeling uncomfortably waiting for a small mouthful of weird, lukewarm green tea."

Mitch, Yoshiko, and I escaped from the concreteness of Tokyo to visit a Buddhist temple high on a hill in a cedar forest. Carved trunks of trees formed the temple walls and small black waterfalls spilled into deep pools. The soothing sound of the water, the calm gardens and the rolling onomatopoeias of shining, timeworn gongs washed over me in the gentle afternoon garden light. Inside the temple slips of paper predicted your fortune and you tie them to the twigs of trees to make them come true. We joined the line to collect ours. My future was decreed to be mediocre which was a little disappointing.

Near Hakone we visited an *onsen*, a series of outdoor wooden baths overlooking a river valley. The water from a natural hot spring continually filled the baths. It was evening when we arrived and cicadas chirruped in the trees. Men relaxing after a hard week in the office sat on tiny stools and washed themselves at a row of hot taps before entering the baths. Others, standing at the balcony or sitting in the baths looked out over the dark valley lost in thoughts, chatting quietly, wafting themselves with fans and enjoying the warm water.

Knowing my fondness for sport, Mitch took me to a football match and, of course, to the sumo. At FC Tokyo the teams were introduced in English to anglicise the atmosphere, after that came the club anthem, *You'll Never Walk Alone*, a song more commonly recognised as the anthem of Liverpool FC. That FC Tokyo had so blatantly stolen their identify from another, more illustrious team halfway round the world did not bother anyone. The crowd stood as one and sang along in English with true football passion. It was bizarre and endearing and symptomatic of so much of the Japan that I encountered.

At the sumo championships things were certainly more Japanese, if no less bizarre. I quickly moved from finding the whole performance very comical, to finding it impressive. And very comical. The sumo performance is very ritualised and is as much of a dignified tradition as a combat sport. The day began with the lowest ranked fighters: skinny and weedy or old, flabby and feeble. The programme moved up through the divisions to the top division, the *Makuuchi*, which was the highlight of the day. The fighters spend an age before their bout strutting round the ring, psyching themselves up, sizing up their opponent, stamping their feet, throwing salt, scowling, rinsing and wiping their mouths. The fight cannot start until both fighters are crouched and ready. The moment that both fighters place both fists on the ground at the same time the fight begins. The tension is released with an explosion of wobbling flesh, huge 'wedgies' and surprising speed, power and balance. A few seconds later one man will be dumped on the ground or hurled from the ring, his dignity and dreams of glory dashed. The crowd yells its approval. At a major upset, like the defeat of the top-ranked wrestler, the crowd frisbee their cushions into the ring in delirious excitement or disgust. I liked Japanese people even more when they relaxed and got excited.

Tokyo was a sensory overload, overwhelming and fantastic. After the empty spaces of the past months I adored it. Millions of people streamed around me and above me and underneath me 24 hours a day. I stayed three weeks and wished I could have stayed three years. I earned enough money to ride back home by giving thirty slideshows and loads of interviews, including one for a magazine called *Tarzan* which, I was half-disappointed to discover, did not want me to pose in a leopard-skin thong. I visited several schools and met many interesting *gaijin* (foreigners) and locals. I replaced my old passport as there were no blank pages left. Its photo showed me with sensible haircut, shirt and tie. My new passport had a photo of me in my only T-shirt, with sunglasses on my head and mad hair. I played darts in the stately British Embassy and spent a night with Mitch, trawling tiny bars in a red-light area of sleazy cabaret and Love Motels. The bars were big enough for just a handful of drinkers who squash close together and sip beer and eat soggy grey bits of food, *oden*, from a bowl of warm washing-up water.

As I prepared to leave Tokyo, half of me was looking forward to the impending emptiness and simplicity of China's Taklamakan Desert, while the other half had been reminded of the pleasures of city life and was daunted to return to life alone on the road. My visa did not expire until March, so I had until then to summon the nerve and energy to take on the Asian mainland. Until then I would ride south and see how much of Japan I could see.

I spent a day stopping and starting through hundreds of traffic lights, which eventually led me out of Tokyo and into the countryside, or at least what passes for countryside in Japan. Japan is a work in progress, with construction under way everywhere. Soon Japan will be the most convenient country on Earth to get from A to B, with every hill tunnelled, every river bridged and every road a direct one. The only hitch is that, as A and B will be identical, ugly sprawls of identical shops and identical overworked people there will be no point in travelling from one to the other.

I rode right beneath Mount Fuji, the symbol of ancient, natural Japan. Buried in mist, grey and thick, I saw nothing of the peak and had to make do with viewing more ugly towns, whose only colour was the lights from the convenience stores and *pachinko* parlours. *Pachinko* parlours are very popular in Japan. They are large, bright rooms of noisy, low-skill slot machines that you feed a bucket of ball bearings into and hope for the best. Occasionally you win something. Gambling is prohibited in Japan so you can only win prizes like cuddly toys. When you leave the *pachinko* parlours you can then exchange your cuddly toy for cash. Not a particularly subtle way of getting round the law.

Riding down the Pacific coastline after three weeks of concrete and neon I really enjoyed being back on my bike. For a few precious hours I saw only beaches, trees and dunes. I enjoyed the combination of fresh air and a bicycle rolling onwards, carrying everything I owned. I rode up a narrow, wooded valley, leaving the main road to take the old service road that ambled along the valley floor. The valley sides above me were woven with overlapping bridges, tunnels and train tracks that criss-crossed the sky, imposing order onto nature and hurling traffic into the black holes of tunnels through the hillside, disdainful of the geography or contours. I preferred to potter slowly up the leaf-strewn winding road down in the valley. The arches of the bridges overhead were painted red and they reminded me of the red gateways, *torii*, at the entrance to Shinto shrines. I wondered whether the golden arches of McDonald's and the red concrete motorway bridges were perhaps the symbols of the new Japan superseding the old Shinto shrines and Buddhist temples.

Kyoto, compact and flat, wriggles with cyclists weaving down the pavements on identical granny-type shopping bikes. Everybody cycles in Kyoto and everybody rides fast. I raced one morning in the wake of a pair of very tight jeans and tall stilettos. I could barely keep up with her, but it certainly made a pleasant change from trundling slowly across Siberia behind Rob's backside. Kyoto's few homeless people lived under bridges down by the river, in improvised dwellings roofed neatly with blue plastic sheeting. There were tidy rows of pot plants outside and you could tell when someone was at 'home' by the shoes lined neatly outside each shelter.

Squashed into Kyoto is a city with thousands of religious sites, a city of the old geisha culture and a city of modern, busy Japan as well. Kyoto's 2,000 Buddhist temples and Shinto shrines are testament to the depth and antiquity of Japanese society. Today they echo to the shuffling feet of tour groups and the beeping of cellphone cameras. Souvenir shopping and group photographs, ideally with everyone striking a Winston Churchill V-sign pose, dominate the modern Japanese spiritual experience. Kyoto is the cultural heavyweight of Japan but early impressions disappointed me. With the help of Paul who hosted me I managed to sneak an insight beyond the tourist honeypots.

I cycled with Paul through the greyness of dawn towards the Ryosen-an temple, the sky just starting to blush pink and blue. It was cold and the streets were empty and we zipped easily down roads that were normally crowded. The monks at the temple strove towards enlightenment through calm meditation and an ascetic pathway of being the best person you could be, causing no harm to others. I thought of life in old Kyoto when the temples were the focus of life, not just a quaint tourist photo-opportunity. Seeing cultural changes and shifts in people's priorities is often easier in places that you are not familiar with. Observing the massive changes in Japanese society over the past 60 years was a good opportunity for me to think about my own culture, the path it is taking, how it has changed, and how I felt about it all.

A few mornings a week Paul rose early to go to Ryosen-an and study meditation with the Buddhist teacher, Matsunami-*san*. He welcomed Paul warmly, and was happy for me to join the morning session. My mind was far from empty Nirvana as my knees protested at the uncomfortable sitting position. We were cross legged, our hands cupped in our laps, tongue resting on the roof of the mouth to drain the saliva without needing to swallow, back straight, eyes almost closed. We tried to completely empty our minds of all the superfluous clutter of our lives in order to reach one-ness, a state of peace and relaxation which would lead to raised awareness, spiritual purification and, ultimately, enlightenment. We breathed deeply from the abdomen, for good things such as laughter stem from down deep in our bodies, while stress and anger come from higher up, typified by shallow, angry breathing. I sneaked peeks at the monk opposite me who was timing the meditation session by the burning of a pencil-grey line of sweet smoke rising straight and steady from an incense stick. The dawn sun shone wanly on his shaven head, his body muffled against the cold with thick white scarves. Outside birds sang softly in the garden sunshine. Eventually Matsunami-*san* struck the bell and the sweet sound rolled round the cold *tatami* room bringing all our minds back together and into the room. We walked quietly outside into the crooked, gnarled trees of the garden. My mind had raced restlessly out of my control throughout the session and yet just acknowledging the whirling in my head had helped me feel calm and focused as we thanked Matsunami-*san* and left to ride back through a waking Kyoto for breakfast.

Shikoku Island was a respite after the densely populated island of Honshu as it is the least populous of Japan's four main islands. I rode round low wooded hills, rocky coastal bays of clear green water and white fishing skiffs. Steep hillsides bright with blossoming orange trees were dotted with bonneted old women, hard at work. Hedgerows gashed with fragrant yellow flowers smelled sweet as I rode by. They were the first flowers I had smelled since six months of winter, and I inhaled with a new appreciation.

The Iya Valley was my favourite glimpse of a pristine, natural Japan, a gorge of tumbling green water racing through the cloud-filled valley, high hills of trees reaching above the mists. Even in this uniquely pretty valley, the villages were hideously ugly. Houses were roofed with corrugated metal and wires ran in tangles to the rooftops from unsightly substations.

To my disgust the weather turned and snow came again. From the bottom of my panniers I dug out, once again, my wet weather gear and I rode through days of rainstorms, sleet and soggy snow. My gloves were full of holes, the zip was broken on my rain-jacket and I was wet and frozen and fed up by the time I pedalled into Hiroshima.

The road into Hiroshima was busy, modern and very ordinary. Like anybody who arrives in Hiroshima for the first time, I was thinking of only one thing, fascinated and horrified that on one normal August morning in 1945 at 8.15am human hell had been unleashed here.

Nuclear attacks ended the Second World War and made both Hiroshima and Nagasaki famous. Sixty years ago Hiroshima was a busy, lively city spread over a flat, seven-fingered delta. Today it is once again a busy, lively city spread over a seven-fingered delta. Hiroshima is a wonderful example of regeneration, a reminder that bad times pass and that there is always hope for the future. The city of Hiroshima is now a powerful and vocal campaigner for nuclear disarmament and for peaceful solutions to international disputes. The bomb still defines modern Hiroshima. Nagasaki's history is older, and unique in Japan. Cobbled streets run down its steep hills to cafés, cruise ships and a waterfront area charmingly lit at night. For centuries it was the only city in Japan where foreigners were allowed to live and trade. Determined to maintain its isolation and independence during the Mediaeval era, Japan allowed only one Dutch ship a year to visit Nagasaki. Today Nagasaki is eager for international tourists to come to a beautiful historic city first, and a bombed city only second.

The sleet stopped and the sun came out as I visited Hiroshima's Memorial Peace Park. The museum in the Peace Park was a gruelling but necessary ordeal, a few hours that left me numb, sick and sad. The superb museum, admirably neutral, and candid about both the Japanese role in the war and the awfulness of the bomb, was filled with shuffling ranks of subdued Japanese school children and quiet Japanese families. Dotted around were tall *gaijin*, more conspicuous than ever, immersing themselves in the horror and avoiding each other's eyes.

The museum highlighted the horrific suffering that the sparkling scientific minds who created the nuclear bomb had worked so hard towards. It also explained Japan's role as the aggressor in the war and the effectiveness with which the bomb ended the war. I was very impressed and moved by the forgiveness and by the regeneration of modern Hiroshima as well as the determination not to let the lessons be forgotten.

I asked myself whether I would have wanted to survive in the inferno of flattened streets and hellish fires. Fires that melted roof tiles and glass bottles. Stumbling round with my body hanging with melted flesh and a thirst impossible to quench in the corpse-filled streams, the grotesque radioactive black rain that fell in floods from the mushroom cloud. I felt it would have been preferable to have simply disappeared instantaneously into death that sunny morning. This spontaneous eradication of people did occur, with the only sign of their existence being their shadows that were seared into the pavement by the extraordinary heat of the blast. I would not have been brave enough to choose life.

I left the museum with a real craving for sunshine and fresh air, as if to reassure myself that all was well now. Close to the museum is a building known as the 'A-bomb Dome.' Virtually all of Hiroshima was flattened by the bomb blast and the fires that followed, but a few buildings survived. Close to the hypocentre of the blast, this one building has been left in the condition that it was in after the bomb fell, a skeletal reminder to us all.

Sadako Sasaki was two years old when the bomb fell on her city. Like so many residents of Hiroshima, Sadako developed leukaemia a few years later. As her health deteriorated, her best friend urged her to fold 1,000 origami paper cranes. Japanese legend said that if she did so then her wish to become well again would come true. Sadako died after folding 644 paper cranes, just another young victim of a war already over. Her classmates folded the remaining 356 paper cranes on her behalf and perhaps the most powerful symbol of Hiroshima was born. Today there is a Children's Peace Monument to remember all the children who died. All around it are hundreds of thousands of colourful paper cranes, folded carefully by passionate, idealistic children from all over the world as a cry for peace. Schools worldwide fold 1,000 cranes, thread them onto string and send them to Hiroshima.

I had wanted to ride the length of the main islands of Japan, but I had enjoyed so many *onsen* and *Asahi* and *teriyaki* with so many people that I was fast running out of time on my visa. Like me, Rob had been riding down Japan, unwinding and regrouping after Russia, enjoying the independence and the relaxed life after the pressure-cooker of our mad Russian dash. We were both now eager to meet up again, to share our experiences of Japan.

One afternoon Rob persuaded me that some naked riding would be an entertaining diversion. I had no idea how the Japanese would respond to two *gaijin* hurtling through suburbia, howling with laughter, in their birthday suits. Reluctantly I agreed to give it a go. After a couple of minutes I lost my nerve and got dressed again. Rob appeared keen to cycle starkers all the way to Sydney, but he too stopped and got dressed. We were just in the nick of time because then three police cars pulled up. They began questioning us. Fortunately the policemen did not speak English. It is far easier to tell fibs when you do not understand each other. We played dumb and denied everything. But then some plains-clothes policemen arrived and demanded our passports. I began to worry. They spoke a smattering of English. I said that it was a very hot day, but they didn't fall for that. So we fell back on the old fail-safe card that we were just two *gaijin* and therefore prone to weird and inexplicable behaviour. We apologised a lot and said that we had not known that naked cycling was not common behaviour in Japan. The police decided that we were just harmless fools and let us go. We carried on our way fully clothed and laughing.

The end of my visa came in Fukuoka. I had not managed to find a yacht to leave on, but a shipping company kindly gave me a place on their ferry to China, complete with sloshing on-board *onsen*. It was a shame that I only had time for a single day walking the wide, light streets of Fukuoka. As well as street stalls selling an array of hot snack food, Fukuoka also had easily the most beautiful women in Japan, giving even Colombia a run for its money. But it was time to leave.

With a few hours to wait at the ferry terminal, I gazed sightlessly across the sea, thinking back, looking forward. I daydreamed about the last three months. Japan had re-awakened me after the struggle of Russia. I was feeling triumphant, excited and curious once more. To my surprise I had come to love Japan, a country in which I had no previous interest. Japan had been so easy, fun, safe, hospitable, interesting and so charming. It was completely bonkers. It was weird, ugly and annoying too, but overall I had really liked it. I had been submerged in unfamiliarity at first, I had no idea how to speak, eat, read or bow and I knew nothing of the people, land, history or culture. Yet there was also a comfy cushion of familiar affluence to reassure me and ease myself in. Like Britain, Japan is a developed country. There is a functioning infrastructure, people wear similar clothes, and material things in Japan are familiar. The Japanese people are like an extreme version of the British; harder working, more insular, more reserved and more conservative. Yet I felt that Japan was the most different, surprising and fascinating country I had visited.

I phoned home from a pay phone, unsure how easy things like that would be in China. I still had no feeling in my toes, a lasting souvenir of Russian winter, and I carried on my toe-wiggling exercises as I chatted with Mum about what we had both been up to. My bike leaned against a wall outside, but I knew that it was safe in Japan. I was trying to get my head around what may lie ahead. I was melancholy for what I was leaving, and excited about a new country. I always began new countries on my guard, alert to what may go wrong. I was excited about China, but anxious about another beginning.

I was approached by a backpacker, another *gaijin*, who asked if I spoke English. He was German, had just stepped off the boat from China, and needed to find a bank as he had no Japanese money. I bought him a coffee and we swapped information, the usual essentials of backpacker's lives: drinkable water, exchange rates, places to sleep... He talked, a lot, about his travels. I listened to his tales of China, lapping up information that eroded some of my nerves about what awaited me.

"China! Oh boy!" the backpacker threw up his hands, "It's crazy. You'll love it!"

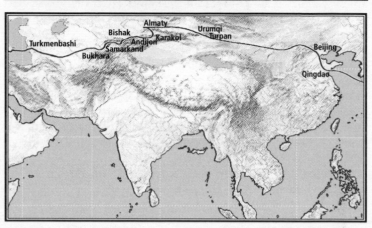

Beijing to Turkmenbashi

I like Chinese

I like Chinese, I like Chinese.
There's nine hundred million of them in the world today.
You'd better learn to like them; that's what I say.
   – 'I like Chinese,' Monty Python

The slow boat to China was fast. I looked out to sea and saw China right in front of me. Skyscrapered and in my face, we had arrived 24 hours sooner than I had expected. I was daunted. It felt like a long way to Yorkshire. As we approached Qingdao we passed a rocky cape with a lighthouse and red roofed Germanic buildings, remains from the old German port. Then the coastline became dominated by tall modern skyscrapers. The sea was a heavy grey and I was fidgety and nervous. I would be happier once I got through customs and past all the police and potential for problems. They did not look very friendly in their smart green Communist uniforms, as they waited for us to disembark.

I rode out into China. After the sterility of Japan my senses exploded into action. It was biting cold and windy, the streets were dirty and potholed and the traffic a whirlpool of hooting chaos. Taxis and buses raced among pedestrians weaving across the wide streets. Excitement welled as I rode into the pandemonium. Memories bubbled of the mad places in the world, the buzz of travel in unknown lands where every day is novel and every trivial task a hurdle. At the same time I thought nervously of how massive and foreign China was. My stomach churned through these emotions as I slipped unthinkingly from Japanese cycling mode (stay patiently in your lane, stop at traffic lights) into the riding mode that most of my favourite countries run on (ignore lanes, ignore traffic lights, ignore everything, get stuck in). I embraced the madness in those first few minutes, making snap comparisons and observations. 'Poorer than Japan... richer than Russia... driving worse than Mexico...' As I concentrated on surviving the hectic streets of Qingdao, my mind took in the grubby old apartment blocks, shiny skyscrapers, McDonald's, street stalls, foetid gutters, mediocre cars, clunking bicycles, rude drivers and potholes. The noise, the chaos. And I used to think Japan and China were pretty similar.

I was greeted off the ferry by two local journalists who wanted to interview me. I have no idea how they knew that I was coming; perhaps the ferry company had told them. I was happy to help them and in return I asked them to guide me to where I was supposed to be staying. I had to ride at top speed across the city to keep up with their taxi. I had made contact with Walter, an Australian, through a travellers' website. He had helped me plan the Chinese chunk of my ride and was happy for me to stay with him and his Chinese girlfriend, Ruidi, for a couple of days whilst I sorted out the tiresome logistics of arrival in China.

Ruidi's family owned a restaurant. As the taxi bumped, beeped and swerved its way to the Chinese restaurant (though I suppose it was just called a restaurant there) I was very nervous about cycling away alone into all this madness.

Everybody in China agreed that it was a good thing that I had left evil, dangerous Japan and reached safe, friendly China. They detested the Japanese. The focus of their dislike was the Nanking massacre in 1937–38 where around 300,000 Chinese were raped and murdered during the Japanese occupation of the city. I tried to tell people how much I had enjoyed Japan and how good the people had been to me, but nobody believed me. I wondered for how long I would compare China against Japan. They certainly acted differently. There was a sloppy informality at Chinese meals, unthinkable in Japan. Chopsticks were far longer in China and table etiquette very different. At the end of a meal in China the table would be strewn with spilled rice and tea. People smoked heavily whilst they ate and chewed amazingly loudly. The noise in restaurants was like a battery of rattling typewriters. But the food was delicious, and the portions massive.

Qingdao was a very small city in China with only seven million inhabitants. I was daunted as to how I was ever going to find an inch of space to put up my tent once I began riding through this crowded country. It was also bitterly cold and a horrible wind sliced through the city. I gave an interview to a TV channel, then got on my bike to cross China.

An hour later I realised that I had ridden in a circle and was right back where I had started. Chinese signposts proved tricky. I tried again and this time made it out of the city. The road passed through countless small towns and in each one I would lose the trail and have to start again, asking people to point me towards Beijing. Everyone was very friendly which was a relief as I was nervous and felt totally at sea. Drivers were terrible, hooting pointlessly and meandering from lane to lane. The headwind was fierce and I only managed 120 kilometres that first day. I had no idea where I was. I hoped that I might be on the road to Weifang.

A day later I discovered that I was quite considerably north and west of where I thought I was. I was nowhere near Weifang. It did not really matter if I knew where I was, only that I knew where I was going. I had given up on the signposts and taken to asking people for directions. I soon became sceptical of the directing skills of the Chinese and began asking three separate people for directions as opposed to the traditional two that I asked in most countries. I learned that showing Chinese people a map with the place names written in English would get me only blank faces. Handing them my other map, with the place names in Chinese, would result only in a large crowd gathering to have a good old chat about what a pretty map it was and to show each other where they came from. The Chinese are the most hopeless direction-givers in the world, so I was much better off to smile, point down the road and say, "Beijing?"

If they nodded then I would point in the opposite direction and ask, "Beijing?"

If they still nodded, I knew that the person had not understood a word, and I would search for somebody else to ask.

That first evening it was hard to find a hidden camping spot. There were clusters of poor houses dotted everywhere on the cold, dusty plain. The road was busy and I was always close to a settlement. But I had been doing this for so long that I knew that I could always find somewhere to hide and sleep, a little sanctuary away from the world. I needed only a tiny concealed place to set up my tent, a slight dip away from the road, or a bridge to drop out of sight beneath. Failing that I could always just wait until it was dark and then lie down safely virtually anywhere.

My biggest worry about China was not where I would sleep, or my safety, but my complete lack of language. I forced myself to spend that first night amongst people. The sooner I learned to relax in China the better. I had noticed that Chinese petrol stations seemed to have a little row of outbuildings for accommodation. Foreigners in China are supposed to stay only in hotels authorised for the use of foreigners, i. e. expensive ones. The hotel then registers your presence with the police. I could not afford to stay in the hotels deemed suitable for foreigners, but anyway, large areas of China are off-limits to independent foreign travellers, especially those on bicycles, so I did not want any dealings with the police. I rather hoped that a squalid truckers' rest-stop which was probably also the village brothel would keep me under the police radar. And be very cheap. So I pulled into a petrol station to take on my first interactions with China without an interpreter.

The staff were shocked when I walked in the door. On top of the surprise that I always caused, they had seen me on television that morning. For me to then walk into their petrol station really threw them. One man, his face comically creased with confusion, pointed slowly at me and then at the television and then back at me. I understood, and grinned. I wheeled my hands in a bicycling motion: it sufficed worldwide as a way of explaining my life. They all laughed and began chattering loudly. They dashed outside to look at my bike. I decided this was the chance to ask for a place to sleep. I was on my guard and ready to haggle rip-off merchants. I mimed that I would like a bed for the night. We established that a room for the night at the petrol station cost 60p so I didn't feel the need to argue. The room even had a light switch that worked.

I dumped my bike in the room and set off on foot to enjoy the sunset in my first village in China. I felt a surging excitement as I realised that I was going to do just fine here. Goats strolled along the road, small boys crouched around a vocal game of marbles, men cycled to-and-fro in blue flat caps, some with enormous loads on three-wheeler trailer bikes. I was only an hour's drive from Qingdao, but already a world away from broadband internet and the glossy, superficial facelift that will persuade the world at the 2008 Olympics that China is a lovely, successful place. After the cold trudge of Russia and the ease and luxury of Japan and North America I felt that I was back doing what I loved best. I was trusting myself to fate in a foreign land, curious and learning. I was interacting with people who were happy for me to be briefly in their lives. I had no idea where I was, but I felt so fortunate to be there, in a random dirty village in China. I had no idea where I would be the next evening. Nobody at home knew where I was, but I had a safe place to sleep and a road heading out of town to lead me somewhere exciting and new in the morning.

I returned to the petrol station and went to the little café next door for some dinner. Before leaving Qingdao Walter had helped me prepare some flash cards. I had thought of a few essential phrases and he had translated them into Chinese. It was time to test them out. I strode into the café, smiled at everyone and whipped out my cards.

'I am very hungry!' I flashed. 'I want to eat something large and cheap!'

It worked beautifully. After some hilarity and passing round of the card I heard giggling activity in the kitchen and minutes later a large steaming plate of food arrived in front of me. Meat, vegetables and noodles in a thick, tasty sauce. What more could I have asked for, China was going to be a breeze.

As well as flash cards like, 'I am on a long journey and very tired. Please can I put my tent here for the night?' and 'How many kilometres is it to the next food and water?', I also had my newly translated Magic Letter. It provoked much nodding of heads and many thumbs-up signs. I had also cut out the newspaper article about me from Qingdao. I had no idea what it said, but it provoked mirth and free bowls of noodles wherever I produced it.

My flash cards were too specific. They always led to a volley of follow-up questions, so I set about modifying my approach. In the back of my diary I drew up a list with two columns. On one side, beneath a smiley face, would grow a written list of calligraphic squiggles that revealed foods that I had enjoyed eating. When I ate something tasty, I would ask somebody to write for me the name of what I had just eaten in the happy column. In the column beneath a picture of a sad face I would ask somebody, not the cook, to add foods that I didn't fancy eating again. This tactic worked better than I could have imagined. When I showed people the list of foods that I had enjoyed they seemed to regard it as a personal challenge to produce a tastier dish than I had eaten in all of China. To get their dish added to the tasty column was a great honour and very amusing for people. I was rarely allowed to pay for my food in China. Instead I was usually presented, free of charge, with a far larger and more elaborate meal than I had ordered. It was as cheap to eat in cafés as to cook myself, and as the chefs were considerably more skillful than me, I ate almost every meal in a café. I ate less well between meals in China: fruit was scarce and expensive on the remote desert route I rode, and bread and jam did not really exist. Between cafés, I subsisted on stale, budget bags of not-very-nice cakes and not-very-tasty biscuits bought at petrol stations.

My night in the truckers' hotel was a success and helped quash my nerves about China. So on the built-up road to Beijing I often stayed in similar hotels where, after haggling, I always seemed to end up with the same rate of 60p per night. Each night truck drivers would come into my room, without knocking, to have a look at me. Or a couple of ladies from a nearby café would push in, or an entire family. I would also have to convince a procession of prostitutes (hair dyed ginger, plastic thigh boots, blue mascara, bad teeth) looking to branch out from their truck driver niche that I was very tired after cycling all day and would actually prefer to sleep alone. They would return later with a friend to have a chat and giggle about my funny eyes and big nose. I would end up shoving my bed up against the door to keep it closed so that I could get some sleep. I could think of little that was less romantic than a 60p hotel room with phlegm on the walls, filthy sheets, random live wires sprouting from the walls and a naked light bulb dangling from the roof.

I once had to share a room with an old man who spat loudly onto the floor when I was put into his room. He did not look particularly pleased to see me. Later I would discover that he was the loudest snorer I have ever endured. He was the classic image of a Chinese Old Man, dressed in a blue blazer, blue cloth cap, simple dark trousers and plimsolls. He walked with the in-turned toes, rounded shoulders and down-turned eyes typical of China's rural peasants. He was smoking, as all Chinese men seemed to be. The old man's breath stank of salami and his voice growled slowly as he read my Magic Letter to himself, savouring slowly every strange calligraphic syllable. I sat on my bed and waited for him to finish. I felt bad about disturbing his afternoon peace and quiet so I hoped he would be happy with what he read.

Finished at last he questioned me, his foul breath washing over me. His questions were slow and frustrated and he did not comprehend that I could not understand him. I could not speak the only language he had ever known. He pointed at the page to sentences that interested him, but nor could I read what he was showing me. Eventually he returned to reading my note through again, his voice low and slow and packed with pauses. A young white guy sharing his room had arrived on a loaded bicycle, with a letter talking about places completely out of his normality. He was completely baffled.

I enjoyed dawn breakfasts at stalls on grubby jumbled brick pavements. I began riding very early each day as I feared that I may need to cover 1,000 kilometres per week to get across China before my visa expired unless I could obtain an extension in Beijing. After my dehydrated instant noodle marathon in Japan it was fantastic to eat proper meals for 15p once again. At the stalls men washed their hands loudly in basins then hurled the water on the ground and spat. Steam rose from hunched heads slurping spicy bowls of tofu soup and fresh-baked discs of flat bread. Bunches of chattering children cycled to school, silhouetted by the low yellow sun, billowing clouds of breath from the effort as they pedalled hard in the cold morning air. Their chains squeaked, as did every bicycle chain in China. A young man slapped dough balls between his hands as his wife carried a bowl of soup and hot bread to my table with a smile. She paused to pluck a hair from my bowl with her grubby thumb, flicked it onto the ground and then turned to the next table that was shouting for service. Apart from a few stomach-turning hygiene technicalities the food was invariably delicious. Fresh dawn air, cockerels, blushing sky, people sweeping yards and a steaming bowl of soup by the roadside: I loved this life in this kind of world. I was deeply appreciative of my position. If I was eager to get home more to pursue new, exciting challenges it was not because I wanted this one to end.

We all think that we are important. Visiting China is a good way of deflating that balloon. I was surrounded now by a billion people to whom I could now say, "Hello, one, two, three. I don't understand. Thank you. Goodbye." China made me feel small. Small, but not alone. I was back in a land that found me fascinating and was not embarrassed to show it. I began generating some of my biggest staring crowds since Ethiopia. At least in China nobody demanded money from me and I rarely had to haggle for a fair price. Eating, shopping, asking directions, sitting still: whatever I did provoked jollity and astonished staring. It was all good-natured and fun. My greatest audiences came whenever I sat at a street stall and ate noodles... with chopsticks! My, oh my, what mirth!

"Quick! Quick! Come look at this!"

What fun to watch the weird white man, the *laowai*, eating with chopsticks!

"Look how he eats!"

"Look at his big nose!"

I had always considered myself to be quite a competent chopstick user but I clearly had a lot to learn. Chopsticks are such daft things. Ted Simon summed it up, "why choose the slowest way of eating and then become so painstaking proficient at doing it quickly?" At one street stall I watched a man demonstrate to the crowd how, in my land, I would use a knife and fork to eat with rather than chopsticks. There was much laughter at his demonstration, and even more when I pointed out that he was holding his imaginary knife and fork in the wrong hands.

Every day people gathered to watch me eat, and fiddle with my stuff. I was strict as always at enforcing a simple, 'please do not touch,' policy for my bike, although I occasionally let people have a ride. It was normally policemen or café owners who wished to try. But I didn't mind people messing with whatever I had on the table; my map, diary or books. There was no concept of privacy, personal space or personal property in China. Grown men would huddle round me to watch me writing my impossible-looking squiggles horizontally across the page from left to right. Others would pull my reading book from my hands to have a closer look. My map entertained people enormously. My Magic Letter, flash cards and precious newspaper article would be snatched from hand to hand. Occasionally I was happy to not speak a word of the language so that I could just quietly mind my own business and let the crowds enjoy their stare-athons in peace.

Chinese driving was a nightmare. It is easy to drive Chinese-style. You could try it this evening on your way home from work. Enjoy these strategies either one at a time or simultaneously:

1. Set out to be as annoying as possible. Bear that in mind at ALL times.
2. Meander from lane to lane as your fancy takes you.
3. Drive very fast in the slow lane, or very slow in the fast lane.
4. Beep your horn at all times.
5. Never use your mirrors.
6. When you have to pull out into traffic, do just that. Pull out into the traffic. Waiting for a gap is for wimps. It is preferable to force a fellow driving at top speed on the highway to hoot in panic and swerve wildly out of your way than to wait a few seconds for the road to clear.
7. Occasionally drive the wrong way down the carriageway. Get annoyed if people get annoyed at you. Beep at them.
8. When you tire of these games go fetch a flock of sheep and wander down the road with it.

I was putting in long days, eager to reach Beijing as quickly as possible and to resolve my visa concerns. The fields were brown and bare after winter and stretched endlessly on to hazy horizons. Broad canals crossed the land, black, stagnant and stinking. China had managed these mighty constructions despite the poverty of individuals and the lack of skills, simply through the vast work-force. But it was hard to see what the 5,000 years of history that

China was so proud of had achieved. Almost everybody was still extremely poor. I was cautious about China's latest 'Great Leap Forward' that has been so talked about in recent years. Progress is surely about more than a miniscule fraction of the population becoming rich. America need not fret too much yet.

Riding into Beijing was exciting. The city centre was even shinier than Tokyo and skyscrapers soared. Scores of simple kites soared even higher than the modern buildings. It was always a thrill to arrive by bicycle at iconic places, and Beijing's superb bike lanes made it even more fun to ride into vast Tiananmen Square. A screen in Tiananmen Square counted down the days, hours and minutes until the 2008 Olympics. I was surprised how many Chinese tourists were there and how few Western ones. Fixing a puncture drew my largest-ever crowd of 'watching somebody repair a puncture' on-lookers. I believe I may even have outshone Mao himself for those few glorious minutes. But the many, many policemen in the Square were not happy with the fun that our group was having and they moved in to break up the show.

Alex said, "Meet me beneath the portrait of Mao in Tiananmen Square." What a place to meet a friend I had not seen for years! Alex and his girlfriend, Sommer, welcomed me with relaxed generosity into their spacious apartment high in one of Beijing's brand-new, middle-class apartment blocks. My room looked out over a skyline of concrete and cranes through beautiful, pollution-induced, lemon yellow sunrises.

I was very fortunate that Sommer's mother, who was born in Taiwan, agreed to accompany me to the enormous government building for visas and other such tiresome bureaucracy. She navigated the queues and the unhelpful paperclip shuffling civil servants at high speed. She yelled at a few people on my behalf and soon I was the delighted holder of an extended three-month visa.

I also needed to finalise plans for Central Asia. After visiting Russia I was alert to the idiocy of the Soviet Union's paperwork fetish, so I knew that I needed to be well organised and ensure I had exactly the right pieces of paper. I was not yet certain which route to take towards Europe. I had weighed up a few options, each with advantages and difficulties:

1. Through China, Mongolia and Russia. (Mongolia sounded

fun, I would like to see Russia in the summer, and I enjoyed riding in Russia. Few visas needed. Direct route home-wards. But would miss India and the Stans.)

2. Through China, Tibet, Nepal, India, Pakistan, Iran, Turkey. (Sounded good.)
3. Through China, the Stans, Iran, Turkey. (I had dreamed for years of riding through Central Asia, especially Afghanistan and Uzbekistan.)
4. Through China, the Stans, the Caucasus, Turkey. (Would be a shame to miss out Iran, but it was essential to always have more than one possible route when considering this region's labyrinth of bureaucratic pedantry and the odds of being refused visas.)

I loved the thought of riding through India, but I thought I should probably choose the Central Asian route. I knew that I would visit India later on in life and the chances of visiting Kyrgyzstan or Turkmenistan for a holiday seemed slimmer. Kyrgyzstan, known to be the safest and simplest of the Stans, had just experienced riots and a coup. The paperwork for Tajikistan was making me inclined not to bother, Turkmenistan would only allow me a five-day visa unless I hired a personal escort, and Iran was bound to be problematic. And I could only really go to Afghanistan if I was able to get out the other side into Iran.

In the Kazakhstan Embassy I enjoyed hearing Russian spoken once again. I had to stipulate the exact date on which I would enter Kazakhstan; no mean feat when the border was still 4,000 kilometres away. I also applied for a visa at the Uzbek Embassy and began trying to get an invitation to apply for an Iranian visa. It would take a week or two for the visas to be processed.

Beijing is such a cycle-friendly place, especially in rush hour when wide streams of bicycles flow and special traffic-directing officials are assigned to control the cyclists. I rode round the old neighbourhoods of Beijing known as *hutongs*. *Hutongs* are areas of old courtyarded residences separated by narrow dirt streets that form clustered mazes busy with daily life. Today the *hutongs* are knocked down at a pace, to make way for tower blocks. That year

20,000 homes had been destroyed in Beijing's *hutongs*. That is a staggering number of families whose lives had been disrupted. But the government does not care about anything except presenting a shiny, successful sheen to the world in 2008. The destruction of the *hutongs* is a real pity, many of them are centuries old and fascinating. Away from the giant roundabouts and flyovers and eight-lane highways it was relaxing to potter around their narrow and dusty streets peeking through doorways into people's courtyards and lives where paper lanterns hung from trees and caged birds tweeted cheerfully from their tiny homes.

I had relaxed in China. I felt safe and I felt welcome. I knew enough about what things cost to know if somebody was trying to rip me off. I was excited about riding west and chasing the sunset homewards alongside the Great Wall. But, as always, I was growing anxious about my next departure. I knew that I would enjoy the ride, but could not help growing glum and nervous as I prepared to leave Beijing.

The realisation that I was going to complete the ride was creeping over me. I had begun because I had wanted to do something that I would certainly fail if I did not commit every ounce of myself to it. I had been contemptuous of my too-easy life. But now the too-oft-imagined end was becoming almost tangible. I was no longer lapsing into scheming how to escape from the treadmill with pride intact. No more did I seem to be in an impossibly vast hamster ball. In less than a year it would all be over. I had no idea what I would be doing, but I would not be doing this. I was on the last lap of the calendar. Never would I be so free again. I promised myself that I would appreciate those final glorious months.

Just a day's ride took me from palm pilots and McDonald's and back centuries or millennia. Farmers in their fields straightened slowly from wooden ploughs to stare and wave at me with surprise that creased their faces into cobwebs of wrinkled smiles as I greeted them. Hills had been carved into terraces for cultivation. Destitute villages of mud-brick homes were the same drab colour as the earth and the hazy sky. It felt more natural and comfortable than the showpiece construction trophies of Beijing. I was fit and I was travelling light. I felt safe and confident and I relished testing myself in China, riding hard and fast for weeks on end. On most days I covered 90 miles or more, about 1° of longitude, rising with the first birds of dawn and riding until the sun set in front of me. The world was creeping tangibly beneath my wheels.

One day began with a few small raindrops on the tent and a good excuse to go back to sleep until seven. But by the time I reached a large coal mining town a blizzard was in full flourish. I was soaked and frozen. The ditch beside the road filled with crashed vehicles as mad drivers drove at top speed through the snow that was carpeting the road, limiting visibility. I pushed through the town and rode on miserably for a couple more hours, hoping for a roadside café to escape into.

Eventually a café appeared through the snow and I stumbled inside, cold and wet and with no feeling in my feet or hands. I sat on a bench and sipped tea in a numb, self-pitying slump. A puddle of melting snow from my clothes spread beneath me. After a bowl of noodles sprinkled with extra MSG and a pot of tea I warmed up and felt guilty about not riding on. The sleet continued unabated and I stood feebly at the door for a while, reluctant to step outside again.

Before I plucked up the resolve to depart the café owners' children returned from school. They spoke a little English which was unusual in China. Pathetically my spirits picked up at being able to moan to two young boys, aged 14 and 11, about how cold and wet cycling in the blizzard was. I snatched at the excuse to sit back down. I had another pot of tea by the hot stove and helped the boys with their English homework. Their textbook included photographs of Big Ben and a red double-decker bus, exotic sights they would probably never see for themselves. Mind you, neither would I unless I got riding. Their Dad spoke a tiny bit of English but really not enough for us to talk. This was hard as I did not want him to lose face if I did not understand what he said. I needed to be pretty intuitive as we talked,

"I life Lady Dee."

"Lady *Di*?"

"Yes, Lady Dee die. You life red and white?"

"Yes I like riding a bike."

"You white?"

"No, I am not married – I do not have a wife."

Instead of riding I helped the boys practice their English further by asking them to find me a place to sleep for the night. By chance the house across the road had a few spare rooms around its courtyard that they let out. The boys helped me move my bike across the road and I promised to return to their café for dinner after a few lazy hours of blizzard-free sloth.

My room, which looked out onto the squalid central courtyard, was adjacent to the pig's room. She grunted and shuffled on the other side of the thin wall. But my room was dry, there was a coal stove and a bed. An old man, after bustling over the stove, spent a very, very long time in silent perusal of the Magic Letter. A black dog, dusted in snow, tried to poke his muzzle round the door but the old man kicked it and it fled with a yelp. We haggled gently over the price of the room, but more because it seemed to be the thing to do rather than because either of us really had the stomach for it.

The old man showed me the pair of planks in the garden, perilously slippery, that spanned the hole that served as the toilet for his family. He mimed that there was no specific place to pee and that I could just go wherever the fancy took me in his courtyard. He left me alone in my little room, listening to the snuffling pig and the sleet on the corrugated iron roof. The naked light bulb highlighted the damp, mouldy walls and the various shades of grey grime on my mattress. I felt like a king and relished the guilty pleasure of a whole afternoon off.

Outside the snow sat a few inches deep. With a chewed and dirty fingernail I traced on my map a glorious route across China that would set the heart of all intrepid souls racing. In a couple of days' time I should reach the Great Wall. I brushed aside biscuit crumbs and looked at the Yellow River and Inner Mongolia, the land of Genghis Khan. On through Gansu province and into Xinjiang I continued. It showed all of that on my map, and a ring from my coffee mug, and my finger traced the expedition in my imagination. Maps are an invitation to adventure. Snow was falling and I was in a grubby, windowless room next to a pig. That was not on my map. Nor were the black muddy alleyways between the snow-covered mud-brick homes grimy with coal dust. Men were slewing homewards on mopeds, their blue workers' hats and jackets covered in white. My socks were steaming and stinking on the stool beside the hot coal stove. None of that was on my map. A map is an idea, nothing more, a framework of geography for an adventure germinating in the back of your mind. From the frame of the map you hang your own discoveries. A blizzard curtailing a day's ride, a pigtailed girl on a red moped, a quirky smile and a wave from a blacksmith. None of that day was on my map. If it was then I could just have stayed at home and read my map. But those small details and glimpses of lives are what will stay with me in years to come.

On the wall of my room was a piece of broken mirror and I was struck when I caught a glimpse of the strangest face I had seen in a while. A tangle of fair hair, not shining and black; big eyes, pale and round; a long nose like a beak; scruffy stubble surrounding straight white teeth; pale white skin… Was it any wonder that people stared at me from their flat, round, brown faces? That glance in the mirror showed me that people were not being unkind in their curiosity: the face in the glass made me pause in surprise as well, until he flashed me a grin of solidarity.

A couple of hours later the old man came to poke my coal stove for me. I wanted to tell him that I knew how coal stoves worked and that I could manage. I wanted to tell him that I grew up with a coal fire at home and tell him about Yorkshire and ask him about China. But I couldn't say any of that so I just let him poke the coals for the mysterious *laowai*. I said thank you and he walked back out into the snowy afternoon to do his own everyday things that he could not tell me about. At dusk he returned once more, carrying a tray with a flavourless gruel with a dredge of grey grain in a metal pint mug, three hard-boiled eggs and two deep fried pieces of bread. And chopsticks. What were the chopsticks for? I saved the eggs and the bread for the road. Dunked in sugar, I hoped the bread might pass as a doughnut. I swallowed the tasteless soup out of politeness and went back to the café across the road for some *gyozo*, fried meat dumplings dipped in soy sauce.

The night was dark and wagons thundered along the rough road, crashing through the thick slushy puddles. The blizzard was over. The stars were bright. It was bitterly cold. The grubby, coal stained homes were now whitened with clean snow. Not for the first time on my journey I thought, 'What on earth do all these people do out here in the middle of nowhere? What is the point of their lives? There is no hope. What is the point of my life?'

Then I pushed open the door to the warm, light café. I ate a tasty meal as kids leaned all over me and hung off me and practiced their English. They showed me another English text book. 'I have a robot. It can walk. Do you have a robot?' it taught, usefully. We looked at another picture of Big Ben and a Scotsman in his kilt. Their Mum smiled and my meal price dropped from six *kwai* to four *kwai* and the Dad came over to share a beer with me. They played a pirated *Backstreet Boys* tape for me as they thought it would remind me of home. They even tried to give the tape to me as a present. By the time I left I was thinking, "perhaps I'd like to live out here for a while."

I woke and the sky was shining bright and cold. I peed in the nice man's courtyard and wheeled my bike back onto the road. Nobody else seemed to be awake. The fields were white with snow but traffic had kept the road clear, if wet. I had been a bit of a wimp taking a half-day's break because of the storm but I was feeling far more positive now. I thought of something Ewan McGregor had said during his motorbike ride round the world when he was having a tough time in Mongolia. "I've got to get tough with it. I'm not going to become a big moany, pansy-arsed arsehole just because it's become hard." Quite right, Sir!

I turned onto a small country road with fewer hooting trucks. Clusters of huts, buried into the flanks of hills, were roofed with insulating clods of earth like primitive Viking hovels. I waved at an old lady hobbling on tiny, bound feet and she snarled at me, and spat. I arrived on the banks of the Yellow River (which was grey) as it scoured deep through a wide, dusty, terraced valley. But there was no bridge over the river. The road simply stopped. No clues were given as to how one's journey may continue.

I faffed around for a couple of hours trying to figure out how to cross the river. Nobody I met was very helpful. Some pointed downstream and talked a lot in Chinese. Others pointed upstream and gave very elaborate explanations about something. I was growing angry at the frustration of not being able to understand anybody when a truck driver went out of his way to direct me down a steep track to the river bank. At the bottom of the track were three men on motorbikes, also waiting to cross the river. After a while a rickety old barge appeared and carried us across.

On the other side I sweated up a steep sandy track to the lip of the river valley and suddenly a city with a massive, belching power station was in front of me. The city was brand new, built from scratch and was not even on my map. The rate of China's industrialisation was staggering. I was beginning to amend my initial cynical view that the Chinese drive towards world domination stopped on the outskirts of a few major cities along the coast.

The city had put up new road signs, which will be useful when the roads are built. I knew that I needed to head for a town whose Chinese symbol looked like a chameleon sticking its tongue out. I had no idea what the town was called, but it was west of where I was and therefore an ideal place to head. It was distinctive and easy to spot on the signposts.

Construction projects were springing up in all the big towns I rode through. They would be overseen by men in slacks and fake leather jackets, with shiny sunglasses and shiny shoes, a cellphone and a shiny black VW Santana with blacked-out windows. The Santana is the car of choice for successful Party Officials who haven't quite reached the status of a Mercedes with blacked-out windows. They puffed on cigarettes and shouted loudly into their phones about how rich they were becoming.

I was away from the crowds of the East now so I stocked up with enough food and water for a few days. I rode out into a brown, dusty world with only occasional villages. Mangy two-humped Bactrian camels scowled at me as I called out cheerful "Good mornings" to them. They understood me as well as anybody in China so it seemed churlish not to chat. The extraordinary faces of old men you see in photographs of China were the norm in every village; distinctive and creased, with smudged spectacles on wonky frames, drooping eyelids, gappy teeth and nut-brown skin. They each looked so different except for their matching blue jackets, trousers, cap and plimsolls. They sat in groups smoking and played loud games of *mahjong,* slamming their pieces down and shouting. Toddlers tottered with holes cut in the seat of their trousers to minimise 'accidents' in the absence of nappies. It was weird to see hi-tech fighter jets flying in formation over those poor villages. It was a good example of the dichotomy of China. The government ambitiously buying jet fighters and hundreds of millions of citizens still in poverty.

The villages were dirty and squalid in a way that was unusual in most parts of the world. I thought particularly of the villages of Africa and the proudly swept areas of clean earth outside the huts. In China, people cleared their throats loudly in front of you, coughing and dragging great gobs of phlegm from their pollu-tion-and-cigarette-battered lungs, which they then spat at your feet. A lady who was cooking my lunch dredged up a foul gout of green slime and spat it out as she cooked. She didn't stop stirring my noodles.

That cold and wind-whipped plain, where the distances and the sky seemed timeless, endless and motionless, claimed Genghis Khan as a son. In Genghis' shadow I marauded westwards across Inner Mongolia, sharing the headwinds and dust and sleeping on the same hard ground. I rode alone, an army of one, the noon sun on my left cheek. Headwinds made for torturous progress and grated my lips to scabs and filled my eyes and nose with sand. My nose oozed blood at night as I slept. I paid the wind the highest possible compliment, describing it as of "Patagonian proportions." Unable to ride at all into the gale one morning I pushed the bike for a few hours before surrendering and hiding out for the day in my tent, sheltered in a drainage channel under the highway.

Idiot drivers skimmed past me at speed and blasted their horns in irritating greeting. The Chinese seem to honk just to prove that they exist. "I honk therefore I am." Shouts of "Halloo! Ha! Ha! Ha!" from every single lorry driver and their incessant beeping really grated. It was worse even than Peru which I had always held to be a benchmark of idiotic claxonnabulation. I knew that I was in a bad mood but the blank-faced staring that had begun to replace the cheerful greetings of a few weeks ago was beginning to annoy me. It was odd that, in the past week, people had become noticeably less friendly and more boorish and stupid. For the next few hundred kilometres there was a large proportion of annoying, unhelpful, unfriendly people. No smiles, no hellos, just gormless staring, hacking, phlegming and spitting, or idiotic leering and calling out "Hallooo!" behind my back. Perhaps living in a hovel in Inner Mongolia was not conducive to being friendly and chirpy. Combined with the endless smoking and spitting and shouting, I was finding it oppressive being in such close proximity with so many people and began looking forward to the Taklamakan Desert.

My annoyance with the people of China accelerated when in one town four morons pointed me down the wrong road and I only realised my mistake at the top of a ten kilometre pass. I wished that I knew some juicy Chinese insults as I turned around, rode back down into the town and out the other side on the correct route. I resolved to stick to steering by the sun. It had been around longer even than the Chinese and was a lot more reliable.

I was followed by a crowd of about 50 in a market as I bought food, tasteless biscuits and two expensive apples, for the next 200 kilometres of rutted, hilly dirt track. I was in an unpronounceable town in a valley not shown on my map. The homes were dirty and dirt-coloured, clustered round a factory that spewed gruesome yellow-grey smoke. The air reeked of sulphur, and the streams and drainage ditches were stinking, frothing and viscous.

After a few days people became friendly once again. Moronia was a thankfully small region. My route crossed the line of the Great Wall. The Great Wall of China is the most famous man-made object that cannot be seen from space. It surpassed my expectations, and it was a thrill to walk along and to camp on. The road had been bulldozed right through the huge earth ramparts of the snow-covered Wall, a very Chinese thing to do. The cold hills were covered with snow and reminded me of home. My eyes followed the line of the Wall snaking ever further away and over the horizon in all its silent and crumbly majesty. I rode parallel to it for a while and then the road veered away or the Wall deviated to follow a ridge of hills. At times the Wall disappeared altogether, as it was not built as one unbroken entity. Rather it was a strategic series of walls built at different times and places. Not only was I following the Wall, this was also the fabulous Silk Road whose landscape had changed little in centuries. Once upon a time traders leading long caravans of camels laden with valuables relied on caravanserais for rest and re-supply during their long journeys. It was exciting to follow along behind. For today's traveller in China the caravanserais are as vital as ever, though nowadays they are called petrol stations.

Further west the Wall was made of mud, as there were no stones in the desert to build with. The Wall, in all its guises, is hugely impressive. I felt as though I was following the dragon's spine across China. The wind blasted in my face as I slogged up long hills. The Wall looked a bit how I felt: worn down and ragged, but still going. It marched on over the horizons of crinkled blue hills, and I gave chase.

I slept sheltered behind the Wall as the yellow plains stretched away. There were a few herds of sheep dotted over the plain, and shepherds with scarves wrapped round their heads against the wind. They wandered with slingshots over their shoulders as endless generations must have done. Deep caves had been carved into the Wall as sheep pens, dark and stinking. I sat barefoot on top of the Wall, fixed a couple of punctures and brewed a cup of tea to help disguise my latest bag of biscuits which tasted unmistakably of cigarette ash. I always liked being barefoot, feeling warm Arabian sands between my toes, damp green grass in Chile, fields by the Danube, hard baked African dirt, the soft seashore of California, Canada's cold clean rivers and now the crusty hard mud of the Great Wall.

The Wall ends officially at Jiayuguan, 2,300 kilometres from Beijing. It had cost me $40 to ride its length, money I had earned in Beijing, substitute-teaching an English class. An impressive fort stands at the end of the Wall, although it was completely renovated. I was a Wall snob by then, and I liked mine rough and crumbling. Unhindering to the imagination. The fort had a less than scenic backdrop of electricity pylons and a huge cement factory, an apt location for the factory, I supposed. I was pleased to see that, although this was claimed to be 'The End of the Wall,' the Wall itself rolled on disdainfully westwards as before, past the fort, across the plain and away into the distance towards the beautiful mountain range that my road paralleled.

The weather was warming now and I slept without my tent at night. I lay in my sleeping bag beneath a full moon and a clear sky. I rode for thousands of kilometres without taking a day off and I was weary. I was eating vast amounts of food and feeling permanently tired, but I was loving the momentum that I was building up. I was making tangible progress around the Earth. Even on my inflatable globe I could see my progress every couple of days. It was exciting to be lying out there on my own, in China, on the Silk Road where so many others have lain on the earth, resting on their own journeys. A heavy orange moon eased up through the trees. When I woke during the night I could estimate how long I had slept by the movement of the moon. It was a full moon all over the world and I thought of the people I missed, and wondered whether they too had noticed the splendid skies that night.

The monochrome of moonlight changed to the colours of day. The sun was just about to breach the horizon. I had overslept. I rolled over, lit my stove and put some water on to heat for tea. I stood up, stretched, peed and packed my sleeping bag. I toasted some bread in the flames of my stove, spread it with honey and stirred some Chinese tea leaves into the water. I faced the rising sun and listened to birdsong as I ate. I shoved my stove and sleeping bag into a pannier, pushed my bike across to the empty road and began to ride. My shadow was long before me on the road, eagerly dragging me onwards, a foreign devil on the Silk Road.

I was pleased to see my first mosque in China. It was a sign that I was making good progress away from Beijing and towards western China. I was seeing less Han Chinese people and more who looked Central Asian. There were Uzbeks, Kazakhs and many Uighurs, the predominant Muslim group of Xinjiang province. They were far quieter and more polite than the Han. I no longer drew such crowds. They didn't even spit much. The mosque had clusters of bicycles outside for it was noon on Friday, the most important weekly prayer session. Men wore white skull caps and the cafés had posters of Mecca on their walls. I was happy to be back in a Muslim area, safe, fascinating and welcoming as ever. I watched a man outside a café preparing noodles. He held a ball of dough in both hands which he pulled out as far as he could and made one long sausage. He folded it in half to make two and stretched it out again. He folded that in half (to make four strands) and repeated the process over (eight) and over (sixteen) and over with nonchalant speed and skill until he had produced an armful of long, thin noodles which he hurled into a cauldron of boiling water. I decided to give him some business. I sat at the table outside his café and gave him the Muslim greeting, "*Salaam aleikum.*"

His surprised grin was enormous as he replied, "*Wa aleikum salaam.*"

The noodles were delicious, they were thick and soft and served with a really spicy sauce. I learned the name of the noodles, *lagman*, and a word to describe the spiciness, *la*. From then on I would explain in cafés that I was a bit of a wimp and wanted my *lagman* less *la* than everybody else's. My scabby lips really suffered eating those Uighur noodles and I would sweat profusely in what was already becoming very hot weather. I would take the opportunity in cafés to drink as much tea as possible to rehydrate. Tea was served automatically at every meal in China. Its style varied with the regions I passed through, from green tea to black tea to a more herbal-flavoured tea that floated with large leaves which stuck in your teeth.

The days were hot and the land, for a few days, was lush with bright green spring crops carpeting the small irrigated fields. Black rocky mountains with apricot dunes rose behind this narrow belt of fertile land. And then I was in a surprisingly smart town, with tree-lined streets, designated bike lanes, parks and travel agents advertising flights all over the world. I was coming to believe in this Chinese explosion.

I decided to pause for half an hour to check my emails. It was always a real treat to read messages from home. Internet cafés are very common in China, they were also easy to find as the Chinese character for 'Internet Café' was easy to distinguish: to my eyes it resembled a football goal with two X's standing between the posts.

The internet cafés were darkened rooms thick with cigarette smoke, loud pop music and people spitting on the floor. Spotty teenage boys slaughtered each other in computer games of eye-opening violence. I would squeeze amongst them to read news from home, and to see how Leeds United were getting on. I sent a quick email home to reassure my family that I was fine. The BBC website was blocked in China and other websites took an eternity to load, so throughout China I relied on the *Sun* newspaper's website for my news.

I stopped and washed my clothes in a muddy but unusually rubbish-free irrigation channel. I felt much better as the hot sun dried the clothes on my back. It was fabulous to be warm again but I knew that soon I would be too hot. I was excited to be heading into another desert, this time the northern fringes of the Taklamakan Desert. 'Taklamakan' means, "he who goes in shall not come out," which sounded exciting, if a little daunting. Graves were marked in the desert by a mound of stones and a ring of stones about 10 metres diameter around the grave. As I rode I wondered why I love deserts, where every day is the same, but I hate sitting at desks for the same reason. The Taklamakan Desert is not particularly fearsome these days. Certainly it is very hot and the distances between water stops should not be taken lightly, but the road is paved and there are cafés with water and bowls of *lag man* every day or two.

Despite having washed my clothes in a ditch I was still filthy. My face was caked in dust from the road and my hair was spiky and wild. As I finished my lunch one day a lady emerged from the kitchen with a basin of warm water and insisted that I wash my hair! It was quite embarrassing. She gave me some shampoo and lent me her husband's comb. I pedalled on westwards smelling like a summer meadow with a very crisp parting in my hair.

One day the crosswind was simply too strong to ride. Instead of pedalling comfortably at about 12mph I was forced to walk beside the bike, making only about 3mph into the wind. By mid-morning I decided to give up and hope for better luck the next day. I had been riding through desert for days on end. On the scrubby, shimmering horizon a glorious blue mirage taunted me with dreams of water, memories of swimming and dipping my head beneath blissfully cool water, the surface dancing with diamonds of sunlight. But I gradually realised that it actually was a real lake. I couldn't believe it. A lake! In the desert! With surprised delight I rushed into the wonderful knee-deep water. It was astonishing that there was a lake out there. The lake was shallow but it was hundreds of metres wide and a few fish jumped. There were even seagulls flying around. In a week or two I was due to arrive at the point on the planet furthest from a sea: how on Earth had seagulls made it to that lake?!

Out on that long, hot desert road, I had barely spoken to anybody in weeks and I had not met another long-distance cyclist since Alaska, so I was excited to see a foreign cyclist riding towards me on the dead straight road. The desert stretched away on all sides, the sun was hot and a few fluffy cartoon clouds hung motionless above it all. I stopped riding, excited, looking forward to chatting to someone again. He was on a racing bike, had no panniers and was wearing a full lycra racing outfit. As he approached me he called out, "looking good!" and he rode past. I watched until he disappeared over the horizon. I shrugged, turned back and pedalled silently down the road. No back-up cars followed him and he had no bags or gear with him.

Emerging into greenness from a desert is like seeing land again after a long time at sea. For days my head had pounded and my eyes stung. A desert of monotonous wobbling silence, sterility, absence of life. To come into an oasis, back to life and motion and greens and blues was amazing. Water! People! Senses, colours, sounds. The fragrance of greenery, the sounds of water – surging and shining – in the irrigation channels that conquer the desert and feed families. Men sat squinting, playing cards and smoking pungent cigarettes under shady vines. Children crouched in play and chattering women walked home on roads flanked with tall, shading trees. They waved and laughed as I passed and that was the nicest sound of all.

The more I rode westwards, dragging my weary evening shadow behind me, the more I left China behind. The Central Asian culture, religion, faces, voices and smiling welcomes began to dominate. Xinjiang province was wonderful, a jumble of races and languages amidst beautiful desert, mountains and grasslands. The towns had more in common with the Middle East than the China I had arrived in. The crescent on mosque rooftops, the tinny noise of Arabic music from cassette stalls, the thump of heat when you emerged from buildings onto the street. The dusty, lumpy pavements, the potholed roads and open drains blocked with litter, the fumes from sputtering motorbikes, the kids cycling slowly through the chaos in flip-flops, wobbling as they tried hard to push the pedals on their too-big bikes. Vines shaded homes from the sun and street cafés with shaded tables were too tempting to resist. I would buy naan bread from the sellers on the street, hot and fresh, pinpricked with patterns of concentric circles, and studded with sesame seeds, poppy seeds and cumin. Then I would rest from the sun on the terrace of a café with a pot of refreshing tea.

One morning I was blessed with a fabulous tailwind. I stopped for breakfast but, watching a flag flapping wildly, I regretted stopping. I should have been using the wind before it turned. I was letting so much race past unused. The ride into Turpan was beautiful, past Flaming Mountain's red sandstone cliffs, striped and windworn, past dunes and streams with grottoes hewn into the cliffs.

Turpan is the second lowest point on Earth, 155 metres below sea-level, scorching hot, and a lovely grape growing oasis. It was a fine place to rest and relax for a couple of days. My body was weary after the ride from Beijing and my mind loved the stimulation of walking round the crazy markets and being the starer rather than the staree. There were a fabulous variety of hats on display. To my untutored eye they resembled lampshades or great accessories for fancy dress parties. Over the next few months in Central Asia I began to learn the nuances of the headwear styles and what they said about the wearer's ethnicity. In a delightful street in Turpan called Grape Street, little girls played skipping games and old men played cards in the quiet, cool cafés. Closed to traffic, paved with cool tiles and shaded by vines hanging over white columns, Grape Street was a balm for the baking daytime heat. Butchers' tricycles dangled with hanging haunches of marbled red and white flesh which danced crazily as the bikes bounced over potholes. On market stalls the meat lay warming and soggy under the hot, high sun. It was mauled by pudgy fingers, grubby and unwashed, danced on by flies and coated with dust drifting from swerving, beeping mopeds or creaking donkey carts. I resolved to have a vegetarian dinner.

The sun would sink to the horizon, and the colours of the world, bleached by the fierce sun, glowed once more with the early evening light. Shadows darkened over the grime of the town, and lights came on. Pool tables were wheeled into the street. Naked bulbs hung over the tables and moths wheeled round in the warm air. Up and down the streets barbecues smouldered. Flared by fans the coals burnt with red energy and slowly settled, whitened by ash, to a steady flow of strong heat. The dangling, festering, infested, raw and dirty meat was diced into cubes, threaded onto skewers then dripped and spat on the grills. Smoke bloomed, aromas filled the darkening air, and spices and chillies were hurled over the meat. The aroma beat my resolve, and I ordered a few kebabs.

I passed through Urumqi, a city of two million people thousands of kilometres from any other major city. It is the furthest city in the world from an ocean. I rode on to the point decreed to be 'The Geographical Centre of Asia.' Actually I did not make it right to the centre of Asia, as you had to pay to walk the last 50 metres to the monument. I felt that I was probably near enough, and I pedalled on.

The area west of Urumqi, towards Kazakhstan, is closed to foreigners. The area was still sensitive as it was near Russsia and because the Uighur were a volatile lot, always on the look-out for an excuse for a spot of civil unrest. I took what I hoped would be a quiet, inconspicuous dirt track through the mountains to another valley, rather than ride along the main road and risk being caught by the police and fined. Or worse, sent back.

I loaded my panniers with naan bread and treated myself to a carton of milk in preparation for the climb into the mountains. It was a revolting disappointment to gulp from the carton of milk and realise that I had actually bought soy sauce. So, armed with bread alone, I headed for the mountains.

I rode over a mountain pass that had not yet been cleared of snow. I did not realise until it was too late. It was hot at the bottom and it did not cross my mind that there may be snow high up. I ended up having to carry my bike straight down a snowy mountainside, climbing back twice to shuttle my bags down. That day I covered only 4 kilometres, my record low. I was knackered as I put up my tent in a snowstorm.

The clear morning sky revealed my tent in a gorgeous alpine meadow, ringed with mountains. I hurtled down the rest of the mountain towards the valley floor. Arriving in the first village I stopped and tried to find something to eat. The crowd of amazed people who ran to cluster around me and stare was my largest in a while. But I accepted that these villagers had good reason to stare at a foreigner in an area off-limits to foreigners, who had arrived on a bicycle down the road that came only from a mountain pass blocked with snow. I enjoyed their surprise, especially when the crowd ushered me into a small café for a big bowl of hot noodles.

The track followed a stream that broadened into a big river. My shoulders and calves were killing me from all the carrying but the ride was magnificent. Racing blue water, green meadows of flowers, pine forests, snowy mountains, sheep, cattle and beehives: it reminded me of Chile, or Switzerland. Except for the yurts and the Kazakh horsemen. Already the slog through the snow felt worthwhile. This was my favourite part of China.

Three days later, in the next village, a policeman spotted me and escorted me to the police station. I was annoyed as I had been about to leave the village. Inside the police station about ten people were smoking in a room that had a bed with a teddy bear blanket, a kettle and a computer that was not plugged in. Was this where my ride across China ground to a halt? I was just a few days away from the border. I had so nearly made it.

I went into my smiling but stupid foreigner, "nice but dim" approach. I tried to act as though I had no idea that I should have not been in the area. They rifled my diary, read my Magic Letter and studied my passport for ages before asking where I was from. They spoke no English so our discussion was not productive, particularly as my Chinese was still non-existent. I played as stupidly, amiably uncooperative as possible and hoped that they would just give up and let me go.

They made a few calls, flicked through a few rule books and acted bewildered. Nobody knew what to do with me. I was dreading the large fine and the ignominious bus ride back to Urumqi. Some time later, somebody arrived with the local English teacher in tow. I was sure that she would be the key to getting me out of trouble. I explained my round the world journey to her, the snowy mountain incident, and how I was just an innocent little cyclist on my way to Kazakhstan. She translated my story to the policemen. To my surprise they decided to let me go, so long as I promised to register with the police when I reached the town of Ili. I thanked my translator saviour, solemnly promised to register in Ili, and got riding before anybody changed their mind. Leaving the village I turned down the wrong road and a Uighur policeman chased me on his bicycle to kindly point me the right way.

It was a lucky escape and I resolved not to linger in towns again until I reached the border. I was glad the police let me go because China had saved her best for last. I loved the vast green grazing pastures as smooth and neat as putting greens, the horsemen in their rakish flat caps, the running herds of half-wild horses, the amazing sandstone hills striped with bands of all colours of rock, the camels chewing and dumb, the swooping swallows and swifts, the white yurts beside racing blue rivers, the overflowing buckets of strawberries for sale by the road and the snowy mountains all around. I zipped down the valley to Ili, riding as fast as possible past the police station and on towards the Kazakh border.

I had high hopes for the Stans, a region I had long wanted to visit. I had ridden hard and fast across China, making significant progress towards home. Yet I had enjoyed the ride across China so much that I didn't really feel like going home.

I would be sorry to leave China behind.

The middle of nowhere

*I would rather wake up in the middle of nowhere
than in any city in the world.*
– Steve McQueen

Central Asia began with a tantrum. I was ordered to travel in a minibus for the 200 metre-long bridge across the dry river bed that marked the border between China and Kazakhstan. I was even told that I had to pay for the privilege. I shouted at the border guards more than was wise, given their potential for hampering my progress should they choose. The guards were pleasant but they would not bend the rules to let me ride across the border. They let me off the fee for the minibus ride and said, "come back to China in 2008."

The minibus revved up with only me and my bike aboard. We drove 200 metres and I climbed out again. I was in Central Asia.

I entered the Kazakh customs building to fill in the inevitable forms. I explained my route to an inquisitive Kazakh policeman. He told me that it would not be safe to travel to Uzbekistan. The government had just shot 500 people in the city of Andijan. It was the first that I had heard of it. The geography of the Stans is so tangled, with borders twisting wildly around each other – there are even islands of one country wholly surrounded by another country – that I could not envisage what the implications may be for my ride. I would need a good look at my map. I decided to press on to Almaty and make a plan there.

Entering Kazakhstan, I felt nostalgic for Russia, from the first scruffy, Russian-speaking border guard in his preposterous military hat the diameter of a dustbin lid. Signposts were in Cyrillic again, more legible to me than the past six months of Japanese and

Chinese. Shops said '**магазин**' (Magasin), and cafés were called '**кафе**' (Kafe). No longer did I have to guess what a building was. Battered matchbox-shape Ladas rattled past, looking like they had been designed by a six-year-old. No more VW Santanas, alas.

Though just an hour's ride from China things were so different already. The Kazakh villages looked just like Russian villages. I was back in the USSR. It brought back happy memories. The sun shone warm and the gardens were a spring chaos of greenness. The bungalows were wooden and whitewashed, with two shuttered windows either side of a central front door. They looked like the kind of cottage that a small child or a Lada designer might draw. I crossed the shallow Ile River onto a boring windy plain. I decided to try to save myself 50 kilometres by taking what I thought would be a shortcut. I left the road and turned off down a dirt track. The washboard corrugations in the track became worse and worse and made riding difficult. The track began twisting and turning until I had no idea where I was. The plain was featureless and deserted beneath enormous white clouds. I was still moving westwards so I was comfortable that I was at least headed in the right direction. But I had only two litres of water left and up to 70 kilometres until the next settlement.

I camped out of the wind in a ditch, hungry, thirsty and unsure of where I was. I wolfed down three packets of noodles, guzzled most of my water and hoped that I would not regret my decadent profligacy tomorrow. I climbed out of my tent and stood bare-chested in the strong wind and I looked round at an empty world and distant peaks. "Hello Kazakhstan!" I shouted at the top of my voice.

The next morning I began to get very thirsty and puzzled about where the track was heading to when I found a dusty old plastic bottle of water lying by the road. I added iodine to purify the water and, after waiting an impatient 20 minutes to allow the iodine to do its thing, I greedily drained the bottle. I felt better immediately. The power of water is amazing.

That afternoon a jeep approached in a cloud of dust. I stood in the road and flagged down the vehicle. The occupants, three Russian Kazakhs, were rattling their way to a lake for a weekend of fishing and boozing, (I did not enjoy being reminded of the

Russian neck-flicking gesture for 'let's get drunk!'). My Russian was hopeless, but at least I could find out where the track headed to and ask them for some water. Better than water, they gave me a litre of cold Coca-Cola. I rode on a sugar high for the next hour. They also gave me a bottle of *kvass*, a fermented liquid bread, even less pleasant than it sounds. But I was thirsty so I drank it anyway and a few hours later my track popped me back out on the road to Almaty. I rode quickly, relieved to be back on the smooth, easy option once again. I reached a little village and refilled my bottles at the village pump, something I had not seen at all in China. The village **магазин** was open, and the shopkeeper gave me a Coke and a bag of tomatoes as I left with my purchases. I dredged through my brain for the Russian I had learned in order to have something to say. "What is your name, are you married, do you have any children?" was not the most insightful conversation in the world but, compared to my Chinese, it was dazzling.

Leaving the village, I stopped at the memorial to those who died in World War II, the Soviet Union's Great Patriotic War. Standing in an isolated village near the Kazakhstan/China border it struck me just how much of a worldwide war it really had been. I wondered about all those men who had been sent to fight a European war on behalf of the hated Stalin. How resentful and reluctant they must have felt. How sad their families as they waved them farewell. I was not surprised that many Central Asian soldiers had elected to turn sides in the war and fight instead against Stalin, their own oppressor.

I arrived in Almaty in heavy rain. The city began as a normal Soviet village with a few old Ladas bouncing through the puddles and among the chickens. It gradually grew until I was in a city centre busy with Audis, billboards for luxury watches and more white people than I had seen in six months. Europe suddenly felt a whole lot closer than it had an hour before.

I hauled my soggy things up to the fifth floor of an echoing Soviet apartment block and, knocking on the door, hoped that my drowned rat appearance would not put my newest hosts off from letting me into their home. Chris was a Canadian photographer and his Swedish fiancée, Malin, worked for the UN. Chris had emailed me a couple of years earlier to say that if ever my ride happened to bring me to Kazakhstan then I would be welcome to stay with them. Chris and Malin seemed not to care as puddles grew around my feet on their kitchen floor. They began to tell me about Kazakhstan, their life there and the chances of me getting a visa for Iran.

After Mongol invasions and all the exciting history of empires rising and falling, the Russians arrived in Kazakhstan and shaped its modern future. The entire country was used as one of the Kremlin's 'secret' nuclear testing sites. Colossal swathes of steppe were converted into cotton monoculture with long-reaching economic and environmental consequences. In 1991, Kazakhstan broke away from the Soviet Union and began learning to govern itself once more. The leader of the Kazakh Communist party, Nursultan Nazarbayev, became the President of Kazakhstan and set about making himself very rich. The country's economy is booming, despite phenomenal corruption, thanks to gas and oil reserves. The future is rosier in Kazakhstan than in most former Soviet republics.

The dawn was fresh and bright like an English summer morning and I saw for the first time the lovely Tian Shan mountains squashed against the southern flank of Almaty. My body was still on Beijing time. China has only one time zone and so, despite having pedalled more than 10% of the way round the globe since Beijing, the time did not change until I crossed the Kazakh border, so I awoke before most of Kazakhstan. I sat with a cup of tea on the balcony, and thought over the organisation for the next stage of my journey. I was allowed to stay in Kazakhstan for one month, and I already had a month's visa for Uzbekistan. I just had to work out a combination of countries whose bureaucrats would allow me to get through to Turkey, Istanbul, and the road to home. The streets were quiet and I heard the rhythmic sweep of a broom in the park below, opposite the *007* kebab shop. A beautiful blonde woman gazed suggestively at me, no less a woman than Uma Thurman, tempting me with a very expensive watch, her billboard dominating the entire wall of a tower block. Almaty is where the profits from Kazakhstan's oil are splashed, a shimmering, glossy sheen in a country still recovering from the Communist era.

My tranquil morning's relaxation was definitely over when I headed off to see my old friends at the Office of Visas and Registration. New arrivals to the country must register their presence with OVIR within three days of arrival. OVIR is a relic of the Soviet days. I set off clutching my passport and a wedge of cash, ready to wrestle my way through queues, be shunted from one unhelpful, streaky-haired woman to the next, fill in scores of indecipherable tatty forms with a random selection of English words that nobody could read, queue some more, be stonewalled by a few more grumpy 'assistants', told to come back tomorrow, and then be fined tomorrow for not having done it today. I was not disappointed.

Having endured that experience I then turned my focus to my main activity for Almaty: securing a visa for Iran. Britain was regarded very differently in the Islamic World to four years earlier when I had begun. Imminent Presidential elections in Iran did not bode well for my hopes of getting a visa. To boost my chances of impressing the Iranian Embassy I borrowed Chris's suit. I found it quite hard to pedal to the Embassy as the trousers were very tight, and rather short, but I hoped that the Iranians would appreciate my effort.

Optimistic, I put on my biggest smile, produced my Farsi Magic Letter, and asked for a visa. "Come back in a week." I was told.

"Super!" I beamed, "I'll come back in a week for my visa."
"Come back in a week," they repeated, less enthusiastically.

A week later they told me, "Come back in a week."
"Super!" I beamed, "I'll come back in a week for my visa."
"Come back in a week," they repeated.

A week later they told me, "Come back in a week."
"Super!" I beamed, "I'll come back in a week for my visa."
"Come back in a week," they repeated.

And so three weeks of my month-long Kazakhstan visa were spent twiddling my thumbs in Almaty. Fortunately Chris and Malin seemed happy enough for me to hang around. Malin was up and out of the house early, heading off to her office. Chris worked mostly from home and seemed to enjoy having me around as he had become a bit bored of having to play darts against himself. He was working on a gorgeous photographic book, *Stanorama*, documenting his extensive travels round the Stans. I picked his brains about Central Asia and what would be the most interesting route for me to travel. His amazing pictures whetted my appetite for the road ahead. Silk Road cities awaited, alpine yurts, Soviet murals and a host of bonkers presidents. It promised to be a fabulous ride. Each day I studied the Central Asian presidents diligently, as there were posters of all the region's head honchos on the walls in the loo.

We visited the funfair in the forested Gorky Park. The bumper cars there were a chance to relax in calm surroundings away from the crazy driving of the city's streets. The rickety ferris wheel left me very impressed that Yuri Gagarin had made it into space, but even more surprised that he had made it safely back down again. Chris was a veteran of the ferris wheel and he knew to buy a round of beers to enjoy as we rose slowly up above the trees and looked over the attractive city and across to the snowy mountains that awaited me.

Despite the overlap of Kazakh people between Xinjiang and Kazakhstan, the Han in China and the Russians in Almaty made the two places feel very different. At least the *lagman* remained the same. The staff in shops, particularly the women, were notably grumpier than in China, preferring to huff and tut at my lack of language rather than enjoying, as people had in China, the game of trying to figure out what the weird foreigner wanted. There was a notable absence of bicycles in Almaty compared to China, and a preponderance of Mercedes'. The city felt more like being in Russia or Eastern Europe than in Asia. Almaty is a fun, cosmopolitan city with a stunning mountainous backdrop. The attractive streets were lined with trees and there were the many parks common to all Soviet countries, filled with trees and outrageously-dressed Russian girls. There were many newly commissioned statues and memorials dedicated to Kazakhstan's ancient heroes. The country was trying to generate its own history and distance itself from the Soviet era. Lenin's statue has long since been removed from pride of place in the main square in Almaty though he does still linger in some other former Soviet republics. An eternal flame burned at the war memorial and newlyweds came to pose for photographs there and lay their wedding bouquets in tribute. Traditionally nobody marries in May in Kazakhstan so in the first week of June the streets were busy with wedding limousines. Nut-brown gypsy women with gold teeth and bright headcloths had taught their grubby, big-eyed toddlers to follow white people with their hands outstretched pleading for cash, but generally Almaty felt affluent and comfortable.

There were many beautiful women in Almaty, dressed very glamorously. Perhaps because it took them so long to get ready in the morning they always walked at great speed. Musclemen posed as they strutted the warm streets in tight T-shirts, tight white trousers and crocodile shoes that pointed and curled at the toes. There was a pleasant pedestrianised street, popular amongst ice cream clutching families, where delicious aromas drifted from cafés. Skewers of lamb meat, *shashlyk*, grilled over hot coals. Children gnawed at their *shashlyk* whilst fathers supped from glasses of cold beer. Artists displayed their canvases on the pavement and a saxophonist played beside a fountain. The warm breeze blew a cool mist over my face and dampened the red brick pavement. Families, lovers and idlers on benches watched the world stroll by in the hot sunshine. *Babushkas*, old women in head scarves, stood begging on the street, their aged bodies bent like question marks. They chewed their gums and their pleading, resigned eyes shifted in embarrassment. With the collapse of the Soviet Union their pensions had collapsed too and now, in their dotage, the proud workers of the Motherland were forced to beg for coins. Many people did give them coins. Grateful, the *babushkas* would wipe their face with their hands in the Muslim gesture of gratitude.

I went with Chris and a friend of his, David, to the old Russian Public Baths one evening. David was a German travel agent who was helping me with my Iranian visa application. We headed for what I anticipated would be a nice relaxing sauna. The heat that hit me as I followed Chris and David inside was beyond that of any normal sauna I have been in. I found it hard to breathe.

We sat on a wooden bench amongst portly, sweating, naked Kazakh men. One man, seeing the look on my face, told me with manly pride that the temperature was 90°C! I sat wincing and motionless because whenever I moved a limb the hot air that wafted against me burned painfully. My hair became too hot to touch and I understood why the regulars were all wearing conical felt hats to cover their hair. The tough old hands were looking at us to see how the softy foreigners would cope in their sauna. Not very well, I was thinking.

Some caught my eye with intimations of welcome and thoughts of, "what the hell are we all doing in here?" or, "you're not going to stick this out very long, are you?" Just when I was beginning to think that the sauna was not really very much fun one man took it upon himself, with a grunt, to pull open what looked like a Soviet torpedo hatch. He hurled a bucket of water inside and gouts of angry steam fired back out into the sauna. He slammed the door shut with a clanging thud. I think that that furnace was probably the central nuclear heating point for all of Kazakhstan. The heat was absurd and even some of the local hard men scuttled for the exit. But the fun was only just beginning.

David had bought a bundle of birch twigs from a *babushka* outside the baths, and we joined the locals in whipping ourselves on the back and shoulders with the twigs. This would improve our circulation, apparently. I was streaming with sweat and light-headed. I felt as though I was about to pass out, but we were not finished yet. Finally we took it in turns to lie front-down on the bench and thrash each other all down the back, buttocks and legs with the bundle of twigs. When we had had our fill of ludicrous macho suffering we dashed out of the sauna for a reviving cold shower and then into the grand-looking baths where we could properly relax at last. Sturdy columns rose up to a high domed roof and the walls were nicely tiled, though it was all a bit Soviet-scruffy too, around the wide, circular bath of refreshing, cool water. I certainly felt clean and relaxed as we left but I decided that I preferred the less rigorous relaxation of Japan's *onsens*.

I visited several schools around Almaty and did a ludicrous TV piece with several Borat-esque interviewers. They filmed some 'action shots' of me taking my tent out of a pannier in Chris' kitchen, and then more shots of me putting the tent back into the bag. I answered scores of banal questions thought up on the spot. Finally we headed outside for some real action. I rode along a street and the cameraman filmed me out of the window of their Lada. Once they had all the footage they wanted they hooted their horn, waved and drove away. I began pedalling back through the city towards the flat. A few minutes later I was overtaken by their Lada zooming back down the hill and screeching to a halt in front of me. The interviewer leaned out of window and asked, "Sorry, what is your name by the way?"

Whilst out visa-bagging I met two American cyclists at the Kyrgyz Embassy, confusingly also called Marlin and Christine. They were just beginning their trip and planned to pedal to Kyrgyzstan and over into China. I went with them one evening to watch Kazakhstan play Turkey in a crucial football World Cup qualifying match. It was terrible. The football was painful. But I enjoyed the national anthem, full of trumpet fanfares, and the view from the stadium of snowy mountains and sunset. Kick-off was more than an hour late, our view of the pitch was obstructed by the massive hat of the policeman in front of us and Turkey walloped the Kazakhs 6 0.

My steady rolling progress across the enormity of China seemed like just a happy dream as I sat and wasted time waiting for the Iranians to make a decision. Waiting for weeks to pass sapped any lingering wanderlust, reducing the elixir of pure travel to a sludge of tedium, bureaucrats' whims, visa regulations, dwindling funds, boredom and the awakening of negative thoughts about what was the point of it all. But time wasting is not always time wasted. When the tourist sights of Almaty were exhausted I managed to catch up on the Brazilian soap operas that I had really enjoyed in Siberia. They were a brilliant combination of over-the-top Latin glamour and drama dubbed in a monotone by a single Russian man who 'acted' all the characters, both male and female. I could watch the A-Team too, repeated daily on Kazakh TV. And I sat in parks reading books and marvelling at the summer girls in outfits so outrageous they appeared to have been sprayed-on. Almaty was more about LA than Allah.

My Kazakh visa was running out so it was make or break time with the Iranians. To enter Iran I needed an 'invitation' from somebody within Iran. I had paid David the travel agent to pay a travel agent in Iran to pay someone for a little piece of paper. If I did not get a visa for Iran then my next two options were so much harder. There was also the disappointment of missing out on Iran, a country I had particularly wanted to experience.

If I could not go to Iran I could try to ride 1,500 kilometres across Turkmenistan to the Caspian Sea within the duration of the five-day transit visa that was the best I could hope for from that paranoid autocracy. Alternatively I would have to ride north for weeks across the empty Kazakh steppe to the lonely city of Aktau and wait for the fortnightly ferry across the Caspian Sea to Azerbaijan. Not very appealing options.

When I returned once more to the Iranian Embassy they told me to try coming back in another week. My Kazakh visa would expire before then so this was not possible. I had to take the hint that the Brits were not particularly flavour of the month in Tehran and that my visa was never going to arrive. I resolved to pedal to Kyrgyzstan and apply again there. If Homer was writing today then surely Odysseus' epic ten-year voyage home, during which the Gods hurled every possible challenge and obstacle at him, would also have included the delights of applying for visas in Central Asia. I got ready to ride again, and set off for the hills towards Kyrgyzstan, where the peasants were apparently revolting.

A BBC correspondent told me he thought it unlikely I would be allowed to ride through the Fergana valley in Uzbekistan. In the wake of the Andijan shootings were rumours of tanks gathering outside Tashkent, and the US Embassy was already being evacuated. Meanwhile CNN told of revolutions in Kyrgyzstan, a pre-election bombing in Iran and a crowd of 20,000 demanding the resignation of the government in Azerbaijan. I had an interesting few months ahead.

Marlin and Christine were also riding to Kyrgyzstan and so

we left Almaty together. We would ride together as far as Karakol on the shore of Lake Issyk-Kul. It was the first day of their journey and chaos reigned in the apartment they were staying in. Kit was strewn everywhere and the challenge of fitting all their gear for the next two months into just a few small bags was proving difficult. We did not leave Almaty until 4pm. We rode out of town and then camped in an apple orchard carpeted with thick clover. Everything that they had successfully squeezed into their panniers had to be emptied out once again as the search began for all the stuff they would need for the evening. My shoes came off, flip-flops went on and my tent went up. I laid out my sleeping bag and mat. My cooking gear and food I placed here, my toothbrush just there, my diary and book nicely to hand; everything had a place. It was simple and efficient. My routines were so slick, my days so ordered. It was ironic to think that I had begun the ride to escape from regular routine! I sat back to watch, as Marlin and Christine tried to find things and laughed with the excitement that comes at the start of all adventures. We sat outside and ate fresh naan bread with sweet tomatoes, red onions and fragrant dill.

We rode through land that reminded me of perfumed English greenness; tangled hedges and lush green meadows. Ladies with colourful headscarves and gleaming gold teeth sat at the roadside selling sweet smelling fruit; buckets of strawberries and pyramids of pale plums, rinsed and shining. Villages were busy with idle men watching the world, little children staring safe under the watchful eyes of the entire village and *babushkas* working in their fecund gardens. The walls of the quaint steep-roofed, whitewashed Soviet cottages that had so often been my salvation back in the brutal Siberian winter now clambered with summer roses. Girls filled metal churns with cold water at the communal hand pumps spaced along the single street villages. We waited our turn to fill our bottles and soak our heads under the clunking spout. The temperature was about 40°C so those water stops were very welcome.

One petrol station where we refilled our water bottles had two pieces of graffiti scrawled in English on the wall, *Beckham is Best* and *Genghis*. Kazakhstan swirls with cultures: Soviet and traditional nomadic and new capitalist oil wealth. From all that the young nation is trying to decide what it wants to be. Will they look east to Asia, west to Europe or north, back to Russia?

The Kyrgyz border guard still wore a hammer and sickle on his cap though the flag flying in the stiff wind was the flag of the new Kyrgyzstan emblazoned with a sun and the crossed lattice smoke hole of a yurt. The policemen at the border were grappling with a new computer and an array of complicated-looking aerials. Their American allies had supplied them with some brand new satellite-linked computers to monitor border traffic as part of their Global War on Terror. Sadly it seemed that, like a Christmas toy without batteries, this gadget was set to prove a disappointment. The barely-literate officials, who I imagine had never used a computer before, had no idea about installing new operating systems. They copied our passport details down onto a piece of paper instead.

After a couple more days we arrived at the shores of Lake Issyk-kul, the second largest alpine lake in the world and rode into the small town of Karakol. Marlin and Christine were heading for the mountains and China. I was heading for the Iranian Embassy in the capital. So I rode on alone down the southern shore of Lake Issyk-kul towards Bishkek. In Almaty I had asked the Iranians to forward my application to their Embassy in Tashkent, Uzbekistan, rather than beginning the whole process from scratch again. They must have felt that I was a man who could not take a hint but they agreed to my request. Giving the application process a few weeks head-start seemed one way to perhaps minimise the time-wasting of waiting. I intended to apply for a visa in Bishkek too just in case they were a bit nicer there than in Almaty. But on TV I had seen yet another pre-election bombing in Tehran. I realised that I needed to stop pinning all my hopes on securing the Iran visa and begin seriously planning the alternative options.

It was fiercely hot as I rode along the lake, past fields of crops and apple orchards. The region is the birthplace of apples; 'Almaty' means 'father of apples.' The shaded orchards were a welcome shelter from the sun, smelling of sage and humming with honey bees. Fields of pink flowers carpeted the valley below the chunky snow-covered peaks that reached high into the hot sky.

Sweating men with tanned torsos swung scythes in the knee-deep meadows. They looked as though they were practicing their 9-irons out of the rough. Other men heaved armfuls of the cut grass onto trailers piled several metres high. Tractors towing these trailers trundled past me along the road and I could easily grab onto the back for a gentle tow, giddy with the sweet summer smell of cut grass. I closed my eyes and dreamed of cover drives. On days like those I could ride for ever.

In the evening sunshine I found an empty beach hidden behind trees, deserted and wonderful. I stripped off and swam into the lake, blissful after such a hot day's ride. My head pounded from the day in the heat, my eyes stung and I was sticky with sweat, so I dived down and swam deep through the cold, clean water. I had overlooked two important things. First, the determination of Russians to drink themselves into oblivion. Second, the ubiquitous little Lada cars that still cough and bounce around the former Soviet Union are indestructible and able to travel anywhere. As I paddled merrily out in the lake, I watched an ancient Lada bash through the bushes and small trees, right onto my private beach. Eight Russians unfolded themselves from the tiny car, four sturdy middle-aged women and their scrawnier menfolk in flat caps. The women were ready for a paddle. The men clutched vodka bottles and were ready to drink.

Swimming stark naked, I had a dilemma. I knew that I couldn't swim around until they went home: Russians do not have the concept of a quick, quiet drink or two. They would be here for hours. Nor could I wait for them to collapse into a sozzled sleep: the Russians are no lightweight drinkers.

I tried to think of an alternative to walking out of the lake to the Russian's sunset party in the fashion of Ursula Andress in Dr. No, or Botticelli's Venus. In the end I swam away from the Russians until I was just about out of their line of sight behind a bush at the very end of the beach. I swam ashore, and then streaked the whitest bum in heathendom at light speed along the beach and into my shorts! Undetected, I pushed my bike quickly along the shore and looked for a more secluded campsite.

I arrived in Bishkek, one of the sleepiest little capitals I had ever visited, to be greeted by several hundred soldiers in riot gear milling around the central square. I had missed, by about half an hour, the latest storming of the parliament buildings by an angry mob. I manoeuvred through the post-revolution chaos and found the family's house I had been invited to stay at. Soon afterwards I was sitting on a rug on the lawn with a group of ex-pats, now battle-hardened veterans of their second revolution. It seemed that your second revolution was much less of a big deal than your first revolution. They were all stoically enduring having been sent home from work at lunchtime and were now busy eating lollipops in the sunshine.

I borrowed another suit, pedalled off to another Iranian consulate to apply once again for a visa and then settled down to test my patience against the Iranians again.

One of the families I stayed with in Bishkek arranged for me to give a talk at the terrifying-sounding 'International Women's Group of Kyrgyzstan' at the very grand Hyatt Hotel. I was very conscious of the holes in my T-shirt as I stood up to speak, not to mention my aromatic shoes. One German lady was particularly disappointed by my talk on 'Cycling Round the World.' She had understood that the theme for the talk was going to be 'Recycling Round the World.' I also gave a talk at the American Embassy. It was not a great success as only one person turned up. And that was the husband of the lady who organised the talk.

Apart from the riot police and the protesters scaling the fences of parliament, Bishkek was a docile little town. I watched a lot of television, read books in the parks where yummy nannys pushed babies in strollers and red squirrels scurried around. I talked with Saffia Farr, the writer, about writing books. She had invited me to stay in Bishkek. She was working on a book, *Revolution Baby*, about having a baby and bringing up a family in Central Asia. The last few weeks of revolution made excellent copy for her final chapters, as lampshade-hatted young men stomped and shouted in the streets, and little Kyrgyzstan had its 15 minutes on the world news.

As well as occasional visits to the Iranian consulate to confirm that they had achieved nothing since I last saw them, I would also phone them to check on their lack of progress. I cannot imagine that they had the sense of humour to have deliberately chosen the tune that played when they put you on hold; it was the tune for the old terrace chant of "here we go, here we go, here we go." I didn't seem to be going anywhere.

Iran was going to have to wait for another journey. It was time to turn to Plan B. It was time to ride over the mountains to Uzbekistan, the Embassy of Turkmenistan and the daunting probability of a repeat of all this bureaucratic nonsense with them.

The day I rode out from Bishkek seemed to be 'National Waterfight Day.' Kids were hurling water at each other and at passing cars. I was a target sent from heaven. Fortunately it was 40°C and the riding was hot and hilly so I was quite happy to be soaked by every child I passed. I fought back as best as I could, spraying children with my water bottles as I rode through villages.

It was mid-summer and by noon each day my handlebars were hot to the touch, my saddle was hot under my bum and my head throbbed with the heat that hung over everything. I would try to stop at a tea-house, a *chaikhana*, to hide in the shade for a couple of hours until the worst of the heat had seeped from the sky. *Chaikhanas* are a long-standing feature of Central Asia and, reclining on the carpet of the low seating platforms, *tapchans,* I imagined people doing the same thing centuries ago as part of a magnificent Silk Road trading caravan. Strings of camels laden with trading goods had trudged their robotic way along the very roads I was riding today, bound for the famous trading bazaars at Tashkent, Samarkand and Merv. The places I was bound for now.

At night I would camp wild as always, hiding out of sight of the road in depressions in the undulating, open grasslands or tucked away beside a turquoise river. Every so often on my ride I remembered with a little surprise that I was alone at the ends of the Earth and how fortunate I was to be there. At the top of a 50 kilometre climb I raced down into a gorgeous broad valley, a vast unfenced meadow with lush flowers and silver streams splintering across the meadow down towards the fast, blue Susamyr river. Cloud shadows folded themselves over the contours of the hills.

Yurts dotted the pastures, the *jailoo*, like gigantic mushrooms. I enjoyed being invited into yurts for tea and a chat and to spend my evenings comparing my life with theirs. I enjoyed less their friendly offerings of *kumis* and boiled sheep's head, cooked on fires of dried animal dung. The dawn scent of their smoky dung fires reminded me nostalgically of Africa.

Shepherds on the high *jailoo* told me that the town of Toktogul was full of bandits and gangsters. I did not find it that bad but people were quite curt there. I wondered why one area was friendly and another less so. Is it an economic effect, a reflection of hard lives in hopeless jobs, a small difference in the levels of politeness expected of young children each generation by their parents, or a gradual evolution towards dourness or cheerfulness? The road climbed and dropped steeply, the brown roadside grass shrilled with crickets and kids sold huge, smelly lake fish humming with flies. Toktogul Lake was ringed by bare brown sculpted mountains, crumpled like a satin sheet. Apparently '*narcotica*' were grown covertly on the inaccessible heights of the plateau above. Ranks of sunflowers shone on the shore and small villages were hidden amongst dark groves of fruit trees and poplars.

As I rode beside the lake a car pulled alongside me. The teenagers inside had been swimming at the lake. They handed me a slice of watermelon and invited me to their house a couple of miles further along the road. Their directions were easier than usual to follow, as one of them spoke very good English. I pulled off the road to their house, shaded under a grove of plum trees. I was immediately invited to stay. The extended family had driven south from Bishkek to stay with their uncle for the weekend and passed me on the road a couple of days earlier, climbing a mountain pass. The uncle was helping to promote President Bakiyev's cause in that weekend's election. They were in high spirits for their man was sure to win, especially here in his southern homeland.

We sat cross-legged on cushions and chatted on their *tapchan* under the trees. We drank tea and ate juicy watermelon and tart crabapples. The 20-year old son, Barman, translated between me and the family. Barman had been a policeman and was now doing a Ph. D in Moscow. Among questions about my trip, they told me about their family and asked about mine. The brothers brought out their family photo album. I enjoyed sharing a glimpse into that family's life through their portraits. There were the stern faced, rigid poses typical of Soviet pictures and there were happy family snaps and weddings and parties, just like my family's albums at home. As we looked through their family snaps they were all troubled by how long I had been away from my home and family.

The family were Kyrgyz and the journalist father was very keen to point out that the chain-smoking Russian man at the corner of the *tapchan* was his driver and that the Russian worked for *him*. He relished this example of the new Kyrgyzstan. As so often in the world they asked me about religion, about mine and that of my country. In turn I asked about their interpretation of Islam.

There was a political meeting in the house that night and about 30 men arrived in their *kalpak* hats to shout and laugh and talk excitedly about the upcoming election. The country was in a volatile position and nobody was sure what the future held. I was relieved that surprisingly little vodka was drunk during dinner, a feast of boiled mutton, noodles and mutton broth with chunks of bread. I slept outside on the *tapchan* while the meeting went on for hours inside the house. I was woken at dawn by a cockerel crowing. I reached up from my sleeping bag for plums to throw at the cockerel until it went away.

As I loaded my bags back onto the bike, one of the brothers came out of the house looking concerned and apologetic. He told me that his friend who had just arrived had heard on the radio of a bombing in London. He didn't know any details and I didn't think too much about it. I assumed it was something small and irrelevant, and that London would be on such a high after winning the Olympic bid that it wouldn't really be a big deal. I waved the family a fond farewell and wished them luck in the elections.

About a week later I connected to the internet in Uzbekistan and learned of the July 7th bombings and the 52 commuters who were murdered by my fellow Yorkshiremen. Men who had grown to feel more sympathy for Muslims in far-off lands than for the people of the land they had grown up in. Men who felt that Muslims in far-off lands would approve of their actions.

The centre of civilisation

The wilderness, centre of civilisation,
Uzbekistan, Tamerlane's nation,
Once the centre of scientific culture,
Now the prey of a Western vulture.
— Roland Christopher

I decided to try to cross the border into Uzbekistan on the road to Namangan. I was worried that I would not be allowed to enter further south in the Fergana valley following the government shootings in Andijan. At the control post five young, feckless conscripts loafed in a squalid metal container that served as their accommodation. They were dressed in grubby vests and combat trousers and were lazing amongst dirty plates and full ashtrays. They said that I could not cross the border. At first I thought that they were simply too lazy to process my papers, but they managed to explain to me that foreigners were not allowed to cross here. It was for locals only. I gave up, turned around, and continued riding south.

I guessed that I may have to ride for two or three more days to Osh. It promised to be hot, hard and un-interesting. Late that afternoon I reached a small road that turned off to the right. Uzbekistan lay in that direction so on a whim, I took it to see where it led. After about 30 kilometres I reached another border crossing, as I had hoped. Would they let me across? The border village was sleazy but friendly. People ambled back and forth, palming money in handshakes with the guards as they crossed beneath the permanently open border fence. Regulations seemed slack. To my relief I was stamped quickly and easily out of Kyrgyzstan. I rode on quickly before anyone could change their mind.

Uzbekistan had made the international news recently following the police massacre in Andijan. Their government has a horrible human rights record with boiling of torture victims allegedly a favoured tactic. Still, as they were good allies in our Coalition of the Willing's Global War on Terror I hoped that I would be allowed to pass freely through the country. I rode a few miles from the border through an area of open cotton fields. Finding somewhere to hide and camp was going to be hard but I was too sweaty and tired to have the energy to stay in a village where I would have to talk to people. I also wanted to stop short of Andijan for the night as I did not know what the situation would be like there. I did not want to be there after dark.

Two lines of bushes ran between the road and the edge of the cotton fields. I kept my eyes open for a particularly bushy bush then dragged my bike through the bush to hide for the night between the two lines. Cars and lorries thundered past a couple of metres away from me, and on the other side of me cotton workers made the most of the last of the evening light. Nobody knew I was there. I lay in the grass reading a book and waiting for darkness to fall completely before putting up my tent for the night. The sun set for the first time in my fiftieth country and I fell asleep, shining with sweat and happy that one more border hurdle was behind me.

I rode into Andijan feeling refreshed and clean having taken a wake-up dip in a drainage canal in all my clothes. A minibus driver hooted as he overtook me. He waved at me, trying to get me to pull over. I just waved at him, smiled and carried on riding. I was so bored of answering the same old questions. I pedalled away from the minibus for I was faster than the rush hour traffic. But the driver caught me again and hooted and gestured again and I was annoyed now and waved him off dismissively as I pedalled through the traffic. The third time that he tried to stop me I gave in and stopped. I glowered at the driver as he got out of his minibus and approached me. And then he held out a handful of money gesturing that I should use it to buy myself some breakfast! He had been chasing me, despite his bus full of passengers, to give me money to buy food and yet I had been rudely trying to shrug him off!

Andijan was waking up and getting ready for the day. Streets were being swept, shutters opened on shopfronts and children queuing for the school bus. With the money the bus driver gave me I bought hot naan bread studded with cumin seeds. I sat in the sunshine on a swept pavement to eat. I watched the peaceful, pleasant town busying itself for an ordinary Tuesday morning just a few weeks after several hundred people were machine-gunned across the road from where I sat.

At day's end I sat by the road. I had stomach ache from eating too much watermelon, drinking irrigation canal water, 40°C riding and inadvertent sunburn because the tree I had lain beneath at lunch time, my shirt serving as a pillow, turned out not to have been a 100% UV-proof certified tree. Storks stared at me from their scruffy nests, their beaks clattering like castanets as I waited for darkness to fall. In the dusty sunset two young boys in flip-flops and baseball caps stood in their donkey carts and thrashed the poor animals down the road in a wild, excited race, whooping at me as they passed. I raised my watermelon rind in salute.

I stopped in a village to collect water. As I queued at the well I remembered, for no apparent reason, a well that I had used in a village back in Lesotho. It was another village focussed round the central water pump, queueing with cheap metal buckets and chatting to friends and neighbours. They were two villages separated by thousands of miles and language and culture and religion. Yet they shared all that was really important: water, relationships, laughter, self-respect. So much of the world gets their water by waiting their turn at the village pump and it felt totally normal to me now. Just another road, another country, another year. I filled my bottles, sharing the water of yet another village and rode away, leaving lives behind and heading towards others. Would my old life feel normal when I returned to it, with showers and taps galore? How many more villages must I ride through before I reached my own village?

Climbing out of the Fergana valley the road wound steadily up a long, uninteresting pass with no shade for respite. I was push-ing hard to reach Tashkent in time to get my visa applications started before the weekend so I put in a long nine-hour day up the hot road. On the steepest part of the pass I overtook a crippled boy limping slowly up the hill. He was sobbing with frustration, leaning on his stick and hoping that somebody would give him a lift towards wherever it was he wanted to go. I wished him luck as I pedalled past with my limbs all functioning fine and enough cash in my pocket to buy myself a bus ticket if I wanted to. He smiled at my greeting and paused briefly to watch me riding up the hill away from him. Sometime later he found a lift. As the vehicle he was in drove past he gave me the thumbs-up sign through the back windscreen. I grinned and returned the gesture. Unfortunately the lift was only for a short distance, as about an hour later I overtook him again. He was limping bravely onwards and once again I pedalled past, legs spinning easily. I wished him good luck again and he gave me an encouraged smile, but he still had a long walk ahead of him.

I thought for a long time afterwards about why I had not given that boy the money to flag down a Tashkent-bound bus. Certainly if he had been a stranded Western backpacker I would not have thought twice about helping him. In fact I would actively have wanted to do so. But I had spent so much time in the last four years trying to persuade people that I was just an ordinary human being and not a millionaire redeemer miraculously arrived in their lives with cash to throw at all problems. I recoiled from the common preconception that all Westerners were rich and led effortless, hedonistic lives thanks to their nations' thieving colonial eras and dastardly foreign policies. Instead I tended to swing too far the other way. I did not help people when I could so easily have made their day better by slipping them a banknote or two. At times it was hard to find the appropriate balance.

I experienced the unpleasantness of travelling in areas where well-meaning tourists before me had handed out pens and goodies to children or had paid too much for things thinking that they were doing a good thing. I witnessed the aggressive begging by people who saw demanding money from foreigners as an easier option than working. I wanted to interact as much as I could with all that I encountered, but I did not want to upset people's stability for the sake of a short term fix. Instead I tried to be decent to people, to smile and to talk with people about the realities of our different lives. I wanted to be just another decent human rather than a Victorian squire doling out alms that would not really solve any problems. But as I pedalled away from the struggling crippled child who I had not helped, I wondered where I wanted to position myself on a scale that runs from interfering do-gooders determined to help the Borrioboola-Gha tribe whether or not they actually want helping along to the other extreme of a war photographer who can take a picture of a dying child, feel a thrill at snapping a prize-winning photograph, and walk away.

The day should have ended with a long glide down a river valley but a strong headwind made it an unpleasant fight instead, pedalling hard downhill. I listened to music as I rode and daydreamed about home. "Here I go again on my own. Going down the only road I've ever known." I was thinking about the end so much now. I had a few more hard weeks' ride ahead of me, but once I disembarked in Baku I really would start to get excited about the end of the road. I couldn't believe that I was actually going to pull this off.

People had been very friendly in Uzbekistan. A greeting of, "where are you from, brother?" and a gentle handshake were standard as well as invitations to their home for food and tea. My ride was dotted with tea breaks in people's homes across all of Central Asia. I rode hard and fast in those final few months, enjoying the challenges of the road and the time to reflect and make plans, but I was beginning to decline invitations to stop for tea and meals and to stay the night with families. It was just not new and stimulating anymore. I realised that I was jaded, I had been on the road too long. I felt a bit sheepish about my desire to be an enquiring, open-minded, curious traveller when all I really wanted to do was camp alone, footloose and fancy-free, on a quiet hilltop. I wanted to read my book and watch the sunset in peace and quiet. I had just about reached saturation point for new encounters and experiences. I was on autopilot now, churning the miles to home.

Through the long, hot tedious outskirts of Tashkent and into the pleasant city centre. Rows of cheap apartment blocks, the mechanics, the thickening of noisy traffic, the buses, the disorientating tangle of streets. There were tree-lined streets, parks, fountains and a grand statue of Timur the Lame, Tamerlane. Genghis Khan's descendant had been chosen by President Karimov to be the modern-day icon of Uzbekistan's history. After all my waiting around in Almaty and Bishkek I had no desire for cities or for waiting and so I planned to be in Tashkent for as short a time as possible. I gave up on my Iranian application. I applied for visas at the Kazakhstan, Turkmenistan and Azerbaijan embassies. I filled in forms, paid fees, handed over numerous photos of myself and retired to the British Council to read the English papers and start to learn more about the bombings in London.

I paid for the Kazakhstan visa but really hoped for a Turkmen visa instead. I did not have the time to wait for consecutive rejections, so I applied for them simultaneously. After more tedious waiting, I received a transit visa to Turkmenistan. This was certainly good news.

The transit visa, however, meant that I was allowed only five days to cross Turkmenistan. An impossible proposition. I begged and pleaded and cajoled the official behind the small barred window at the office in the Embassy. Eventually, in order to get rid of me rather than because he gave a damn about my predicament, he changed the date on the visa with a scribble. Delighted, I looked at the visa. He had given me permission to be in the country for seven days. There was no way that I could cycle across Turkmenistan in seven days. I began trying to explain once again, but my time was up. The official ignored me and turned his attention to some papers on his table. No central Asian official ever did anything with their piles of papers, so I knew it was a bluff. I decided to be grateful that I had got a visa at all, and trotted off to the Azerbaijan Embassy to see how things were going there.

Things were going rather well at the Azeri Embassy. When I arrived I was welcomed into a large reception room by the ambassador himself. On the wall was a huge map of Azerbaijan and together we talked over what might be the best route for me to cycle across his country. He asked me how long I would like to spend in Azerbaijan. I knew absolutely nothing about Azerbaijan or the Caucasus, and I was excited to have a look around, not least of all because I was apparently a Caucasian myself.

I decided to aim high. "A month?"

"No problem!" he replied, clapping me on the back and marching off into his office to stamp my passport. The Asian maze of bureaucracy was over. I had weaved my way to the end of the labyrinth, and now I needed no more visas to get back to England. If only I could get through Turkmenistan fast enough and find a boat across the Caspian Sea my path home was almost clear.

The golden road at last

To learn the age-old lesson day by day:
It is not in the bright arrival planned,
But in the dreams men dream along the way,
They find the Golden Road to Samarkand.
   – Flashman at the Charge

While I was trying to make up my mind what to do after graduating, four lines of a poem caught my eye and my imagination. It was a regimental motto in a book about the British Army. I tracked down the poem, James Elroy Flecker's *The Golden Journey to Samarkand*. My fascination with Samarkand was born. *Samarkand* it sounded so exotic. But where was it? Out came my atlas and I tracked down Samarkand; Silk Road trading city, capital of Timur's empire, busy modern city and World Heritage Site. Samarkand lay between gigantic mountains and inhospitable deserts at the end of the civilised world. Yet for centuries it had been wealthy, cultured and powerful. Samarkand sounded like the most remote, exciting place on Earth, and I dreamed that one day I may visit. As I trundled through my degree I realised that, more than the challenges and adventures of a career in the Army, I wanted to see the world on my own terms, and to test myself on the open road.

Now, after so long, I was almost at Samarkand. I was so excited to reach that landmark on my journey that I polished off the 200 miles from Tashkent in just a day and a half. The road wasn't very golden: it was hot and ugly and potholed and every single person yelled "*Otkuda? Otkuda?* Where are you from? Where are you from?" and kamikaze boys chased me on rattling bikes bombarding me with questions I didn't understand.

The land was semi-arid brush, the horizon featureless and shimmering. Villages were charmless and uninteresting. It was a wasteland as primitive, I imagined, as when the great works of Samarkand were built. What had been achieved in the last seven centuries here? The roadsigns I passed were a list of awesome-sounding places, each one of which I would have loved to cycle to: Samarkand, Dushanbe, Kabul, Tehran, Aktau and Baku. They were a reminder for me of the powerful magic of the road and of the charms and delights and new places that all roads offer up if only you keep riding long enough. I thought of the Uzbek man who had died in the fire in Russia. His death had reminded me to seize life and treasure it, to make the most of my time and to be thankful for every opportunity. The morning after he died I had made a promise that I would ride the road to Samarkand with a smile on my face. I had thought of him often over the past thousands of miles and I thought of him now once again as I rode into Samarkand.

To crest a hill and see Samarkand, Timur's capital before me, was a real thrill. I had built Samarkand in my mind into the apogee of my travels. I was hit by the noise of swarms of tiny, buzzing Daewoo taxis, pedestrians and vendors' pushcarts and then, the glorious, astonishing lapis domes above all the earthly chaos below. It was the Registan, one of the spots on the planet I had most looked forward to. After 40,000 miles I had arrived, and I had arrived by bicycle.

The blue domes were delicious beyond my imaginings, with a white stripe of sunshine seared down the flanks of each dome like curved scimitars. The hot sky, paled by summer dust, seemed feeble against the blue tile work; blues of kingfishers, glaciers, tropical shallows, Patagonian rivers and the deepest oceans. Even the brickwork was intoxicating. Like both the world and travel in general, the brickwork was not so dramatic up close, being flawed and not quite as perfect as how I had imagined it. But the overall impression and effect of the simple geometric patterns was mesmeric. The tilework inside the curved alcoves of the quads was much more intricate. Tendrils of yellow vines intertwined and flowers burst from curved vases. Excited Arabic calligraphy swirled around and I was intrigued to imagine what it may say. Ecstatic lions pranced and a cheerful pair of suns peered with expressive faces from behind the beasts. Such beauty, such skill, there at the end of the world.

Samarkand was once a hub of learning, philosophy and astronomy. The columned courtyards of the madrassas reminded me of an Oxford quadrangle. I tried to take my mind back through the centuries to the heyday of this region with great academies and splendid places of worship. Nowadays the quads were busy with nothing more than a score of desultory tourists, a few gift shops selling postcards and silly hats, a cut-out you could put your head through to make you look like an old Emir and a sign saying, '*Herr spricht man Deutsch, Nous parlons Français,* We speak English,' and, I guess, the same thing repeated in Japanese.

For days I kept creeping back to the Registan to sit quietly and stare. One night I returned to the Registan to enjoy the buildings in the cool quiet of a full moon. But a *son et lumière* was in full swing for a coach load of middle-aged French tourists. Instead I climbed a minaret at dawn and watched the sun creep above the same brown horizon that I too had crept over. Colour and warmth oozed into the city below me.

The mausoleum of Tamerlane, the Gur-e Amir, was a magnificent, immortal monument to man's mortality. I took a photograph there of a young Uzbek who was impressing his girlfriend by scratching his name into the tilework with a shard of stone. I asked him to stop but the two of them just laughed at me. Was this a snapshot for the progress of this part of the world? Centuries ago men were clutching at immortality through 40-metre minarets and soaring domes. Today, just a crude scribble of graffiti.

From the lofty beauty and magnificence it was never too far back to the grubby frustrations of reality. I scrummaged through crowds as the central bank opened at 9am, with everyone pushing and shoving to try to get some cash. Economic crisis was brewing in Uzbekistan: the value of the largest banknote was 1,000 Sum ($1) and there weren't very many of them around. The bank drew down its shutters about an hour later: they had run out of money. We should come back to try again tomorrow. We all turned around and trudged, irritated, out of the bank which locked its doors behind us. I made sure that I was leading the charge the next morning, changing $20 into a fat wad of Sum. I had decided that it was probably sensible to get all my money for the rest of Uzbekistan at once rather than attempting this whole process again in a different bank on another day.

I met a man in the queue, a Tajik called Jonny who spoke excellent English. I agreed to meet him again that afternoon. We shared a beer and crisps together in the park and by the end of the afternoon I really liked him. I felt sorry for him too. He was 26, divorced from his forced marriage and was trying to care for his two-year-old son on a $30 monthly income. He had just returned to Samarkand from working in Russia. His earnings had been better there but he had missed home and decided to give Uzbekistan another try. He was a motivated and clever man with an engineering degree, but he was unemployed and had been for three months. He said that his friends, when they returned from Russia after a few years away, looked at modern Uzbekistan with shock and asked each other, "what has gone wrong here?" We talked until sunset about our families and our lives and ambitions. He was so honest with me about his life that I didn't feel I could be honest about my life. I could not bear to tell him that because I had a degree and a British passport I was never going to struggle to find a job. I could earn more in an hour than he did in a month. And, if I was unemployed and had a two-year-old son, my government would give me money, shelter and medical treatment for as long as I needed it.

We parted at sunset as Jonny had to pick up his son from his ex-wife's house. I walked slowly back to my hostel. The next morning Jonny tracked me down again. He had presents for me, a baby's Uzbek skull-cap ("for your son one day") and a silk shawl "for your girlfriend, if she is still waiting for you, from the Silk Road." Jonny gave me a hug then walked off down the street and I fought to hold back tears.

Back inside the backpacker hostel I had treated myself to stay in I sat in the vine-shaded courtyard and listened to the conversation bouncing around me between the backpackers. An American, the first I had seen in the region, held forth at high volume about the epic nature of his backpacking trip and the dangers he had faced. A Swiss couple interrogated everyone in detail about the safety of the road from here to Almaty. I could have helped but everyone else was enthusiastically sharing their own experiences of the road. People from five or six nations were sitting around comfortably, chatting in various accents of English and boasting gently about their escapades.

I listened to the conversations but did not speak much. I was sitting back on my haunches in the shade, my feet bare on the warm concrete floor, my trouser hems frayed and my blue shirt faded by sun and sweat to almost white, my hair tangled and sun-bleached, my eyes creased by miles of bright sunshine. I was calm and relaxed and comfortable with whatever environment I found myself in. I was confident and knew my weaknesses. I listened to their tales of adventures, happy that I was, at last, in control of myself and my journey. I was going to get home. I was going to succeed. I had come through stronger in every way. I could look forward to the end with pride and with gratitude for the lessons I had been exposed to and could learn from if I took the chance. The sunshine was dazzling white and hot and I edged further backwards into the shade. I had hung on through but I had nothing to brag with these people about. I had been humbled by the road. I had only just made it through. Now I just wanted to get home safely and begin whatever the next challenge would be.

Fitzroy Maclean, adventurer, soldier and diplomat extraordinaire, wiggled his own way through the labyrinth of Soviet bureaucracy to visit Samarkand in the late 1930s. His book, *Eastern Approaches*, was one of my favourites. He was young, energetic and fancied a bit of adventure. He was impressed by Samarkand, though he lamented that,"two or three incongruous modern buildings in the Soviet style have already made their appearance and will no doubt be followed by others." He worried, as people have done before and since, that he was witnessing the last gasps of a glorious civilisation before it was swallowed by modernity."But it is only a matter of time before all there remains of a bygone civilisation is swept away," he wrote. "Chancing to look into the courtyard of a house in the old town, I was not surprised to see some 20 little Uzbek girls of three or four years old being marched briskly up and down in fours and made to sing hymns to the glorious Leader of the People."

We visited Samarkand 70 years apart, either side of the Soviet Union's heyday, yet Maclean's fears did not appear to have materialised. Despite the Kremlin's best efforts to stamp out indigenous identity, destroying mosques and using magnificent buildings as mere granaries, I still saw much that Maclean had seen. I saw the glory of the architecture. I shopped in, "the open bazaars (where) great heaps of fruit were offered for sale: melons, apples, apricots and grapes," that Maclean described. I saw countless Uzbek men who, "wore their national dress, long striped quilted cloaks and turbans or embroidered skull-caps," and I too sat and drank tea with, "turbaned and bearded worthies squatted on raised wooden platforms strewn with fine carpets, gossiping and sipping bowls of green tea." Nostalgics like me perhaps need not fear quite so much the end of our world.

Before I left Samarkand I had one small but important task to complete. My Turkmenistan visa was due to expire on the third of August. I decided that, with a bit of cunning calligraphy, I could easily turn the three into an eight. This would give me five more days in the country and a fighting chance of not only getting in but also getting out the other side before it expired.

I knew that getting caught falsifying a visa in my passport would not be pleasant, and that the success of this plan depended on the Turkmen officials not having a computerised record of my details. I decided it was worth a try, grabbed my pen and changed the date before I had time for second thoughts.

I rode through a boiling headwind to Bukhara along a bumpy road through flat cotton fields. Energetic boys raced their rattling bikes beside me, pedalling wildly to keep up with my more practised spinning of the pedals. They fired questions at me as they rode. Men, idling in patches of shade, whistled and shouted "*Otkuda? Otkuda?*" Fields were fertile and green thanks to a controversial irrigation policy that was contributing hugely to the drying up of the Aral Sea and the ensuing environmental catastrophe there. Cotton, notoriously thirsty, corn, wheat and fruit covered the land just as it had done in Fitzroy Maclean's time.

Bukhara had two other British visitors 160 years ago, Colonel Charles Stoddart and Captain Arthur Conolly. Stoddart had come on behalf of the British government in an attempt to persuade the Emir that it would be preferable for Bukhara to become a British dominion rather than a Russian one. The Emir had other ideas and imprisoned him. Conolly staged a rescue attempt but was himself imprisoned. They were dumped in the Emir's horrific 'Bug Pit' prison, a deep well infested with insects, reptiles, rats and human bones. It is difficult to imagine their suffering, nor how they would have felt when forced to dig their own graves before being publicly beheaded so far from home.

Bukhara, thought of as a strategic pawn in the great political games between Britain and Russia in the 19th Century, and a powerful Silk Road city, was a stirring place to ride into. I climbed off my bike when I reached the imposing walls of the fortified citadel and wandered slowly through the small town. I ambled with my bike through a market where lively debates raged over the prices of rolled carpets, through the surprisingly cool dome-covered markets, past a central tree-shaded water reservoir flanked by three magnificent buildings and on finally to Bukhara's showpiece, the Miri Arab madrassa and the 900-year-old, 46 metre baked brick minaret that has survived wind, earthquakes and Communism.

My visa for Turkmenistan stipulated the exact date on which I must enter the country so I had time to linger. I spent a couple of days in Bukhara. It was a pleasant place to relax and to store up some energy for the dash across Turkmenistan. Bukhara felt very old and the least Soviet place that I had been to in Central Asia. There were narrow unpaved alleys with mud and straw walls. The wooden doors were fixed with big metal rivets. Open, they revealed glimpses of courtyards and gardens. Only the corrugated metal roofs were any different from the times when Fitzroy Maclean or, indeed, Stoddart and Conolly were there.

The old communal water pools, stagnant green and smelly, floated with leaves and old Coke bottles. The sun burned bright and the winds were hot but the shaded markets were cool. There were very few tourists and yet much of the centre of Bukhara was geared to tourists, with rug and hat sellers politely yet persistently trying to make sales. Savvy, cheeky, confident girls who spoke many languages buzzed around, polite and charming in their attempts to persuade you to visit their shop. I sat in the lee of the minaret drinking in the incredible sight of the Miri Arab madrassa opposite and chatting with a handful of the children who had gathered to try to sell me stuff. They thought me very weird – "dirty and smelly," they said – and found it very funny when I told them that normally I slept in a tent. They did not believe me and thought I was joking: foreigners are rich and they stay in smart hotels with air-conditioning. But they enjoyed listening to me telling outrageous lies such as that I had cycled to Bukhara all the way from the Great Wall of China.

It was an unkind irony to be gifted that rarest of cycling combinations, a screaming tailwind and a flat road, and yet be only 100 kilometres short of the Turkmenistan border which I would not be allowed to cross until morning. Instead I stopped and read my book in a shady ditch by the road as the wind blew fiercely and the afternoon edged by.

I left Uzbekistan easily and then waited in a line of Turkish lorry drivers for the Turkmenistan border post to open. The Uzbek and Turkmen checkpoints had not synchronised their opening hours which left various annoying times when one office was open and the other closed. The drivers shouted through the fence, telling the officials to open up. A policeman with a snarling dog stormed out of the office to tell us all that they would open at 9 o'clock so we should all just shut up until then. It was already 9.15. One of the lorry drivers caught my eye and we both shrugged our shoulders and grinned at the general ineptness.

Eventually the police opened the gate. The policeman carefully copied down my visa dates from my passport into his official ledger, a school exercise book with puppies on the front cover. A few more officials repeated the process in their own files and then

I was away. So far so good! The lorry drivers hooted cheerily at me over the next hour as they too negotiated their way through customs and continued their long drive back towards Turkey and home.

I crossed the historically pivotal River Oxus, now called the Amu Darya, shallow and silted, and the Karakum Canal, wide, straight and perfect for swimming. The 800 mile Karakum Canal is the largest irrigation canal in the world. It is vital for the agriculture of the region. Unfortunately, because of its shabby construction it leaks almost half of its water and is the chief culprit in bleeding the Aral Sea dry. The volume of the Aral Sea has dropped by 80% in recent decades and is now an environmental tragedy.

Turkmenistan. It was time to pedal, and pedal hard. If I was to get to the Caspian Sea without resorting to taking a train I needed to cover big miles day after day, even though the temperatures were at least 45°C. My visa tampering had given me a chance, but it was still going to be difficult. I was concerned to find police checkpoints placed literally every few kilometres along what was the only road across Turkmenistan. Scores of virtually illiterate young policemen laboriously copied the details from my passport and visa with varying levels of inaccuracy. It was all a good test of my forgery skills which seemed to be holding up quite well.

After the sophistication of Almaty, the green mountains of Kyrgyzstan and the splendours of Samarkand, Turkmenistan was certainly different. Unfortunately the desert was not beautiful and romantic as I had hoped. It was flat, scrubby and smudged with only a handful of cheerless towns.

Yet I always enjoyed arriving in countries that I knew absolutely nothing about, particularly bit-part countries that scarcely featured on the world stage. Invariably I would discover (with a surprise that is perhaps a sign of the arrogance of the English), that there were people in that country, millions of them, who saw it as home and the centre of their world. I, of course would find that the country had its own history, language, music, culture, infrastructure and food. Only very occasionally in the world did arriving in a country make me grateful to not live there. Turkmenistan was one of those select few.

Turkmenistan is a big country but most of it is inhospitable, lunar-like desert. Its history is one of empires washing back and forth across its land, the most recent being the Soviets. Guerrilla resistance, desert irrigation and massive cotton projects dominated the 20th Century. As the USSR disbanded Saparmurad Niyazov was elected president, supposedly with 98% of the votes. He began creating a powerful, if bizarre, personality cult and his parliament declared him 'President for Life.'

Even by Central Asian standards, Turkmenistan is hot, and its food dreary. But its President was completely bonkers by anyone's standards. President for Life Niyazov's smiling, seemingly benevolent portrait was everywhere. A country with more portraits of the president than road signs has surely taken a wrong turn somewhere. He had named cities, a month and even a meteorite after himself. He had penned a very odd book of his version of history, religion and the meaning of life which all citizens were forced to study. A copy of this holy book, the *Ruhnama*, had even been fired up into space for posterity. Statues of Turkmenbashi, 'the father of the Turkmen,' were everywhere but the pick of them was in the capital city, Ashgabat. There, in the city centre, stood a 12 metre gold statue that revolved through the day to follow the sun. He was so absurd that he reminded me of the tale of the Emperor's new clothes.

Turkmenistan was also poor. The roads were the worst in the Stans and there were almost no signposts. That did not matter too much as there was really one road across the country. In the first village I reached I went to the market to load up with bread. Turkmen bread was denser and heavier than the delicious naan bread of Uzbekistan. The bazaar was poor but the mood was fun and lively. I posed for a picture with a wrinkly gold-toothed granny but she resolutely refused to flash her magnificent gnashers for my camera despite grinning wildly most of the time.

Well-loaded with food and water I rode along the empty, melting road past a roadsign for camels crossing the road and a landscape of coarse bushes scattered across an undulating vista of rolling sand and gravel. It was great to camp wild with no people around, to sit on a dune and let the breeze blow away the stresses of the hot hours, the wind, the bumpy road, the beeping horns and the fact that in a country with only one real road I still got lost in every horrible town.

Near to the town of Mary was the old oasis of Merv, one of the greatest of ancient civilisations, described by the Persians as 'the cradle of the human race.' Slabs of ruined mud walls were all that hinted now at former glories. Beneath the crumbling walls was a market whose stalls hoped for shade beneath flapping strips of cloth worn ragged in the permanently strong wind. Dust flew and women wrapped their bright scarves tightly across their faces as they tended their small pyramids of tomatoes and heaps of watermelons. Old men meandered slowly with their utterly impractical big black sheepskin hats on their heads. The market was poor, dirty and listless. It was a pitiful sight, a pathetic snapshot of the modern Turkmenistan struggling to survive in the lee of far grander times which in turn had failed and crumbled to nought. Round the decay of that colossal wreck, boundless and bare, the lone and level sands stretched far away.

It was fiercely hot in Turkmenistan, the hottest I had been since riding through Sudan. Sweat dried instantly so I did not feel wet, only salty. My shirt and trousers grew stiffer and stiffer with the salt. Whenever I crossed an irrigation canal I would leap in in all my clothes to rinse away the crust of salt. I soaked my sunhat to cool my head. Minutes later I would be completely dry and over heating once again. Heat pulsed upwards from the tarmac so that I felt I was enveloped in heat. I was drinking around ten litres of water each day as well as pausing in the hottest hours to rest in a *chaikhana* and drink pot after pot of green tea. Turkmenistan was so cheap that I was even buying Coke sometimes, diluting it with water in my water bottles. This expedition was becoming extravagant. Small settlements also had little stands beside the road selling 'gas water,' a shot of colourful fruit-flavoured syrup with fizzy water. I would slug a couple of those whenever I could to boost my sugar and water intake. I learned to avoid the stalls that sold fizzy camel's milk.

The extreme temperature felt far easier to deal with than it had back in Sudan. Perhaps back then I had less concept of what the world's weather could throw at me and so was less prepared to deal with it? Perhaps I could now also appreciate the relative ease of travelling in extreme heat having experienced extreme cold. It was certainly preferable to be too hot than too cold. There was also the major bonus that in Turkmenistan I was riding on tarmac rather than dragging my bike through deep sand.

The centre of Ashgabat had more soldiers than civilians and not a single other tourist. It was very weird. There were enormous, ostentatious buildings and impressive ministries. There was a gold domed palace and I was shouted at by two different policemen as I tried to take a photograph of it. The vast Arch of Neutrality proclaimed Turkmenistan's position as a neutral country. Atop the statue stood the gigantic golden statue of the illustrious leader, complete with billowing cape, that rotated through the day to follow the sun.

Away from the showcase nuttiness of the centre, Ashgabat was just another Soviet town, identical in style from the Pacific to the Baltic. There were no internet cafés in Turkmenistan but it seemed as though satellite TV was permitted from the dishes on the sides of the tower blocks. Ashgabat had been completely rebuilt in 1948 after an earthquake killed 110,000 people and destroyed the city. The Communist party leaders in Moscow were horrified that something as unplanned as an earthquake could happen in their land. So they simply cordoned off the city and denied that anything had happened until the city was re-built!

I was approached in a village by a young man who spoke good English. Begench invited me to spend the night with his family. Begench took me to meet Matt, one of the few Peace Corps volunteers in Turkmenistan. I was surprised to meet another foreigner. The Peace Corps is the American version of VSO, with thousands of mostly young Americans sharing their particular skills with the communities they are placed in for a couple of years. I don't know what Matt was like before he had been sent to Turkmenistan for two years, but by the time I met him he was very odd. He was delighted to see me and be able to talk at speed once again. And I was happy to see him because he had got hold of last week's *Guardian* newspaper from somewhere and I could read the cricket results. Begench's mum was happy to meet the sweaty stranger her son had picked up at the market and taken home for the evening. She ushered me off to the bathroom for a welcome bucket shower, a nice improvement on my usual dips in the irrigation canals. The night was so hot that after supper, Begench, his two brothers and I climbed a ladder onto the flat roof of the adjacent shop to sleep under the stars. We hoped that it would be a little cooler up there than inside. Dogs barked, an occasional train rattled slowly past and some boys raced their Ladas up and down the main street. Begench snored with a carefree cacophony and I could not sleep because of a rash of itchy insect bites from the night before when I had slept sweating and naked amongst some sand dunes. I walked to the edge of the roof to watch the drunken boy racers and the rising midnight moon. Where better to be in the world than a moonlit rooftop on a warm Turkmen summer's night?

I was only about 500 kilometres from the end of Turkmenistan, with three days still left on my visa. Everything was going to plan. I had savoured my English newspaper, reading every word and rationing it for days. It felt disconnected to be hunched in the shade behind a bush in the desert reading about British business, share prices, ballet and terror alerts in a country whose people knew nothing and therefore cared nothing for all that felt important to me.

I escaped the fiercest hours of heat in a bus shelter. The road had become even more empty west of Ashgabat. It didn't really go anywhere and I had not seen many buses in recent days. There was a small village a few hundred metres off the road, but I could not see another person and the shelter was empty. It was covered in broken glass, but it was the only shade for miles around. I swept away the glass with my foot then sat and sweated in the shade. The tarmac on the road was sticky with the heat. In my diary I wrote one of my occasional lists of, 'Reasons to be Cheerful':

It's +45°C not -15°C
Only two more days to the ferry
Nice people

Safe country
Flat
Good road
Visa forgery seems to be holding up to scrutiny

One thing a bored male cyclist may hope to write on a list like that whilst sitting bored and lonely in a bus stop is something like, "approached by a woman begging to sleep with me."

But when it actually happened I was a bit thrown.

I'm not sure if it was the gold teeth or the monobrow, or the fact she was about 40, or that the ditch she suggested as a venue for our union was not in the shade and I didn't fancy cycling on a sunburned bum, or that it was simply too hot for anything but sitting gormlessly and sweating, but I found myself thinking quickly of excuses.

I said I did not pay for sex. She said, "no problem."

I said she would have to pay me. She said, "no problem."

I said it was too hot. She said she could wait awhile.

I asked if she did not have a bus to catch. She said it would only take a minute.

I said I had a ferry to catch and got back on my bike and put some miles between us.

In the morning a farmer sent his child sprinting across the open ground from his house to intercept me at the road and present me with a gift of three small cucumbers. I thanked the boy and looked over towards his father. He saluted me, thumped his heart with his fist and pointed defiantly down the long, straight road on my behalf. I repeated his gestures back to him to acknowledge my gratitude as tears spiked at my eyes. I was riding alone, but I certainly was not alone.

I treated myself to a breakfast of eggs and tea in a truckers' café. But nobody spoke any Russian so it was time, yet again, for a doodle of a chicken and an egg (which to draw first, I wondered?) and yet another word to learn that meant 'egg' to the people I was amongst. But the lady in charge grasped my arm and led me into the kitchen to choose instead from various piles of still-steaming stomach lining and a simmering pan of the guts of a just-slain goat. There were no eggs.

A truck driver in the café hassled me to give him $10 because "we were friends." There had been so little of that in Asia which had been an extremely safe, hassle-free and friendly continent. Some Iranian drivers told him to leave me alone and invited me to join them instead. I explained, with sign language and charades and waving my passport around, how much I had wanted to visit Iran but how I had been prohibited from doing so. They told me how beautiful their country was and paid for my breakfast to apologise for their government.

Later that day a policeman took a fancy to my sunglasses, an expensive pair that I had been given by Oakley in Japan. He asked how much they cost. I told him that they had cost $5. His eyes lit up with greedy delight at their phenomenal expense. I had made a mistake, telling him a price clearly exorbitantly high. If anybody else asked I would say that they cost $2. He suggested that I should give them to him as a reminder of me and England. I told him that I would swap them for the uniform cap he was wearing, one still bearing the hammer and sickle of the Soviet Union. He declined the deal and I pedalled on.

I spotted a potentially disastrous problem with my back wheel. Four of the holes where the spokes attach to the hub had split which meant that I was already riding with four less spokes supporting my wheel. The added strain would accelerate the rate at which others broke. It was a time bomb waiting to ruin my wheel. I could only hope that it would survive until I was out of Turkmenistan. I was not convinced that Azerbaijan would have many bike shops, but at least I would have a month there to try to solve the problem.

I reached the Caspian Sea and the small ferry port of Turkmenbashi. I had until morning to get on a boat and get out of the country. I rode to the port and found that a ferry was due to leave shortly for Baku. Delighted, I bought my ticket. There was lots of stupid paperwork and pointless shuttling from window to window, but as long as I could get on the boat I didn't really care. I didn't even get too annoyed that foreigners had to pay vastly more for their ticket than anyone else, or that I was made to pay $5 for my bike and another $12 to put the bike onto the boat. I passed through baggage controls where the police checked my bags out of sheer curiosity rather than security interest. I was almost there. But then, at the last hurdle, the man at the passport desk spotted that I had not registered with OVIR in Turkmenistan. I smiled and nonchalantly told him that it was no longer necessary and I tried to take my passport and glide invisibly away towards the boat and freedom. But he just smirked, gripped my passport and told me that I had a problem, a BIG problem.

I asked him how big the problem was. He told me the fine would be $480. Now it was my turn to grin.

"$480?" I checked my Russian was correct. "That is a big problem." It was probably more than any of them earned in a year. It was an enormous, and impossible amount for me as well.

I settled down to out-stubborn him. He told me to sit on a bench and wait until all the other passengers had been dealt with. I sat down with a sigh.

I was called into the passport office and I got ready to argue. My trump card was a photocopy of a *Lonely Planet* guidebook page highlighting that the law had recently changed so that tourists no longer needed to register with OVIR. It was a tenuous trump card perhaps, but I persisted in waving it round, along with my Magic Letter. I was not surprised that the guidebook was more up to date than the officials. I pointed at the ferry and I pointed at the clock on the wall (which had stopped, I noticed). I pointed at my passport and suggested that, whilst this had all been lots of fun, I really did have a boat to catch now. But they were not yet ready to let me go. I sat quietly and waited. The optimism of the magnitude of their 'fine' was still amusing me, though their pointing out to me that the ferry was about to leave without me was rather sobering. Smoke was billowing from the funnels and its departure had already been delayed by an hour just to wait for me!

Our arguing reached an impasse. Nobody really understood what the other was shouting about. The ship set sail and all but one official went home. Looking back at this incident it seems funny how confident I felt about having the moral and legal superiority in the argument, convinced that I had done no wrong. The fact that I had forged the dates on my visa and, if caught, would doubtless have been in more than $480s worth of trouble seemed to have completely slipped my mind. If it had not I would probably not have argued so loudly and determinedly.

Eventually the town's OVIR specialist turned up at the port, summoned from some carefully hidden, obscurely located office. Actually, as it was early afternoon on a weekday, he had almost certainly come from relaxing at home. Fortunately he was a decent, intelligent man about my age. He spoke good English. I showed him my photocopied guidebook page and my Magic Letter and he quickly let me off.

Fortunately I had only eight hours to wait until the next ferry. I lay down on a patch of floor that the world's slowest floor sweeper had actually swept and snoozed for a few hours. Then I went back to the ticket office to change my ticket, but the lady in the booth said that I would have to pay $2 for her to re-stamp it. I was livid at this and stomped off to shout at the police who had made me miss my last boat. I was having a good old rant (I had eight hours to kill) and they probably sensed that I was unlikely to leave them in peace. Eventually one of them said, a little impatiently, "Look, if you pay $2 you can leave Turkmenistan." That sounded like a fair deal to me! I paid the 'fee', boarded the ferry and sailed out of Central Asia.

Turkmenbashi to Yorkshire

Dancing my way through

They burn,
They kill,
Shout, laugh and sing
They dance their way through history.
– Roland Christopher

I dabbed a forkful of sausage and bacon into the dollop of HP sauce on my plate. Mouth full, I topped up my mug from the teapot of PG Tips and turned my attention to the sports pages of The Sun newspaper. I had found it difficult to fall asleep the night before. My bed had had clean sheets, the toilet paper had perforations, the room was air-conditioned and the television was showing the Liverpool-Everton football match. Everything had been too perfect to waste on sleeping.

I arrived in Azerbaijan at nightfall. Some friendly boys at a cigarette stall helped me phone Derek who ran the Red Roofs Hotel in Baku. He had kindly said that I could stay for a while at his hotel which catered mainly for British oil workers on temporary postings to Azerbaijan. His hotel was a home away from home for its customers, hence the baked beans and English newspapers.

I was out of Turkmenistan safely and this mysterious land I had arrived in seemed to be full of wealth and mystique and promise. Bright lights and the trappings of wealth that go with an oil boom glittered all round. It was all quite a shock after the Stans. I rode along a boulevard beside the sea and past a park with a large ferris wheel. There were graceful old buildings and banks with ATM's. I gave one a try. It actually had money in it, unlike those of Uzbekistan. It whirred and spewed out some notes, a new exchange rate and a new set of colours and crests and national heroes for me to get used to. Evidently my bank account was not yet totally empty. The frugal years had paid off as my money seemed likely to last until the end. Back in China my friend Alex had given me some money to buy a meal in the first McDonald's that I passed after leaving Beijing. After several months and thousands of miles I was back in the shadow of the golden arches once more. I kept my promise to Alex.

Boutique window displays gleamed, Mercedes and BMW's hummed. It was Friday night and rich, beautiful people were enjoying the warm evening in cafés and bars. The men wore slacks, wide-open shirts, pointy shoes and a gold bracelet or two. Women seemed dressed for a Dynasty theme party. I was filthy, stinking and sitting on a pavement fixing a puncture when a black Mercedes stopped beside me and a blacked-out window opened. The driver was in his forties with gelled hair, a smart shirt with gold cufflinks, strong aftershave and, this being 9.30pm, dark glasses. In the backseat were two beautiful young women.

"Good evening!" I said in Russian, not yet knowing a word of Azeri. "Welcome to Azerbaijan," replied the man, in excellent English. "Is there anything I can do to help you? Anything at all?"

"Erm… No, I think I'm OK, thanks," I stammered, taken aback.

"Well, enjoy our country then." He smiled, gunned the accelerator, and was gone. I should have replied, "I was just wondering where I could get hold of a fancy car and a few babes to cruise the streets with on a Friday night." Over the next hours, days and weeks I thought of many clever replies that could have led to all sorts of adventures.

With the morning sunshine I saw that Baku swung round a tree-fringed bay in a crescent of high buildings. I looked down the hillside from the hotel pool over a jumble of roofs and out over the Caspian Sea. I was so happy to be able to stop and to relax mentally and physically now that the physical and logistical hurdles of Central Asia were behind me. It was nearly over. It was not until the next day that I summoned the energy to even leave the hotel and head out to explore Baku. I needed to find a new hub for my wheel. I visited the few bike shops, and even Azerbaijan's national velodrome, in an attempt to track down a suitable hub. I found several young mechanics working with skill and enthusiasm on old, simple track bikes. They loved cycling but acknowledged that it was not very popular in Azerbaijan. Newly-affluent Azeris wanted cars not bicycles. Unfortunately my wheel had 36 spokes rather than the usual 32 so they could not help. They felt sure that there would be no chance of replacing it in Azerbaijan or Georgia. So I had a choice: either I ordered a new hub from England and waited in Baku for it to arrive, or I pedalled on towards Turkey with fingers crossed that the wheel would hold out.

That afternoon I checked my emails. I had a message from someone called Steve. He had been a few years above me at school and had heard about my trip through the school's magazine. He was working as an environmental consultant for BP in Azerbaijan and said that I was more than welcome to stay with him when I arrived in Azerbaijan. So I called, and he invited me to join him, and his fiancée Becky, for a barbecue with their friends. After the barbecue we moved on to a fantastic nightclub. The dance floor was outside, under the stars and busy with rich men and expensive hookers. Photography was banned in the club to prevent the risk of incriminating evidence against their clients. The crowning glory was that the club also had a go-kart track, an active encouragement for the Soviet propensity for drink-driving. Racing Russian prostitutes in fast go-karts drunk beneath the summer stars was the sort of thing I would miss when all this was over.

Steve and Becky kindly said that I could stay with them until I fixed my bike. On top of that, somebody from their company was due to fly out from England in a couple of days time and could bring the part with them. Steve and Becky even insisted on paying for the hub themselves as their sponsorship of my ride.

When one door closes you just have to find another one to open. If I had been allowed into Iran, I would have missed the Caucasus. As well as the go-karts and friendly Mercedes drivers, Baku had a beautiful old town, a World Heritage Site that was a chaos of narrow alleyways, cafés and carpet shops squeezed inside stout city walls.

Just outside Baku however, the landscape was grim. By the late 1800s, Baku had become the world's leading producer of refined petroleum. The remains of man's early infatuation with the black gold, the devil's blood, are still an ugly scar on the landscape today. The pollution around the old oil fields is revolting. Old cranes and derricks and scaffolding lie tangled on a barren and stinking landscape slick with oil.

We drove through the hot lunar landscape to visit some mud volcanoes. Mounds of solid mud, ten or twenty feet high, belched hot liquid mud from their cones. Large bubbles of methane brewed under the mud then burst like grotesque farts. We put burning sheets of newspaper on the bubbles and as they burst they blazed with a ball of fire. The land was saturated with valuable fossil fuels, Azerbaijan's get-rich-quick ticket. If corruption and incompetence could be overcome, as well as the strife over the Nagorno-Karabakh region, then the future for Azerbaijan could be bright. They are large 'ifs' but, despite the inequality of wealth and the government's silencing of dissidents there was optimism for the future and even bold talk of one day joining the EU.

Once my new hub arrived it only took a few days to cross Azerbaijan. Apart from the terrible, arrogant, aggressive drivers it was an enjoyable ride. On one long climb I tried to truck-surf a heavy lorry, grabbing hold of its bumper as it passed. All was going well. But the lorry driver became very angry when he eventually spotted me in his mirror. He started yelling at me to let go. I grinned at him and held on. So he began veering his lorry wildly back and forth across the road attempting to shake me off. As the hill was winding and narrow and he kept swerving onto the other lane of the road, I decided it was prudent to let go and continue the ascent under my own steam.

The road from Baku climbed steadily for about 100 kilometres through a golden-brown emptiness; part desert, part moorland. One day, I discovered that a mouse had built a nest in my pannier overnight. I felt sorry to move him and his house, but he had built his house on my house and I wasn't planning on stopping. I carefully moved the intricate ball of woven grass over to a bush and left him in peace.

A disadvantage of small countries is that they don't take long to pedal across and so I got to know them far less well than bigger lands. I was enjoying learning about gas pipelines, hating Armenia and loving a dead President but then I was into Georgia, another country, another treasure trove of juicy issues, another land I knew absolutely nothing about.

The border crossing was simple as, for the first time since Japan, I needed no visa. To get an early feel for the atmosphere I stopped in a village café for food and to meet the locals. I did not know a word of Georgian and the menu was indecipherable as Georgia has its own unique alphabet. I pulled out one of the banknotes I had changed at the border, worth about a dollar, pointed to my belly, grinned, and gave the money to the lady behind the counter. She looked at my bike, gave it an enthusiastic thumbs-up, and disappeared into the kitchen. She emerged soon afterwards with a steaming bowl of lamb stew and a glass of local wine. On taking the first mouthful my eyes lit up with surprise. It was delicious! After the mundane daily task that was eating in Central Asia, the stodgy mediocrity of the food and the congealing of mutton fat on the roof of my mouth, my taste buds now leapt back to life. Spices! Garlic! Textures! And wine too! I sang a happy song as I pedalled off into the sunset and Georgia.

The narrow, hilly road ambled through villages. Georgian village homes were large, cube-shaped buildings with steep roofs of zinc and decorated guttering. The roofs extended a long way forward covering a large balcony that ran right round the house. Gardens were full of fruit trees, vegetables and vines. Hazy blue mountains lay in the distance. Life seemed to be lived outside as much as possible. Old men sat in the sunshine, their trouser legs rolled up to the knees. They clicked backgammon pieces as young men chatted on mobile phones. Pretty girls, their blue-black hair spilling over their shoulders, washed pots in the water fountains that were spaced regularly through the villages. When somebody dies in Georgia a fountain is often installed as a memorial. I waved good morning to an old woman dressed all in black sitting in a wheelbarrow beside the road. She was clutching her stick and selling watermelons, aubergines, peppers, peas and peaches. The streets smelled of cows and cockerels crowed from gardens.

Georgia was rural and dilapidated and great fun.

Between settlements the countryside was beautiful. The sun was bright on crags and truly ancient little churches perched on hilltops. Georgia became a Christian land back in the year 337. Throughout Georgia I looked round small, pretty churches; in villages, beside rivers, on hilltops. I removed my cycle gloves in awkward reverence. I passed monks with huge beards and black-clad nuns in peaceful villages. I walked round rural churchyards and peered at the swirling inscriptions on the gravestones and tombs, faded and obscured by lichen and wonky with age.

Tblisi was a gorgeous ramshackle city set on a river. Urban rivers are usually tamed and uninteresting but the Mtkvari river was a proper river with boulders, banks, little beaches, curves and rapids. It was an ideal river for a future journey by canoe, I decided. The old town of Tblisi was woven with narrow streets of winding smooth grey cobbles, quiet alleys and more charming aged churches. The newer part of the city was more indicative of Georgia's drive to align itself with Europe, busy with McDonald's, trendy urbanites and modern shops. A pedestrianised shopping area was busy with street basketball and live music.

I rode up a forested gorge away from the main highway, following a river that contoured through the hills. I was riding towards the aptly named town of Gori, the birthplace of Stalin. Upon arriving I was amazed to discover that even today Stalin was still their favourite son. A sizeable statue of him enjoyed centre stage in the town. Stalin, perhaps the greatest murderer of them all, stood tall and proud outside the Gori town hall.

Each morning I stacked up on calories with a *khachapuri*, a fantastic hot cheese pasty. After protracted discussions between a *khachapuri* seller who I asked about the road ahead, and passers-by who joined in the debate, it was announced that I would be spending the entire afternoon riding uphill. I was relieved when, after only an hour and a half's climb, I reached the summit of the mountain and enjoyed a long, gentle descent along a river valley, stopping occasionally to swim. Old ladies sat outside their homes selling what they called "Georgian Snickers." They looked like kebabs in a condom, but were actually hazelnuts and walnuts in a sweet, chewy brown goo. An ancient woman with crooked gold teeth ripped me off terribly, but I didn't feel that I could argue with such an old lady.

It was summer holiday time and large groups of families had gathered on the riverbank to enjoy the sunshine and the river. Family gatherings and celebrations are important in Georgia which places great importance on strong family ties. White-bellied men with tanned throats and forearms fussed over barbecues and proffered bottles of wine round the tablecloths spread over the grass. Children played in the river, watched by their mothers.

I felt torn in the Caucasus. It was a beautiful, hospitable and fascinating region. I absolutely loved riding through it. Part of me wanted to linger and travel widely. Yet I was also conscious that the end of the journey was not only looking possible, but was actually imminent. I wanted to ride like the wind to get back home again. I was riding around 200 kilometres each day now. The nearest that I got to a compromise was to really relish my brief glimpse of the region whilst pedalling like mad at the same time.

There was an almost equatorial lushness to the Black Sea region. It reminded me of Colombia with fragrant fruit for sale and steep hills covered in thick vegetation and tea plantations. The narrow, winding road was busy with holiday makers who drove like idiots, hurtling past me whilst chatting into their phones with young children perched on their laps as they overtook each other on blind corners. Stunning cliffside mansions overlooked the blue sea. But the beach resorts were nasty, the Black Sea's Benidorm. Crowds of white-bellied Russians strutted their sunburn, shiny shorts, tattoos and gold chains up and down the beach. The beach-front road was a crush of people in towels and flip-flops and people selling ice-cream. The newly-rich still tried their hardest to race their black Mercedes' through the crowds.

The Georgia/Turkey border crossing was one of the most beautiful crossings I had made. It was nestled between a sandy beach on the calm silver Black Sea and steep cliffs green with dense foliage. Georgia had been an absolute gem. I was now at the end of my USSR. It had been a revelation to me and a real high-light. And Georgia had saved the absolute best until last.

Back to the end

And to make an end is to make a beginning.
The end is where we start from...
And the end of all our exploring
Will be to arrive where we started,
And know the place for the first time.
  – TS Eliot

I was in Turkey once more. I was back where I left in November 2001. It was now August 2005. I remembered my first night's camp the last time I had entered Turkey. I was in a forest at the top of a pass near Bulgaria, knackered and hidden in a prohibited military zone. I camped on the Black Sea coast with folds of darkening mountains behind me. I pitched my tent quickly then enjoyed an amazing swim straight out along the golden road of the sunset, swimming directly towards the sun. The clouds were underlit by a ludicrous golden-red light like the sky in a religious painting after a particularly notable miracle. It was one of the best swims of the entire journey.

I was so happy to be back in Turkey. The weather was beautiful and the riding was easy as the road hugged the Black Sea coast. I swam in the sea, gorged on Turkey's baguette-style bread and rode hard and fast back to Istanbul. I was so fit and I was tearing up the miles, reaching ever greaterer daily distances. I was riding for eight hours a day. I felt fabulous. But the physical slog was wearing down my body. I was covered in rashes and horrible little pustules. My hands were numb from the hours leaning on the handlebars and I could no longer sleep lying on my side because my shoulders throbbed with a dull ache. I still cannot.

I began Turkey with a pretty ride through a tea and hazelnut growing region. The pavements in villages were covered with hazelnuts, drying in the sunshine after the outer layer of leaves had been thrashed off. Turkey is developed enough to have obese people and to produce masses of rubbish, but it is not developed enough to do anything about the rubbish. So the roads were lined with cans and bottles and fast-food papers and approaching each town I would pass a huge, smelly, open landfill site. I began to appreciate how much Russian I had subconsciously absorbed during the past months. In Turkey, I realised that I could only remember the words for 'hello', 'bread', 'darling' and 'thank you.'

When I rode into Turkey on the outward leg of my ride it had been the beginning of Eastern excitement and unpredictability and the real start of my journey. Now, however, Turkey felt like the beginning of the amazing luxury and ease of the Western world.

I was surprised by how many minarets there were in Turkey, white and slender and poking up through the jumble of shabby apartment blocks. Turkey had more mosques than I had seen anywhere else in Asia. There were large, conspicuous mosques in odd spots – petrol stations, for example, often had a big one – where there was no chance of them ever being filled. I was surprised also how many women wore headscarves. I was not sure whether there had been an increase in recent years or whether it was just a far higher proportion than I was used to in the Muslim countries I had ridden through recently.

Along the Black Sea coast I began to see a few cars with European number plates; Germans, Dutch, French and British holiday makers. In far-flung lands I used to wave if ever I saw an unusual number plate and the wave would be returned and we would share a brief bond of solidarity in our minority status. But in Turkey the tourists just ignored me and I soon stopped waving. My return to my normality had begun.

Upon reaching Samsun I took the direct road towards the Pontic Mountains and a straight line route to Istanbul. A few big hills, a few days of biggish miles and then the first signpost to Istanbul and the end of Asia, just 622 kilometres away. I tried to rein myself in, to slow down and reflect, to savour the ride back into Istanbul, the city that I had left in such a nervous state 40,000 miles earlier.

I was really relishing the ride from Baku. It was how I had imagined that all the world would be during the years of daydreaming that led to me eventually beginning my ride. All those happy days poring over maps and globes. The dreaming of being fit and free to make my own rules and boundaries. Dreams of riding through beautiful lands in warm weather but not too hot, with friendly locals and delightful campsites. This was what it should all have been like.

I camped at mid-afternoon in the shade of some riverside trees. The breeze was warm as I lay on the grassy riverbank watching darting fish and fat frogs. I swam and prepared popcorn and rambled in my diary about how good life was. A young man strolled through the trees to my tent. He spoke English and he sat down on the grass beside me. I prepared tea on my stove, essential for any social event in Turkey. Tea had been such a common feature of life across Asia, from the pale, weak tea in China, served without sugar, to the green or black tea in the Stans, sometimes sweet, sometimes not, to the samovars of sweet Azeri tea and the sweet, strong tulip glasses of tea in Turkey. The teenager dazzled me with the sophistication of his mobile phone. His phone had video clips and the internet and music and all sorts of amazing stuff. The world had certainly changed in my absence but not only in teenagers' gadgets. Because the final video clips he showed me – after some sexy women in bikinis and before bidding me a cheerful, "Goodbye and good luck!" – were of two men being beheaded in Iraq to cries of, "God is great!"

A couple of days later I felt terrible. I always detested being alone and in the tent when I was ill. I wanted hot water bottles and a toilet and somebody to whinge to. I barely slept a wink as my head and back throbbed all night. I kept bursting from the tent and vomiting and my bowels had a mind of their own. Morning arrived, thank goodness, and I was weak and aching but hopefully on the mend. I loaded everything on to the bike and then realised that one of my shoes was missing! I could only imagine that a dog must have run away with it in the night. After a long hunt I eventually found it in some bushes. I had been amused at the prospect of having to ride in just one shoe to the next town and then walking into a shop and asking whether I could buy just a right shoe.

It was a day for a soft bed, not for a busy road of idiot drivers. The driving in Turkey was frightening. I felt genuinely afraid on a regular basis as cars and lorries scraped past me at speed. The road was narrow and busy and the populace seemed to have mistaken the recent inaugural Turkish Grand Prix for a demonstration of the correct-and-proper-way-to-drive-on-the-public-roads-of-Turkey.

I was still feeling sick and fed up so when an 18-wheeler lorry skimmed just inches past me blasting its air horn I gave the driver the finger. My one-man crusade against idiots hooting their horns backfired as the lorry driver got very angry! Manly traits such as 'honour' and 'saving face' are very important in Turkey but I had not expected the driver to slam on the brakes of his lorry, squeal to a halt and leap out of the cab to confront me. He was a portly fellow, with a grimy white vest and a round belly. His unshaven face was set in rage and I decided that the best thing would be to keep on pedalling and zoom past him. He was brandishing a heavy stick like a rolling pin and he chased after me shouting insults as I accelerated away from him up the hill.

He climbed back up into his lorry and roared past just centimetres away from me. He was screaming insults at me and he hurled a bottle of water at my head. But then he stopped again, blocking the whole lane of traffic and raging with his rolling pin as he waited for me to reach him! By now I realised that I had angered an angry man. I decided to try to placate him. As I approached him I stopped my bike and, with one hand on my heart and a contrite look on my sickly face I offered a hand for him to shake. But he was not in the mood for reconciliation. He was about to start walloping me with his rolling pin when four men thankfully jumped out of a car and restrained Angry Turkish Trucker whilst I made good my escape.

Drawing ever closer to Istanbul I saw, for the first time in a very long time, single occupant vehicles and numb commuters blank-faced and resigned sitting in queues of traffic. I saw busy people running to catch buses rather than just settling for taking the next one that came along. The world was getting hectic and rich and grumpy once again. I must be nearly home.

Built-up areas merged tighter and tighter together, the buildings grew taller, the roads busier. I was entering the sprawl of Istanbul's outskirts. I craned my head over the traffic, eager to glimpse a glint of the Bosporus or the spires of the Blue Mosque. I knew that I had to ride several more hours, but I was impatient.

During those seemingly endless hours of riding towards the centre of Istanbul I remembered back to arriving in Istanbul four years ago, racing down a terrifying motorway after dark. It had been an unusual entry into the historical gateway to Asia but I had crossed my first continent. It had been a sad, lonely and unexpectedly difficult beginning to my journey, but as a friend once said to me after a particularly tough day's ride, "you really face your demons on a bike."

I remembered leaving Istanbul after three fraught weeks re-organising my route after the 9/11 attacks. I had crossed the Bosporus into Asia, a ten-minute ferry crossing which I spent pacing the deck and looking back at Europe. I had tried to imagine how I would feel if I arrived back at this band of water again. That would mean that I had made it right round the planet. The thought was highly improbable. But it still brought tears to my eyes, as did most things back then. There seemed to be no chance that I would be able to keep going for long enough to see it all through. Four years on and I had stuck it out. To my complete surprise I had made it through. I had had the best four years of my life and now I was about to complete the circle.

I arrived at the shore of the Bosporus and sat and waited for the ferry across to Europe. I sat on a bench, writing in my diary and staring across the narrow strait of water, busy with boats, towards the spectacular horizon of the old city. The minarets of the Blue Mosque and Hagia Sophia still speared the sky over Istanbul as they had on the morning I last made this crossing. Europe! Istanbul! I was back again. I had done it. I shook my head and grinned and celebrated with a jam sandwich. Little by little the road had given me everything I ever dreamed of.

For once in the world I did not need a map, or to ask directions, or to spend hours riding around feeling lost. I rolled off the ferry with the crush of other passengers all busily pushing past me and racing on with their lives. I knew where I was. I knew where I was going. I looked at the Golden Horn and the Galata bridge. It was still lined with relaxed men dangling fishing lines. The lower tier of the bridge was still busy with restaurants fragrant with smoky fish kebabs and sweet-smelling water-pipes. I walked through the Istanbul I remembered, market stalls still packed tight together, humanity filling the gaps and huge barrows of fruit or pistachio nuts being manoeuvred impossibly through it all by per-spiring, shouting men; streets of shiny bath taps, streets of rugs; streets of pirated music CD's and DVD's; sacks of spices and herbs seeping their scents; precarious pyramids of pomegranates to be squeezed into juice. Old men still sipped glasses of amber tea, smoking apple-scented water-pipes and frowning at their backgammon boards. There were still sausage stalls and giant blocks of cheese and silver wet fish plucked from the Golden Horn. Old, sunken-eyed ladies hunched in layers of blankets were still selling saucers of grain to feed the frenzied squabbles of pigeons (bringers of good luck) at the entrance to the New Mosque, four centuries old but four years older now. Nothing seemed to have changed in the four years I had been away. Had *I* changed, I wondered?

Last time I had been in Istanbul it had felt like an exotic, exciting opening into the East and all my adventures. Now it looked wealthy, calm, ordered and I felt at ease. So I knew that some of my perceptions had changed out on the road. You don't take a journey, they say, the journey takes you. Istanbul had not changed a great deal, but our world had certainly changed since I was last there. The War on Terror had changed everything. The world was re-aligning itself and finding new enemies and pariahs to fear and loathe. Turkey's ongoing identity crisis was more prominent than ever. Were they to be a European country or a Middle Eastern country? Islam or EU? Officials tried to pretend otherwise but it seemed that they could not choose both. Mecca or Brussels? Tehran or Washington? Which way would they lean? Yet men continued to lean on the railings of the bridge watching their fishing lines and hoping for the best, as they had done for years, and would continue to do. Perhaps the same was true for me, that some things in my life would stay the same whilst other parts would change dramatically. Whilst I felt certain that my ride would have influenced my character, my perspectives and my ambitions in some ways, I also felt that I hadn't really changed that much deep down.

I rode up the short steep hill to the Blue Mosque and my favourite memory of Istanbul. I stopped in a café for a glass of tea so that I could ask the owner to keep an eye on my bike whilst I visited the mosque. The inside of the mosque is a huge, calm orb of light and space. Limpid sunshine filters through colourful stained glass windows around the high dome. Sweeping circles of lamps hang down from long chains to sit in circles just above head height. On the floor lovely silk carpets were portioned into rectangles, one for each worshipper. The calm serenity of the mosque soothed my racing mind.

In Istanbul I stayed once again with the same family I had stayed with four years earlier. Caroline and Gurkan had been so understanding and hospitable when I stayed in their home in 2001 trying to reorganise my entire expedition. I had been afraid and uncertain when I said goodbye at their front door. Surprisingly they were happy to see me again, or perhaps they just had short memories. Caroline's welcoming hug and Gurkan's smiling handshake meant a lot to me.

Whilst I had been riding round in circles, everybody else had been busily rushing forwards with their lives. In their son Eren's eyes, I had been pedalling half his life. Since I had last seen him he had changed from a four-year-old toddler into a bilingual, artistic eight-year-old boy. Their daughter, Alara, had simply exploded into life: from a bundle of baby who I had watched take her first ever footsteps she had become a highly opinionated, extremely loud, charming, fully-functional human being.

And to really confirm that much had changed since I left home, England actually beat Australia at cricket. On one of those precious days in life when everything is perfect I discovered that Turkish satellite TV could pick up the Indian cricket channel. I watched the final day of the triumphant Ashes series and then I had sausage, chips and beans for tea with the children. During the cricket there was an advertisement for a motorcycle company. A man was cruising on his bike through a beautiful wilderness on an empty road. He was revelling in his freedom, the time alone to think and dream and plan and remember. He was high on life and at peace as he mused, "I forgive everyone. I feel like God."

I was keen to visit the Istanbul International Community School where I had given my first ever presentation. Thanks to that talk I had gone on to give literally hundreds of talks to thousands of children in schools around the world. I had made many friends and stayed with fascinating people through that network. It was lovely to return. I got a real buzz when one 18-year-old said that even just a few months ago he and his friends had wondered how I had got on in my journey.

Several of the older pupils remembered the assembly that they received years ago from a guy who was just setting off to ride round the world. They thought it a funny coincidence that they were now having another talk from someone who had just finished riding round the world. They took a bit of persuading that I was the same person, that in all those years when so much had happened in their lives I had just been pedalling obstinately on and on. They did not know whether to be impressed or to think me a bit weird. I was not sure either.

Getting on with it

Is there a time for keeping your distance
A time to turn your eyes away?
Is there a time for keeping your head down
For getting on with your day?
— 'Miss Sarajevo,' U2

I rode for 100 miles from the Bosporus until I found some countryside in which to camp. The last leg was under way. There is a great commonality to human nature. We all share the same feelings and concepts of right and wrong. We could all be each other; our lives could easily have turned out like somebody else's. This sameness in human nature was deeply disturbing as I rode through the murder fields of the Balkans, but endearing when a lorry driver spotted in his mirrors that I had grabbed onto the back of his lorry and gave me a big grin of support, as did everyone in a roadside café that our strange little convoy passed. I was excited about the ride across Europe. I knew that it would be beautiful, fun and easy. I also knew that it was the end of my journey, and possibly the end of all my journeys. I had to savour it.

As I crossed into the European Union in Greece I changed the remains of my Turkish money into the first Euros I had ever seen. I winced at how expensive my meagre groceries were now that I was back in Europe. I camped in an olive grove on a clifftop. I could hear the lone clanging bell and rhythmical chanting from the monastery on the hillside. It sounded fresh and new to me after months of listening to the Muslim call to prayer blasting out, too loud and too early. I was seeing things in Europe now with fresh and open eyes.

The wind in the metal roadside barricades made peaceful

panpipe sounds as I sat eating breakfast on the hard shoulder. This was my tune, whistling me homewards. It was also a lament for the limited numbers of times left when I would sit by a road studying my map to see where the day would take me. The sun was warm on my face and on the golden-brown fields and bush-covered hills. A French couple on their motorbike stopped to chat. They were on their way home from Turkey. I enjoyed being able to speak French once again. My French is poor but it is much better than my Greek (or Turkish, Georgian, Azeri etc.). They gave me their address and invited me to stay if I happened to ride their way on my trek up France. Cheered, as I always was when people stopped for a chat, I pedalled on briskly. A few minutes later the French couple came back down the road towards me, handed me €100, smiled and roared away again without saying a word.

Shortly before leaving Greece I stopped for a roadside hotdog. It was served with tzatziki and therefore became my most authentic Greek experience. The vendor spoke English and he asked me if I thought whether Turkey should be allowed into the EU. I thought quickly, "Do I want a quiet peaceful snack?" But then I replied, "Yes, I think Turkey should be members." His rant against the evils of the Turks began. He also warned me that I would be robbed when I reached Albania by all the thieving Muslims. As he paused for breath and I munched my sausage I tried to change the subject, telling him that I was about to leave Greece and ride through Macedonia. But that only set him off again. Surely I knew that Macedonia was actually part of Greece? Later, approaching the border, I passed a large stone monument engraved in English with the words, 'Macedonia means Greece.' Right across Europe, nobody seemed to get on with their neighbours.

Macedonia passed briefly beneath my wheels – the tang of apples as the road climbed higher through orchards, the chase of aggressive dogs – as I daydreamed of home. A masochistic asceticism and the crushing weight of a road seemingly without end had taught me the value of things that I used to take for granted. Perhaps it would be only a brief thing, but I felt no wanderlust any more. I was ready to stop.

Summer was ebbing fast as I pedalled up towards the charms of a northern European winter. It was raining in Albania. Across the border I squelched into a town just as all the shops were closing. I was hungry and I had no money. So I banged on the front door of the bank which had just closed for the day. To my surprise the staff actually opened the door and let me in. The cleaning lady motioned that she had no problem with my muddy shoes on her clean floor. I reappeared from the bank with a handful of Lek and set off to look for food.

Albania is Europe's poorest country. The rain was thumping down. The people looked hard-up, with bad clothes, sallow skin and tough faces. I was back in a land of beeping car horns, crap cars, potholes and unfinished, shoddy buildings. My bike computer ticked over to 70,000 kilometres and I paused to hide from a cloudburst under a large tree. I shared the tree with a stout woman under an umbrella who was keeping a very close eye on her one grazing cow. She seemed to think I may steal it.

At the top of the third large pass of the day I decided to stop for the night. As it was still pouring down, and as I like sleeping in silly places, I thought it would be a good idea to sleep in one of the disused mushroom-shaped concrete anti-tank bunkers that lie wherever you look in Albania. The lakeshore and hilltops were covered in them. The former paranoid Maoist dictator, Enver Hoxha, built 600,000 bunkers in order to repel attack from whatever quarter it might come. On the evidence of my first afternoon in the country it was hard to fathom why anybody would fight to get IN rather than to get OUT of Albania. Anyway, camping in an old anti-tank bunker seemed like a fine idea: a dry night's sleep and an amusing one too. There was a strong ammonia smell of goat poo in the bunker but at least it was dry. I celebrated by adding my final slice of Turkish salami to my dinner. Little did I know that I was to be feasted on by hundreds of fleas that night, and would itch awfully for days.

In the morning the rain had stopped, the sun was shining and I rode enthusiastically on towards Tirana. Occasionally there is a glory that light up a man. It is a welling deep in his body that flames all of his senses, bubbling through his heart with an almost painful energy. At those moments he does not wish to live forev-

er, he knows only complete satisfaction with that moment. I felt
it that day on the high mountain road from Elbasan to Tirana. I
climbed up and up from a valley dominated by an enormous and
ugly factory, up the craggy limestone switchbacks, up and up until
the air was cool and sweet and smelling of pine. A man standing
by his moped and admiring the view kissed his fingers and gestured out at the world as I passed. Below me the hills rippled to
the horizon in every direction, dark green with trees and interrupted only by rocky outcrops, pale squares of corn fields and very
occasional red roof hamlets. I was very aware of my good fortune.

I had the privilege to visit the work of *Hope and Homes for
Children* in Albania, Bosnia and Croatia. I had visited their project
in Sudan and had been looking forward to seeing their European
work. It was humbling to meet the devoted staff. Working on small
salaries, or on no pay at all, they poured such energy and expertise and loving compassion into changing a regional system of State
Institutions that was decades behind the West in its approach to
orphans, institutionalisation, special needs children and adoption.
The resilient, positive, enchanting children in the homes filled me
with a sense of awe and frustrated helplessness. Their lives had
been so much harder than my mind could ever properly grasp.
Hope and Homes for Children were doing inspiring work but so
much more could be done for those children if only the funds
were available. How could an orphaned child be left in an uncar-
ing State Institution, her chances of leading a happily fulfilled life
shrinking with every wasted year simply because the money needed to finance appropriate solutions could not be found? With the
contrast between my personal light-hearted mood and my frustration at my fund-raising shortcomings confusing me I pedalled on
once more.

The road to Yorkshire pointed out of Tirana past rows of grim
Communist-era tower blocks that have, under the new Mayor's
supervision, been painted in colourful shapes and patterns, rain-
bows, stripes and spirals as part of his bold regeneration campaign.
It carried me on out of Albania and into Serbia and Montenegro
where it led through terraces of olive trees above the Adriatic and
rock-strewn, craggy peaks of bright white limestone.

Cold, heavy rain was a distraction to the beauty of the ride along Montenegro's coastline. It was world-class riding. There were mountains, islands, mediaeval towns, deep blue bays, Roman mosaics, cave paintings and jet-black espressos. Cupped in the massive rough limestone hands of Southern Europe's largest fjord, the small town of Kotor shone like a pearl, even in the rain. The old town is tucked in the tight fold between the sea and the craggy cliffs, and cold green rivers rushed to the sea all around.

Kotor's history is typical of the Balkans: turbulent, dramatic, wild and unsettled. Empires have washed back and forth, battles been fought, religions come and gone and come back again. The fantastic Venetian-baroque architecture, the churches and friezes and the narrow cobbled streets reminded me of a mini Vienna ringed by stout walls or of a rainy, windy Cartagena without the fresh fruit juices. Kotor is one of the best-preserved mediaeval towns in the Adriatic. I rode on along the coast road that wiggled around the contours of the fjord. I really liked Montenegro, despite the rain and wind and it was a pity when my rode popped me out into Croatia.

There were so many fantastic places like Kotor along the Adriatic Coast that I was not very disappointed to be disappointed by Dubrovnik. Dubrovnik is similar to many rich and fashionable women: gorgeous from a distance, rather a let down up close. Dubrovnik was undoubtedly beautiful, but I had become spoiled and selfish and greedy. I liked my tourism to be solitary, unexpected and with a sense of fortunate discovery. In Dubrovnik there were simply too many tourists and too little normal life. Even the fruit market in one of the cobbled central squares felt twee and contrived.

Away from Dubrovnik the road climbed into the hills. The ocean was dark blue far below and dotted with islands, the hill I was hauling up covered with green trees and white boulders. Suddenly a blaring, riotous, happy cavalcade of about 50 cars hooted past me, the cars flapping with rosettes and flags. It was a jubilant wedding procession. They were on their way to a chapel that I could see up ahead. It was honey coloured in the afternoon sun at the end of a white dusty track, its lone bell tolling the procession towards the wedding. It was a gorgeous beginning to a marriage and I cheered the cars as they passed me and then began pedalling just ever so slightly faster towards home. I camped that night in an orange grove and fireworks from another wedding celebration were framed in my tent door as I slurped pasta from my pan. All around the grove glowworms pulsed my own personal silent light show for me.

I fingered the smooth warm porcelain of my second espresso. The first had sparked my nerve ends and ignited my morning but I wasn't yet ready to leave. Besides, it was cold outside and I still had money in my pocket. Frost clung to the outside of the window but inside a pleasant fug of steam and warm breakfast cigarettes weaved rivulets down the pane. It was October now and the 57th country of my ride waited for me a stone's throw down the road. Bosnia. The Great War of 1914-18 that stole millions of young lives used a terrorist murder here as its final mitigating excuse, and Europe's foulest genocide since the days of Hitler and Stalin burst here like a festering boil just over a decade ago. I was a little anxious at what may lay ahead. I emptied the last coins from my pocket onto the table for a tip, the end of my Croatian money, and I walked out into the fresh morning and Bosnia and Herzegovina.

A small queue of vehicles built up behind my bike at the rural border barrier whilst the official dragged on his cigarette and satisfied his curiosity about the colourful stamps in my passport. He raised his eyebrows at me, saw no response in my deliberately expressionless face and lifted the gate to allow me to proceed.

In the former Yugoslavia picturesque scenery, delightful towns, mosques, monasteries, synagogues and churches blend beautifully together. It is its tragedy that the people have not managed to co-habit so harmoniously. What struck me most about the Yugoslav wars was how recent they had been. Whilst I was ambling unconcerned through my teenage years the people of Yugoslavia had been killing, butchering and bombing each other a few hundred miles away.

To further his expansion plans for Serbia, Slobodan Milosevic had successfully re-ignited religious animosities that had been brewing for centuries (and have not been entirely resolved now).

Families, friends and communities tore each other's lives apart. I found it extraordinary that the completely normal people around me had within them the capacity to murder one another. History, of course, has shown that it is a capacity that all of us share.

The river Neretva escorted me to Mostar, a mediaeval town divided by a river. The left bank is Muslim, the right bank Catholic, and for centuries everybody worked and traded together, separated and united by a graceful half moon bridge over the deep green river. Today the cobbles are polished smooth between cafés, souvenir shops, mosques, churches and art galleries. Window boxes splash colour and the river gleams as it slides through the town. It is a very pretty town, except for the streets of bombed homes, still with empty windows and broken roofs, roofs thatched only with sunlight through which trees grow. Buildings whose facades were shredded by bullets as Yugoslavians tried to train their kicking guns on the bodies of other young Yugoslavians crouching at windows and firing back. Mostar had been the scene of heavy fighting in 1993, and much of the town was destroyed.

The rebuilding from war is slow, despite the funding from various agencies of many countries. The mental healing is slower still. A symbolic step towards this was the rebuilding of the old bridge that had spanned the river since the 16th Century until it was destroyed by Bosnian Croats during the fighting. Before its destruction, mad young things bent on adrenaline, vanity and impressing their peers would leap from the arch into the river 21 metres below. Four centuries of testosterone-driven tradition continue on the new bridge and I watched a muscular, tanned young man sitting on the bridge rail in tight grey Speedos with affected insouciance. He had a tattoo of the bridge on his heart and a cluster of excited girls around him. He did not seem to be in a hurry to hurl himself from the bridge so I continued looking round the town. A couple of hours later I returned. The bronzed stud was still on the bridge, slightly more bronze now perhaps, with an even larger giggle of groupies around him. But he did not appear to be any nearer to jumping. He seemed to be quite content standing around posing in the sunshine and occasionally readjusting his very tight trunks.

Then I got road-raged at again! Having learned in Turkey what happens if you give the finger to moronic drivers, I merely waved angrily at the latest car to almost flatten me by racing towards me on the wrong side of the road with an insanely dangerous overtake. A few minutes later there was a screech of wheels beside me. The idiots had gone to the effort of finding a place to turn around and then driving back to rage at me. I was touched.

Three very angry young men leapt out of the car. The passenger, a classic example of Little Man syndrome, suddenly punched me twice in the chest! I was so amazed at the anger on his face that I could not help but chortle. At this the driver kicked me in the stomach! I decided not to provoke this incredibly pointless over-reaction any more so I walked away from them until they finished screaming at me and drove away again.

Apart from the petty violence it was an enjoyable ride to Sarajevo, following the jade-green river through a canyon into the hills. The road and railway weaved back and forth across each other as we climbed higher through frightening unlit tunnels and over bridges. Villages clung to the sides of steep valleys. Conical haystacks stood in newly-mown fields. Less fortunate settlements were now just destroyed carcasses still ringed with red skull-and-crossbones signs warning of uncleared landmines. Their fields were unmown and untouched. People were selling fruit and fish by the road. It was a weird mix of normality and madness. I began my mental struggle once again, trying to twist my brain to accept and comprehend the madness of war. Did that jolly, middle-aged man who sold me those plums suffer the murder of somebody dear to him? Did he himself once kill another man? Why did they start killing each other? How do they return to normality now?

I was worried about camping wild in Bosnia because of the threat of landmines. So I camped on the edge of a solid track that looked as though perhaps it was an abandoned road or perhaps somebody's driveway. I was too tired to be bothered to investigate and at least it was sure to be free from landmines. After I had set up my tent I was discovered by the man whose house was, in fact, up the drive. He was not bothered at all about me sleeping on his drive. He said, "England very good. Sleep: no problem" and gave me a banana. It was a reassurance for me of the relaxed decency of people after riding through a country that seemed set to try to shatter my cheery belief.

Over the mountain pass and I swooped down into the valley of Sarajevo, down the steep hills that made it a fabulous winter Olympic City. A mere eight years later those same hills made equally fabulous strategic sites for the placement of the Serbian guns that besieged, shelled and starved the beautiful city for almost four years whilst UN and NATO forces looked on impotently, their hands tied helplessly by diplomatic waffle.

Sarajevo was a magnificent city and the ride down into its centre from the high surrounding mountains was spectacular. I glided down the long central street formerly known as 'Sniper Alley' where graffiti signs of "*Pazi – Snajper!*" ("Watch out – Sniper!") were daubed on the walls cautioning the citizens of the city who still needed to dash across the street during the four-year siege of the city. 'Sarajevo Roses' were scattered around the streets, concrete scars like skeletal flowers from where mortars had burst on the pavements. They have been filled with red resin and create strangely attractive, poignant memorials as each Sarajevo Rose commemorates a blast that killed somebody.

Ramadan had begun that day and the afternoon cafés were unusually quiet for a Balkan country as I rode into the city centre. I went to the row of bridges over the narrow River Miljacka to cross the stone arches of the Latin Bridge where Franz Ferdinand was shot and the Great War found its excuse and catalyst. In the evening the mosque in the quaint central Pigeon Square was full. The mosque overflowed onto the pavement and each worshipper prostrated in prayer in union. It was an impressive sight in the warm street light.

It was Monday morning. Back on the bike and pedalling out of Sarajevo. Back to work after a week in the company of *Hope and Homes for Children*. I rode 100 miles at about 14mph which was both far and fast in my slow world. I followed the Bosna River valley and the deep red russets of autumn forests dropped steeply down to the riverbank. Herons stood still and stared as I swooshed past. The only difficulty of the day was in staying alive. The

Bosnians earned my nomination for being the most reckless drivers in the world. I collected water from a fountain that was engraved with the names of all the young men from the village who had died in 1993–94. The cold clean water bursting bright and unstoppable from the marble plinth seemed an ideal memorial for all those young lives cut short. I decided that when I die I wanted someone to put up a drinking fountain in my memory. The fountain would have to be in addition to the hilltop bench that I had once decided, when sitting on one, would be a good thing to leave the world.

Dawns broke foggy and I would have my road to myself as I dismantled the dew-soaked tent and began riding at the first hint of light. My toes were cold in the mornings now and I dug out my gloves and hat once again. I was back in Croatia once more. It was noticeably richer than Bosnia, despite the strafing bullet holes still spattered round windows. Whole areas were being rebuilt, funded by the UN, and people were slowly putting life back together. Church towers were still down, resembling jagged bones or broken teeth, a nerve-jangling link back to the madness.

The Children's Home in Lipik was the first building to be shelled and destroyed by the Serbs when they attacked Lipik in 1991. The 80 children sheltered in the cellar for a week until they could be evacuated. When Colonel Mark Cook, the Commander of the British Contingent of troops in Croatia, came to Lipik and saw the destroyed orphanage he promised to return and rebuild it. Out of this project *Hope and Homes for Children* was born. I went for a drink with Goran, the director of the *Hope and Homes for Children* project in Lipik. The small red brick café was playing Croatian love songs and we drank local beer and chatted. Goran told me that the café was famous in Croatia because the Serbs never captured it. The front line was only 100 metres away but the café kept on serving throughout the war. A framed photograph on the wall showed a rag-tag bunch of men and women dressed in combat gear and sunglasses. They were all grinning and brandishing lethal weaponry. The photograph is a vivid reminder of the brave locals who volunteered to become soldiers and defend their town, their homes and their families. After firefights the café would be full and boisterous deep into the night, as the villagers bonded tight through the shared experience of war.

Close to Ljubljana rise the fabulous Julian Alps. Caesar did pretty well to have a mountain range as well as a salad named after him. They were as beautiful as Switzerland but without the caravans. On the way to Italy I visited Kobarid on the beautiful chalk-blue Soca River. "In the bed of the river there were pebbles and boulders, dry and white in the sun, and the water was clear and swiftly moving and blue in the channels." It is the scene of Hemingway's First World War novel, *A Farewell to Arms*

My bike was dying fast. The chain was snapping about twice a day. When you repair a broken chain you lose a link or two of the chain, so it meant that the chain was getting shorter by the day. This adds even more strain to its tired links. I climbed into the Dolomites, a little nervous on the descents for I had no back brake. My front rim was buckled and so braking was an uncomfortable series of violent jolts. The rear rim was cracked, my bottom bracket wobbly and my few functioning gears jumped wildly around.

One day I had three punctures and, as night fell, my tyre started going down again. I had to pump it up every five minutes as I dashed to make the most of the dying light and find somewhere to sleep. In my wet tent that night I spent an hour with my pan filled with water in an attempt to find the hole in the inner tube, but with no success. The next morning I had five punctures before 11am and my chain was now so short that I could use only a few of the gears. The gears that still worked jumped and bounced infuriatingly. My front pannier clips broke and I had to lash the bag onto the frame with string. My gloves had gaffa tape for palms, and my rain trousers had a gaffa tape crotch. My knees decided on sympathy pains as well, throbbing and aching at day's end as I crawled into my damp tent. And my stove kept breaking as well so I had to fix that most evenings before I cooked dinner. The expedition really was hobbling homewards.

The magnificent Dolomites had very civilised mountain passes. Signs told the altitude, how many kilometres remained to the summit and how many more hairpin bends stood between me and the top. They were about as easy as mountain passes ever get. I would climb two or three passes each day, but each one only took a couple of hours to climb so they were good fun. All around was a gorgeous landscape of huge walls of rock and autumnal forests that echoed as I yelled at my terminally sick bike.

My bike was a total contrast to the Sunday afternoon riders of Italy who purred along on carbon fibre dream machines looking every bit the professional in fancy racing outfits. There is a saying in Italy that "it is easier to buy a light bike than to lose weight." Clearly my bike and I were a lower class of being as the thoroughbreds rarely stooped to the level of replying to my greetings. Snobbishness like that was a demand to be overtaken. I got a childish pleasure from accelerating hard with four years of practice and overtaking the posers.

Ahead of me only the top of a mountain still glowed proud pink in the last of the setting sun. I was camping by a cold clean river in a steep autumnal valley. The evening was chilling quickly. Over that mountain pass lay Switzerland. I was at the bottom of the last pass of the ride. I sat on a smooth white boulder, hugging my knees and feeling quite sad. I didn't want all this to end. I could think of nothing better to do with my life than this. I could not imagine anything matching up to what I had done and, in melancholy mood, I anticipated dreary mediocrity awaited once I was over that pass and home.

I paused at the top of the Simplon Pass, built by Napoleon. Cowbells were ringing, the mountains were pristine, the car park was full of caravans. It was vintage Switzerland. It was the last pass in my world. I felt sad that the end was nigh. It was all downhill from there. I wondered whether I should just turn around and ride back down the way I had come and pedal on to Australia. But my bike would never have made it that far so I just rolled on down towards Geneva and from there up into France.

Geneva was so rich, so clean, so perfect. It was about as far as it is possible to be from the chaos of the developing world. I was feeling the first disorientating waves of reverse culture shock wash at the soft sand foundations of the life I had come to know as 'normal.' Wonderful bookshops were crammed with lifetimes of armchair education, provocation and adventure. They showed me the infinite possibilities for our lives. How could I make a choice?

The perennial question of "what shall I do next?" was no longer just a happy excuse for miles of daydreaming. In a few (too few) days' time I would wake up in my bed at home and have to say to myself for real, "I am not riding today. What next?"

In Geneva the traffic, to my constant surprise, stopped for me at pedestrian crossings. 50-seater buses contained no more than 50 people. People waited their turn in the post office. Banks contained money. Lots of it. Street signs told me where I was and where I wanted to go. Manhole covers had not been stolen for scrap metal. Nobody honked their horns or shouted. Traffic flowed. Nobody raised their prices when they saw that I was foreign. There were traffic lights in the cathedral bell tower to help tourists ascend and descend efficiently. The sun was not blotted by pollution. And I saw not one single donkey in all of Geneva. But, lest I seem ungrateful after the years of whingeing, I will whisper this quietly, as quietly as the Geneva rush hour: it was so boring!

During hard times I had often dreamed of cycling in France as some sort of ideal: riding from village to village and sitting in street cafés drinking coffee and reading *L'Equipe* [the daily sports paper]. Within 100 metres of entering France I was sitting in a café making the dream come true, celebrating.

France was a green and pleasant land, and the view from my tent each morning of dew-drenched green fields and hedges and steaming cows was so similar to the England I remembered. I spoke French badly but even so it was a luxury to be able to not only ask for directions, but even to understand some of the replies.

Racing up the N6 through Auxerre and on towards Paris, the land was flat and open. I settled into my own rhythm, rushing along, my nose following the white line ('yuppy style') as my legs span me closer to the end. The mornings were cold and misty and as I rode in a 7am dawn I thought, "how the hell did we do Siberia." I stopped for *café au lait* and *pain au chocolat* at the first village I entered, confirming for me that my resilience had absolutely gone!

I didn't want all this to end. I wanted to turn round and ride for ever, sleeping in forests and filling my bottles at village fountains. I hoped that the sadness I felt and my reluctance to end the amazing, precious experience actually stemmed from a lazy desire to take the easy option, rather than because I honestly felt nothing could ever be so good again. I knew that going back and facing all the new beginnings that I would have to make was a tougher path than continuing with this life I now knew so well.

Entering Paris, I followed the route of the Tour de France's final stretch, up the Champs Elysees and round the Arc d'Triomphe. If Geneva had been a reverse culture shock, the chaotic traffic round the Arc d'Triomphe was a nostalgic reminder of what cycling in the developing world had been like.

In just two more days I would take the ferry to England, and it would be all over. I hoped that my bike would hold up for two more days. My mind raced with memories and I had to try to tell myself that the end of the ride did not mean the end of my life. I had absolutely no idea what I would be doing a month from now, but that was no excuse not to get on the ferry and find out. I was excited about the end, but nervous about the new life that awaited and sad that these momentous years and miles were almost done. But a consolation was that Europe had saved the best for last. The end of all my exploring had been to arrive where I started and know the place for the first time: Europe had been my favourite continent of all that I had seen. Europe has everything for the traveller: landscapes, history, cities, food, languages, cultures at least the equal of anywhere on Earth, and all squashed nice and tight together so you don't have to pedal for a month to get to the next interesting place. If any European country was dropped in the middle of any other continent it would instantly become a dream travel destination.

After 4¼ years and 73,000 kilometres, I came within a whisker of missing the ferry back to England. Across the water my parents and Sarah were waiting for me and I so nearly messed it all up by missing the boat! I had begun that final morning just 99 kilometres from Le Havre and so I had a nice lie-in in my tent. But the

French road signs somehow turned the distance into 140 kilometres. Two hours before the ferry departed I discovered that I actually still had 40 kilometres to go! I was going to miss the ferry. I began riding like a lunatic, sprinting as hard as I could. I was completely knackered. But it dawned on me that it was not possible. I conceded defeat and decided I needed to take a taxi. I was going to end my ride round the planet by cheating in a taxi. But I simply had to catch that ferry. I overtook a taxi at a traffic light, flagged him down and asked him for a ride to the ferry terminal.

Bizarrely the taxi driver refused to give me a lift. "No, I will not take you. If you pedal quickly you will make the boat."

I cursed him, but his strange refusal was a reminder to me of the philosophy that had got me this far. I should not forget it now, not so near to the finish. If you try hard enough, and if you want something enough, then you can find a way to accomplish it. I could not forget that now. I could not just give up and cheat so close to the end. So I continued the sprint, absolutely furious at myself for messing up, for missing the boat and for all the ensuing hassle. Lungs fighting for air, legs burning, heart striving, head commanding me not to yield. This was a bloody ludicrous ending.

I hurtled up to the ferry terminal just as the gates were closing. The ferry was departing in 15 minutes' time. Thankfully they let me through – the final small kindness from a stranger – and I pedalled into the cavernous ferry and the huge doors closed behind me. Exhausted, stressed and shaking, I realised that this was it. I walked onto the deck to watch as we pulled away from the shore, towards the end and back towards where everything had begun. It was all over. I leaned on the railings and cried.

My penguin's egg

If you march your Winter Journeys you will have your reward,
so long as all you want is a penguin's egg.
– Apsley Cherry Garrard

But there is no such thing as 'The End.' For every ending makes a new beginning. It was wonderful to see my friends and family again. It was reassuring to feel as though I had not really been away and that I could just slip comfortably back into old friendships despite having been away for over four years.

I rode from the ferry at Portsmouth to the *Hope and Homes for Children* office near Salisbury. It was a pleasure to meet all the team and I was really touched at the effort they made to welcome me. The weather was appropriate for my first day back in England: it was windy and raining.

The final ride, back to my home in Yorkshire, was postponed briefly for a couple of fantastic homecoming parties. Everything seemed to be happening so fast. I was at the centre of a whirling, affectionate attention from my friends who I had not seen in so long. Yet when I walked the streets or spoke to strangers I was totally anonymous for the first time in years.

The road into Oxford was beautiful and I looked at everything with a deep, and new, appreciation. The grass was stiff with frost and the skeletons of winter trees were dark before a low, yellow sun. The hedgerows were thick and green and lumbering pheasants dashed panicked across the road. The spires of Oxford's venerable colleges appeared on the skyline, nostalgically reminding me of happy times. I realised that England – my home – was as fantastic a country as any other place I had visited. I just had to approach it with enthusiasm and an open mind in exactly the same way I had approached the last 60 countries.

Having said that, England was freezing cold and the sun setting at 4pm was quite depressing. I shivered in my tent in muddy, frosty fields. I really did not have enough clothes for camping in that weather. So, on my final night before reaching home, I made the most of home advantage. I phoned a friend, Rich, who picked me up and drove me to his parents' home. His mum cooked huge steaks and I slept in a warm, fluffy bed. The next day Rich drove me back to where he had picked me up and I carried on riding, for the very last time.

It was a long day's ride, up through the Peak District and Sheffield and across Yorkshire towards home. It was a real thrill to be surrounded by familiar, beautiful scenery once again. To not need a map anymore, to know where I was going, to be going home… It was a beautiful final morning, frosty and blue-skied. I loved the green hills, the grazing sheep, the intricate dry stone walls. The drivers were safe and courteous, there were occasional bike lanes and the road signs were plentiful and accurate. It was good to be home!

My bike was rattling and wobbling horrifically. I honestly expected that I was going to have to just dump it in a hedge and run home. I didn't think it was going to make it. The gear cable snapped so I had to ride the last 30 miles in just one gear, standing up on the pedals to push the high gear round. My tyres were so bald that, coming round a roundabout just 15 miles from home, I skidded and crashed, ripping my trousers and cutting my knee. I had rarely fallen during my trip. This incident highlighted to me that you are in as much danger living your life on your doorstep as you are on other side of the world.

Fame had found me, in the form of my local TV station wanting to film me arriving at my front door (not to mention being invited to turn on the local Christmas lights!). I arrived in the village before my own two hours before the cameraman was due to arrive. So I went to the pub. I left my loaded bike outside and went inside. The warm firelight was welcoming. I knew that nobody would recognise me in that village and I would be able to sit quietly and collect my thoughts. The end was so close! I walked to the bar and ordered a pint.

I took my beer to an armchair beside the log fire. I was cold and tired and the beer tasted good as it slipped down. I warmed my hands and feet in front of the fire. I was about 20 minutes ride from the end of my world. It seemed so long ago that I began. I couldn't believe that it was nearly over, that I had actually made it back home. I could barely imagine a life without all this. I listened to the conversation of the men sitting at the bar. It was good to catch up on local gossip. Around the world I had enjoyed listening nosily into conversations whenever I could understand them. The insight into other people's normality fascinated me. Now I was back in my own normality once again.

"I got a real nice bone for dog from butcher today."
"Oh aye?"

I thought back five years to when I began planning the expedition. My search for sponsorship did not go well. I suggested to one bicycle company that linking its products to a journey across five continents could well benefit them. Their reply was not encouraging. "Do you really think we just got off the banana boat?" said one letter. "Riding a *bicycle* round the *world*?! If you want a bike why don't you get a job like everybody else. Nobody is going to fall for such a ridiculous suggestion."

The urge now to turn up on their doorstep with a large bunch of bananas and a grin was strong.

"It were cold last night. Weatherman says it'll be -10 this weekend!"
"Oh aye?"

But I would not go gloating, partly because *nobody* really expected me to finish what I had started in reckless pub conversations and unrealistic daydreams in the dusty recesses of my mind back at university. For the duration of my ride I carried a sentence torn from an email I received at the beginning from a well-wisher. "I will be stunned if you complete it, " it said. He was not the only one. The biggest doubter was me. From the moment I left my front door until, more than two years later, I sailed out of Colombia bound for Panama, I knew that my plan was beyond me. Self-doubt plagued me. I *knew* that I would quit. It was simply a question of 'when.' The gradual realisation that I was actually going to accomplish my objective had therefore been a constant source of surprise. I had underestimated my capacity and I had learned to aim so much higher.

A new man came into the pub, another farmer in wellies, bringing a wave of cold air and a sheepdog with him. I used to play cricket with him but he wouldn't recognise me now. Someone offered him a beer.

"Crikey! Well, if you're buying I'll have an 'alf."
"No, have a pint."
"Ooh: look who's full of money tonight! Nobody ever buys me a
pint."

I had thought it was going to be impossible for me succeed at my ambition. But, as Mohammed Ali said, with swagger, "Impossible is just a big word thrown around by small men who find it easier to live in the world they've been given than to explore the power they have to change it. Impossible is not a fact. It's an opinion. Impossible is not a declaration. It's a dare. Impossible is potential. Impossible is temporary. Impossible is nothing." I sipped my beer and felt stunned that I had completed it.

"Bought a big lump of belly pork today."
"Oh aye?"

Before I began I had had several motivations for wanting to attempt to ride round the world. I reflected now on the ride, on how it had differed from my expectations and what it might lead to in my future. I had decided to begin as a quest for adventure, to see some of the world and to escape from England and the conveyor belt of my life. I longed to escape from tedious routine (although in fact my life on the road was dominated by repetitive routine). I wanted to challenge myself and to see whether I could follow faintly in the bold footsteps of the great men and women who had gone before me and told mighty tales of adventure in epic books. I wanted to see whether I could do anything remotely similar. There was only one way to find out, and that was by having a go. And I had wanted to do something that I would certainly fail unless I poured everything I had into it. I wanted something difficult. And I got it: this was the hardest thing I had ever done physically, mentally and emotionally.

"It's not cold. Just put a couple of jumpers on, a pot of tea with a drop of whisky and you'll be reet warm."
"Aye but it spoils the tea, that."

I began because I wanted to try to begin a career as a travel writer, as someone living to travel and to write. How the writing would progress I would discover in the coming months as I sat down to test my brain and try to write the book of the journey. I had ridden the ride, now I just had to learn to write. I was pretty disciplined at making myself cycle all day long; whether I could make myself sit still and type all day I was less sure about! Ironically, in the final few months before arriving home and beginning learning to become a travel writer I had felt that I had at last cured the wanderlust that had plagued me for years. Perhaps I didn't even want to be a travel writer at all after having done so much travelling! Or perhaps a few months of computer screens and rainy days would have me reaching for the atlas and the panniers once again.

"I've found this super shop where baked beans only cost 7p."
"7p?! Well, beans are beans aren't they?"

I had over-estimated the physical side of the expedition. My body had gradually strengthened and hardened to meet the challenges of the road. It was a real thrill to have become so fit. To ride 100 miles a day, spending eight hours in the saddle on a laden bike over demanding terrain and to be able to wake the next morning and do it all again, and again, and again was something I was very grateful for. We greatly under-estimate our bodies. People I met used to say to me "I could never ride that far." For most people that was nonsense.

I am no sporting superstar. I was never in any sports teams at school, I realised sadly young that I was never going to play for Leeds United and in Los Angeles I nearly lost an arm wrestle to a 50-year-old woman. But by the end of my journey I was riding for more hours a day than the *Tour de France* cyclists (so I could eat as much food as I wanted to and I would not get fat) and I could sing very loudly as I rode smoothly up Alpine mountain passes. It felt good. I felt tired but satisfied at day's end. Never in my life would I ever be so fit again.

I hoped not to lapse back into the sedentary life of our rich world where even children do virtually no exercise and are prevented from taking risks. We drive everywhere, we eat crap food, we slouch indoors and we forget that doing exercise is something that makes you feel good, not bad. We eat too much, we run too little. Healthy mind and healthy body: how mad we are to neglect our body, the very machine that carries all our thoughts, emotions, ambitions, dreams, fears and our life itself. And yet we still expect to live smoothly, healthily and happily to a ripe old age.

"Aye, well when I'm in Keighley I always pop into bloody Netto to see if they have any cheap peaches."

But if I over-estimated the physical aspect of the trip, I also underestimated the mental challenges. Being away from friends and family helped me to appreciate their true importance. Splitting up with my girlfriend for the sake of the ride made the whole journey so much more difficult. It made me question, on numerous occasions, why I was doing it. I hoped that Sarah may now take me back! Being alone for so long had made me realise that there was even more to life than seeing spectacular places, being carefree and wild and facing fresh challenges and new experiences. I realised that what I really wanted was to share all those things with somebody else.

Being alone meant being completely reliant on myself for motivation. Nobody was checking up on me; nobody praised me if I rode an extra long day; nobody got cross if I slacked off and camped early at 6 o'clock; nobody would know (or care) if I took a bus. Nobody raised an eyebrow if I took an easy option or if I spent frivolously my too-few funds, or if I avoided a challenge that frightened me or if I walked over a mountain pass I could have ridden. Nobody gave a damn. Nobody except me. I understood now the importance of self-respect for how happy you feel within yourself. I knew how tempting it could be to take the easy option. On your own you stand or fall by your own efforts or shortcomings. Trying to persuade myself not to quit, to keep going, not to take the easy options: this was the single hardest aspect of the ride. But it made the end product sweeter. It doesn't always have to be fun to be fun.

"Right, lads, I'm off. Same time again tomorrow?"
"Aye."

The friends at the bar finished their drinks and left. I bought another pint and returned to the fireside. I wanted to savour the sensation of being so near the end for a little longer.

The trip had been a powerful learning experience for me and not only because I had empty hours each evening in which to read hundreds of books. Talking with people of every race, religion, political view and wealth level was eye-opening and helped widen my own horizons. From having to make thousands of snap judgements on who to trust or not to trust I saw that first impressions can occasionally be misleading, but usually they are not. I was helped by so many strangers, many of whom became friends and inspirations and without whom I would never have succeeded. I will be forever indebted to all those people. I learned to trust people, to relax and to believe in an essential goodness to the human race. Almost everybody in the world treated me well. Nobody ever refused me water. I was only refused permission to camp twice (both occasions were in Europe). Everywhere else in the world I was given at least a safe place to camp, and often a bed, shower and feast. Everybody has hopes and dreams and loves. Everyone laughs at something funny. Don't believe what you see on the TV: the world really is a good place.

I finished my drink, left the pub and cycled home.

To be continued...

Look, if you had one shot, one opportunity
To seize everything you ever wanted
Would you capture it or just let it slip?
— Eminem

How much better has it been
than lounging in too great comfort at home.
— Robert Scott

I would never have learned backgammon at a pavement café in Amman. I would never have drunk *tej*, Ethiopian mead, from a vase flask in a dim drinking den. I would never have heaved the helm of a yacht to run down the face of an Atlantic wave along the silver path of a full moon. I would never have camped beside the Straits of Magellan or on the banks of the Yukon. I would never have had my beard entombed in Siberian ice, eaten octopus in Tokyo or sat humbled in Samarkand's Registan. I would never have ridden around the planet if I had not taken the hardest journey of all: stepping out of my front door and beginning the ride. From your front door it's a long way home.

They were the best of times and the worst of times. The thrill of new experiences was tempered by numbing boredom and loneliness. The challenge and privilege of solo travel fought my lazy streak dreaming of sofas and cappuccino. Slums terrified me then surprised me with gestures of welcome. I was afraid of entering violent and dangerous countries yet they often turned out to be amongst my favourite countries.

Being totally fit, riding hard but comfortably over Andean passes with all my worldly possessions in a few small bags, no deadline to make and no persistent phone demanding my attention, the vast freedom of a long adventure and the privilege of time and space to evaluate what is and what is not really important in life. These are the things I appreciate most from my ride.

I never thought when I began that I would actually succeed. But the essence for me was not whether I succeeded in the end. It was whether I gave it my best shot. More important was that I turned a dusty daydream into a reality and reaped the rewards from taking time out from our hectic 21st Century whirlwind to smell the roses, smell the coffee, smell the stinking industrial wastelands, smell our amazing world. In our era of email and Chinese takeaways we glibly say that the world is a small place. That is nonsense: the world is enormous; certainly too big for a single lifetime. Its diversity and variety is staggering. I am fortunate that I took the chance to see a small part of it. For in hauling myself around a thin slice of our world I discovered so much about myself.

Recipes from the road

Grilled Dorado - *Atlantic Ocean*
Ingredients:
  fillets of dorado
  minced garlic
  minced ginger
  lemon juice (tasty and helps prevent scurvy!)
  chopped coriander
  olive oil
  salt and pepper

Method:
  Season the fish with salt and pepper. Mix the garlic, ginger, lemon, coriander and olive oil and rub the fillets with the mixture. Place the fish on a very hot oiled grill (to prevent the fish from sticking) for a few minutes until cooked.
  Serve with mashed potato.

Chimichurri - *Ramón the repair man, Argentina*
Ingredients:
  Olive oil
  Lemon juice
  Fresh parsley, chopped
  Finely chopped onion and garlic
  Salt and pepper
  Chilli seeds (to taste)

Method:
  Mix the ingredients well and allow to stand overnight. Sprinkle liberally over meat before and after grilling.

Empanadas - *Argentina*
Ingredients:
  Dough
  500g minced beef
  1 cup beef fat

2 finely chopped onions
2 tomatoes, seeded and chopped
1 red pepper, finely chopped
2 carrots, thinly sliced
2 hardboiled eggs, diced
pitted black olives
1 teaspoon cumin
1 tablespoon paprika
salt and pepper

Method:

Roll the dough flat and cut into 4-inch discs with a cutter. Sprinkle the disks with a little flour so that they do not stick to each other.

Fry the onion in the beef fat for five minutes. Add the mince, salt, pepper and cumin, and brown the mince. Add the carrots, the paprika, the tomatoes and the red pepper. Cook until the carrots are soft. Remove from the heat, add the pitted olives and the chopped hardboiled eggs. Stir well. Allow to chill in fridge.

Place two tablespoons of the filling in the centre of each disk, moisten the edges with water, fold one half of the disk over the other and press the edges together. Pinch them tightly together to seal them.

Place the empanadas on a greased baking sheet, brush them with a beaten egg, and bake in a hot oven for 10 to 15 minutes until golden.

Quinoa Soup - Peru
Ingredients:

1 cup quinoa
1 chopped carrot
1 chopped stick of celery
1 tablespoon oil
1 finely chopped onion
½ chopped green pepper
2 cloves crushed garlic
1 litre chicken stock
2 finely chopped tomatoes
¼ sliced cabbage
salt and pepper
parsley
a couple of chicken's feet

Method:

In a large pan brown the onions and garlic in the oil. Stir in the vegetables and quinoa for a few minutes to soften them. Add the stock and bring to a boil. Simmer for about ten minutes. Season to taste with salt and pepper. Garnish with parsley and the foot of a chicken or two.

Lomo Saltado - Peru
Ingredients:

500g steak, sliced into thin strips.
2 medium onions, sliced into strips
2 cloves of garlic
2 medium tomatoes, peeled and cut into large pieces
2 chopped spring onions
a handful of cooked chips
oil
1 tablespoon red wine vinegar
2 tablespoons soy sauce
salt and pepper
parsley
cumin
coriander
thinly sliced hot green chillies

Method:

Brown the onions then fry the meat in hot oil. Add all the other ingredients (except for the spring onions) and cook on a high heat for a couple of minutes. Sprinkle the spring onions on top. Serve with rice.

Baked guinea pig - Ecuador
Ingredients:

1 whole guinea pig (*cuy*) per person. Available in markets skinned, cleaned and gutted, split open and always sold with the head.
Chilli powder
Chillies
1 tablespoon *aguardiente* (strong 'fire-water' booze distilled from sugar cane)
garlic
oil
salt and pepper

Method:
Rub the meat with garlic, salt, pepper, chilli powder, *aguardiente* and oil.
Place a chilli in the mouth. Skewer and cook on a barbecue.
Serve with hot sauce, boiled potatoes and salad.
Wash it down with *chicha*, a homebrewed, fermented maize drink

Ceviche - at sea
Ingredients:
Cubes of fresh dorado
Crushed garlic
Salt and pepper
Chopped coriander
Green chilli, seeded and chopped
Freshly squeezed limes, enough to cover the fish
1 red onion, thinly sliced and rinsed

Method:
Combine the ingredients, except the red onion, and mix well.
Place red onion on top and let the ceviche marinate in the fridge for
at least 2–3 hours before serving. The fish 'cooks' in the lime juice and
turns white like cooked fish.
Before serving, mix well and serve with lettuce, cold salad vegetables,
crisps and beer on a sun-soaked yacht with dolphins leaping in the bow
waves.

Tacos - Mexico
Ingredients:
soft tortillas
fillet steak, in thin strips
salsa (see below)
frijoles (mashed re-fried beans)
guacamole
finely sliced red onion
shredded lettuce
coriander
lime

Method:

Tacos: Spread frijoles and guacamole on a warm tortilla. Grill the steak and add to the tortilla. Spread salsa on the steak, add coriander, onion and lettuce. Squeeze lime juice over it. Roll up the taco and eat by hand.

Salsa Mexicana (so called because the red, white and green colours match the Mexican flag): Mix, according to taste, finely chopped tomato, onion, hot green chillies, coriander, salt and lime juice.

Banana Tacos - Sonora Desert, Mexico
Ingredients:
Bananas
Tortillas
(sugar, honey, lemon or rum if you are doing it in style)

Method:

Place a banana, in its peel, under hot coals until hot and soft. Spread banana over tortilla. Add other ingredients if available. Fold tortilla in half and place on hot ashes until crisp on both sides.

Chocolate Chip cookies - Alaska
Ingredients:
250g unsalted butter
150g white sugar
150g brown sugar
2 eggs
3 cups flour
2 teaspoons vanilla essence
1 teaspoon baking soda
½ teaspoon salt
250g chocolate chips

Method:

Warm and beat together the butter and sugar. Add the eggs and beat well. This is your chance to offset some of the calories you are about to eat. Beat in the other ingredients (adding the chocolate chips just before the end). Place cookie-sized blobs of the dough onto a greased baking tray and bake at 180°C for about 12 minutes or until golden brown. Try to allow to cool before eating.

Borscht Soup - Russia
Ingredients:
    1 litre beef stock
    3 tablespoons butter
    ½ finely chopped cabbage
    3 diced potatoes
    2 diced carrots
    1 stalk of chopped celery
    1 chopped onion
    2 finely chopped tomatoes
    ½ diced beetroot
    1 teaspoon vinegar
    dill
    sour cream
    salt and pepper

Method:
In a large, heavy pan, melt the butter and lightly sauté the cabbage, potatoes, carrots, celery and onion. Add beef stock. You can also add chunks of cold beef or bones and any other vegetables you feel like. Add tomatoes and beet juice to stock. Cover and simmer over low heat until vegetables are tender but not soft.

At this point, add the chopped beets and vinegar. Season well with salt and pepper and remove from heat before the beets begin to lose their colour.

Serve with a dollop of sour cream and a sprinkling of dill.

Chankonabe - Japan
If you had not guessed, sumo wrestlers tend to eat well. This is the classic sumo dish, eaten in vast quantities at sumo training school. It is not typically made to a set recipe, but always contains plenty of protein and vegetables. An uncouth person may imagine it is just everything left in the fridge hurled into an enormous cauldron. It is normally served with beer and rice. I have adapted the recipe slightly as Japan has many vegetables that are hard to find in the West.

Ingredients:
    Lots of cubes of chicken breast
    Lots of thinly sliced belly-pork
    Lots of chopped cabbage

Some daikon radish
A large, chopped aubergine
Several leeks, onions, carrots and shiitake mushrooms, all chopped
Plenty of fresh tofu
Pints of pork or chicken stock
Soy sauce, sake, mirin and miso for seasoning
A handful of dried fish flakes
Vast quantities of noodles or rice

Method:
Simmer the chicken and pork in the stock. When the meat is cooked add the sliced daikon, eggplant, and carrots. Add the miso. After a few minutes add the chopped onion, mushrooms, cabbage and tofu. Season with sake, mirin and soy sauce and fish flakes. Serve hot with steamed noodles or rice and beer. Delicious! *Oishi!* Eat as much as you can possibly fit inside you. Then have a nap.

Chanakhi - Georgia
Ingredients:
1kg diced lamb
3 tomatoes, peeled
1 large aubergine, sliced
2 onions, chopped
parsley
basil
2 cloves mashed garlic
2 potatoes, diced
olive oil
salt and pepper

Method:
Chanakhi was traditionally made in a clay pot. Place a layer of lamb in the bottom of the pot. Place a layer of sliced aubergine on top of the meat. Add the garlic, onion, parsley, basil and a sprinkle of olive oil. Add the peeled tomatoes and potatoes. Season with salt and pepper, cover and bake in the oven for 1½ hours.

Kit List

My equipment obviously fluctuated according to the environment I was in, but this is the essence of it.

Bike (two steel Specialized Rockhoppers which were great and then finally a wonderful steel mountain bike with downhill rims – I was sick of breaking wheels – made by a company who wouldn't give me even a tiny discount so I childishly taped over their logos), 4 large Karrimor panniers, 2 large Ark dry-bags, bungees, granny-style shopping basket (so much better than a bar bag), 2 water bottles, Brooks saddle, Jandd Extreme front rack, Blackburn Expedition rear rack, Schwalbe Marathon tyres (1.9s), DT spokes, SPD pedals (one sided), bike odometer (I wanted the Cateye with the altimeter), bar ends, horn for amusing kids and easily amused adults, bell, Topeak Alien multi tool, adjustable spanner, Leatherman Wave, freewheel remover, tyre levers, 2 pumps, puncture kit, 2 spare tubes, spare tyre, spare chain (I switched them every 3,000 kilometres), gaffa tape, superglue, zip ties, string, oil, spare nuts and bolts, strip of sidewall from an old tyre to wrap round the inner tube in case of a split tyre, free-standing Coleman tent, Therm-a-rest, sleeping bag, LED head torch, MSR Whisperlite, pan, spoon, cigarette lighters, mug, 10 litre water bag, iodine for water purifying, 2 zip-off trousers, 1 long-sleeved shirt, 2 T-shirts, SPD sandals, 1 pair of socks, lots of warm clothes in Siberia and none in Sudan, Karrimor rain jacket, rain trousers, thin gloves, waterproof mitts, Buff, baseball cap, helmet, suncream, Oakley sunglasses, cycling mitts, rechargeable AA batteries and charger, tiny First Aid and needle kit, insurance, photocopy of all paperwork, blood group info, dollars cash, lots of credit cards, a pipe, passport photos, maps, books, diary, Olympus digital camera (I wish I had had a tiny digital one and a digital SLR), music, passport. And my toothbrush.

The Magic Letter

I tweaked it and altered it according to each country I was in, but the cheesy essence of the Magic Letter is here. It looks quite excruciating and simplistic written out in English, but I wanted it to be understandable to even the least educated people I met.

Hello!

My name is Alastair Humphreys. I am a 25-year-old teacher from England. I left home in 2001 to try to cycle round the world. Since then I have cycled more than 20,000 kilometres across Europe, through the Middle East and all the way down Africa. I crossed the Atlantic Ocean in a sailing boat. I am now riding from Ushuaia up through South America towards Alaska. From Alaska I will cross to Asia and cycle across Asia back home to my friends and family in England. My journey will take about three more years. I will cross 5 continents and about 60 countries.

This adventure is trying to help young orphans in some of the poorest areas of the world. I raise money to help these children by giving talks and newspaper interviews about my adventures.

To earn money to eat and to live during the journey I write about my experiences for newspapers and magazines. They do not pay much money but my life is cheap: I sleep in my tent and so only have to pay for food. I do not even need any petrol!

I am excited to ride across your country and I apologise that I do not speak much of your language. It is hard to learn all the languages of the world!

I hope that you can help my journey to continue safely and happily. By helping me, you are also helping the hundreds of children that my adventure is helping.

When I get home I will write a book about my journey. I look forward to telling people in England and around the world about the safe and exciting times that I enjoyed in your country.

Thank you!

Alastair

A List of '-ests'

Longest day: 150 miles, Peru

Shortest day: 2½ miles, a Chinese snowdrift

Highest point: 4,900m, Peru and Argentina

Lowest point: -392m, the Dead Sea, Jordan

Longest time away from land: 24 days on the South Atlantic

Furthest point from the ocean: Urumqi, China

Hottest temperature: 45°C, Sudan and Turkmenistan

Coldest temperature: -40°C, Russia

Fastest speed: 50mph, Germany

Steepest road: 35% gradient, Lesotho

Longest Uphill: 2 days, Peru and Argentina

Longest Downhill: 50 miles, Peru

Heaviest bike: gear for -20°C, 8 days food, 18l water, Argentina

Heaviest me: a supersized, well-fed 85kg, USA

Lightest me: a post-Siberian winter 70kg, Russia

Most food carried: 10 days, Alaska and Russia

Most punctures in a day: 15, Bolivia

Most vomits in a day's ride: numerous, Turkey

Longest break from the bike: 2. 5 months, Cape Town

Longest ride without a break: 1 month, 4,200km, China

Longest time without a shower: 1 month, China

Longest time without a conversation (with another person)**:** 8 days, Argentina and Chile

Furthest north: 70°, Prudhoe Bay, Alaska

Furthest south: 56°, Ushuaia, Argentina

Furthest east: 179°, 59, 59: Pacific Ocean

Furthest west: 179°, 59, 59: Pacific Ocean

Acknowledgments

Thank you to the friends who joined me on the road, and the strangers who became friends. You gave so much.

Thanks to Rob and Dave for the miles shared and for being my Best Men.

To those who knocked me back: thanks for fuelling the fire.

To the people who read Moods of Future Joys, *and whose supportive feedback gave me the confidence to write this book.*

To the team at Eye Books.

To my friends and family who continue to support and encourage me.

And most of all, thank you to Sarah: my wife and my best friend. Thank you for waiting!

A Carbon Neutral Book

One of the many things that can be done to address the critical challenge of global climate change, as well as reducing emissions, is to become carbon neutral. Whenever we use fossil fuels, whether by driving, flying, using trucks, heating with oil or gas, or using electricity which has been generated with coal or gas, we cause the release of carbon, which forms carbon dioxide, the Number 1 greenhouse gas. Whenever we use paper that is not recycled, we also contribute to the loss of forests and forest soils, which store immense quantities of carbon, reducing the ability of our planet's ecosystems to store the carbon we are so busy releasing.

What can we do? We can reduce our emissions, and we can render our existing emissions "carbon neutral" by investing in initiatives which will prevent the release of a similar amount of emissions elsewhere, or which support long-term carbon-storing initiatives. The most common method to become carbon neutral involves investing in tree-planting initiatives that will absorb a similar quantity of emissions. The second method involves investing in initiatives which will prevent the release of a similar amount of emissions, such as paying to fit efficient light bulbs, or supporting the use of wind energy.

The production of books produces CO_2 from a variety of factors (forest soil loss, trucking, pulping, paper manufacturing, shipping). The trees themselves are considered carbon neutral, since they have already absorbed the CO_2 that will be released as their fibres or the paper made from them break down and release the stored CO_2 back into the atmosphere. The use of recycled paper releases less CO_2, since there is no loss of forest soil, and less fuel is used in logging and trucking. Carbon is also released through the vehicles used to deliver each book.

Therefore, for each book sold, a donation will be made, through www.climatecare.org, to offset the carbon emissions involved in printing and shipping this book. My journey was virtually carbon neutral, and I would like my book to be also. This is not an issue we can ignore for much longer.

Hope and Homes for Children

*H*ope and Homes for Children is a registered charity working in 13 countries in Eastern Europe and Africa. Our head office is in Wiltshire in the UK. Our Mission is to give hope to the poorest children in the world – those who are orphaned, abandoned or vulnerable – by enabling them to grow up within the love of a family and the security of a home, so that they can fulfill their potential.

Our Vision is A World Where Every Child Feels Loved.

Today, home for more than a million children in Eastern Europe is a bleak state-run institution. These children, abandoned at birth or removed from their families because of a mental or physical disability, are hidden away in facilities that rarely meet even their most basic needs.

At *Hope and Homes for Children* we believe that every child has the right to grow up with the love and care of a family. This is why we are working with governments to not only close state institutions, by moving each individual child into a caring family environment, but also to change outdated attitudes to childcare policy and practice. Closing institutions is just the beginning, not the end, and we are helping governments put in place the alternative care systems that prevent children from entering institutions in the first place.

Children who are alone due to the AIDS pandemic are being given hope. Every 14 seconds AIDS turns a child into an orphan and almost 20 million of these children live in sub-Saharan Africa. We are supporting people with HIV and families who have lost parents through AIDS. Our work keeps families together and, in the case of a parent with HIV, we help to make plans and provision for their children. We are helping to avoid the alternative: children without homes or schools, forced into begging, crime or prostitution in order to survive.

Children orphaned or abandoned through conflict are given a family and a future. In Sierra Leone, Eritrea, Rwanda and Sudan alone, there are estimated to be more than two million children orphaned by conflict. We are caring for children in parts of Eastern Europe and Africa who have been affected by conflict, war or genocide and the social disruption and poverty that result from the hostilities. These children may be living on the streets, in government camps, in local institutions or in impoverished circumstances in the community.

Should you wish to learn more or make a donation please visit the website below. Your donation will help us to change a child's life. Whatever your contribution, it will be greatly appreciated.

To find out more about *Hope and Homes for Children*, please visit
www. alastairhumphreys. com

Thank you.

eyeAuthor

Alastair Humphreys

Alastair's quest for adventure began young. Aged 8, he completed the 26 mile Yorkshire 3 Peaks Challenge and the National 3 Peaks in 24 hours aged 13. At 14 he cycled off-road across England. After leaving school Alastair taught for a year in South Africa.

Whilst at university (Edinburgh and Oxford) Alastair cycled from Pakistan to China, Land's End to John O'Groats, Turkey to Italy, Mexico to Panama and across South America. He ran a charity project in the Philippines and the London marathon dressed as a rhino.

Since graduating, Alastair has cycled round the world for 4 years (the story told in *Moods of Future Joys* and *Thunder & Sunshine*), raced a yacht across the Atlantic Ocean, canoed 500 miles down the Yukon River and walked the length of the holy Kaveri river in India. Alastair also ran the Marathon des Sables, (one of the ten fastest Brits despite breaking his foot during the race) and rowed to France with Major Phil Packer, a soldier paralysed in Iraq.

To fight off the wanderlust back home Alastair managed a sub-3-hour marathon, had a miserable time during the Original Mountain Marathon, the Devizes to Westminster 120-mile canoe marathon and another one during Tough Guy. Travelling round the 2006 football World Cup in a van was much more fun.

After spending a year teaching 10-year-old boys in a school's Special Needs department, Alastair is now training for an Ironman triathlon and preparing for SOUTH, the first unsupported return journey to the South Pole and the longest unsupported polar journey in history.

You can follow Alastair's latest adventure at www.alastairhumphreys.com or follow him on Twitter – @Al_Humphreys.

www.eye-books.com

Got a dream? Live it... Alastair's lessons are an inspiration to us all.

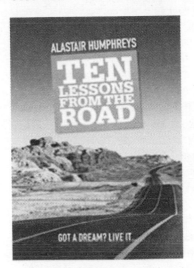

10 Lessons from the Road
£9.99

Illustrated throughout with inspiring images from around the world.

After four years spent bicycling round the world, Alastair knows all about motivation and how to keep going when the going gets tough. In *Ten Lessons from the Road* he asserts that the lessons he learned on his travels can be applied to any goal in life; from doing the washing-up to flying to the moon!

Moods of Future Joys
£7.99

Alastair Humphreys' round the world journey of 46,000 miles was an old-fashioned adventure: long, lonely, low-budget and spontaneous.

This first part of the ride crosses the Middle East and Africa and continues towards Cape Town. The epic journey succeeded through Humphreys' trust in the kindness of strangers, at a time when the global community was more confused and troubled than ever.

www.eye-books.com

eyeSight

Our greatest fear is not that we are inadequate, our greatest fear is that we are powerful beyond measure. By shining your light, you subconsciously give permission to others to shine theirs.
Nelson Mandela

Travel can be a liberating experience, as it was for me in 1990, when I was just one hundred yards from Nelson Mandela as he was released from prison. I watched this monumental occasion from on top of a traffic light, amidst a sea of enthralled onlookers.

This was the 'green light' moment that inspired the creation of Eye Books. From the chaos of that day arose an appreciation of the opportunities that the world around us offers, and the desire within me to shine a light for those whose reaction to opportunity is 'can't and don't'.

Our world has been built on dreams, but the drive is often diluted by the corporate and commercial interests offering to live those dreams for us, through celebrity culture and the increasing mechanisation and automation of our lives. Inspiration comes now from those who live outside our daily routines, from those who *challenge the way we see things*.

Eye Books was born to tell the stories of *'ordinary' people doing 'extraordinary' things*. With no experience of publishing, or the constraints that the book 'industry' imposes, Eye Books created a genre of publishing to champion those who live out their dreams.

Twelve years on, and sixty stories later, Eye Books has the same ethos. We believe that ethical publishing matters. It is not about just trying to make a quick hit, it is about publishing the stories that affect our lives and the lives of others positively. We publish the books we believe will shine a light on the lives of some and enlighten the lives of many for years to come.

Join us in the Eye Books community, and share the power these stories evoke.

Dan Hiscocks
Founder and Publisher
Eye Books

www.eye-books.com

eyeCommunity

At Eye Books we are constantly challenging the way we see things and do things. But we cannot do this alone. To that end we have created an online club, a community, where members can inspire and be inspired, share knowledge and exchange ideas. Membership is free, and you can join by visiting www.eye-books.com, where you will be able to find:

What we publish
Books that truly inspire, by people who have given their all, triumphed over adversity, lived their lives to the full. Visit the dedicated microsites we have for each of our books online.

Why we publish
To champion those 'ordinary' people doing extraordinary things. The real celebrities of our world who tell stories that celebrate life to the full, not just for 15 minutes. Books where fact is more compelling than fiction.

How we publish
Eye Books is committed to ethical publishing. Many of our books feature and campaign for various good causes and charities. We try to minimise our carbon footprint in the manufacturing and distribution of our books.

Who we publish
Many, indeed most of our authors have never written a book before. Many start as readers and club members. If you feel strongly that you have a book in you, and it is a book that is experience driven, inspirational and life affirming, visit the 'How to Become an Author' page on our website. We are always open to new authors.

eyeCommunity

Eye-Books.com Club is an ever-evolving community, as it should be, and benefits from all that our members contribute.

eye-**Books Club** membership offers you:

eye-**News** – a regular emailed newsletter of events in our community.

Special offers and discounts on the books we publish.

Invitations to book launches, signings and author talks.

Correspond with Eye Books authors, directly. About writing, about their books, or about trips you may be planning.

Each month, we receive enquiries from people who have read our books, entered our competitions or heard of us through the media or from friends, people who have a common desire — to make a difference with their lives, however big or small, and to extend the boundaries of everyday life and to learn from others' experiences.

The Eye Books Club is here to support our members, and we want to encourage you to participate. As we all know, the more you put into life, the more you get out of it.

Eye Books membership is free, and it's easy to sign up. Visit our website. Registration takes less than a minute.

eyeBookshelf

THE AMERICAS / ASIA

Category	Thunder & Sunshine (Alastair Humphreys)	The Good Life (Dorian Amos)	The Good Life Gets Better (Dorian Amos)	Cry From the Highest Mountain (Tess Burrows)	Riding the Outlaw Trail (Simon Casson & Richard Adamson)	Trail of Visions Route 2 (Vicki Couchman)	Riding with Ghosts (Gwen Maka)	Riding with Ghosts – South of the Border (Gwen Maka)	Lost Lands Forgotten Stories (Alexandra Pratt)	Frigid Women (Sue & Victoria Riches)	Touching Tibet (Niema Ash)	First Contact (Mark Anstice)	Tea for Two (Polly Benge)	Baghdad Business School (Heyrick Bond Gunning)
eyeThinker		•	•		•				•	•		•	•	•
eyeAdventurer	•	•	•				•	•	•	•		•	•	•
eyeQuirky						•							•	
eyeCyclist	•						•						•	
eyeRambler														
eyeGift	•						•							
eyeSpiritual														

AFRICA / EUROPE

Category	Moods of Future Joys (Alastair Humphreys)	Green Oranges on Lion Mountain (Emily Joy)	Zohra's Ladder (Pamela Windo)	Walking Away (Charlotte Metcalf)	Changing the World from the inside out (Michael Meegan)	All Will Be Well (Michael Meegan)	Seeking Sanctuary (Hilda Reilly)	Crap Cycle Lanes (Captain Crunchynutz)	50 Quirky Bike Rides...in England and Wales (Rob Ainsley)	On the Wall with Hadrian (Bob Bibby)	Special Offa (Bob Bibby)	The European Job (Jonathan Booth)	Fateful Beauty (Natalie Hodgson)	Slow Winter (Alex Hickman)
eyeThinker		•	•	•	•	•	•							•
eyeAdventurer	•	•							•			•	•	•
eyeQuirky								•	•			•	•	
eyeCyclist	•							•	•					
eyeRambler										•	•			
eyeGift	•							•	•					
eyeSpiritual					•	•								

eyeBookshelf

ASIA / AUS

Book (Author)	eyeThinker	eyeAdventurer	eyeQuirky	eyeCyclist	eyeRambler	eyeGift	eyeSpiritual
Travels in Outback Australia — Andrew Stevenson	•	•					
Last of the Nomads — W J Peasley	•						
Prickly Pears of Palestine — Hilda Reilly	•						
Jasmine and Arnica — Nicola Naylor	•	•					
Good Morning Afghanistan — Waseem Mahmood	•	•					
Behind the Veil — Lydia Laube		•					
Siberian Dreams — Andy Home	•	•					
The Jungle Beat — Roy Follows	•	•					
My Journey with a Remarkable Tree — Ken Finn	•						
Fever Tress of Borneo — Mark Eveleigh		•					
Desert Governess — Phyllis Ellis	•	•	•			•	
Trail of Visions — Vicki Couchman	•	•					
Jungle Janes — Peter Burden		•					

EUROPE / CROSS CONTINENT

Book (Author)	eyeThinker	eyeAdventurer	eyeQuirky	eyeCyclist	eyeRambler	eyeGift	eyeSpiritual
More Traveller's Tales from Heaven and Hell — Various			•			•	
Further Traveller's Tales from Heaven and Hell — Various			•			•	
Traveller's Tales from Heaven and Hell — Various			•			•	
Blood Sweat and Charity — Nick Stanhope		•					•
Triumph Around the World — Robbie Marshall	•	•					•
Great Sects — Adam Hume Kelly	•					•	
Discovery Road — Tim Garratt & Andy Brown	•					•	
Death — Herbie Brennan			•				
Around the World with 1000 Birds — Russell Boyman	•	•					
Travels with my Daughter — Niema Ash	•	•	•	•			
Forensics Handbook — Pete Moore	•	•	•			•	
Con Artist Handbook — Joel Levy	•	•	•			•	
The Accidental Optimist's Guide to Life — Emily Joy	•		•				

eyeBookshelf

Discovery Road
£9.99

The first people to mountain bike around the world. It is a fast-moving inspirational tale of self-discovery; full of adventure, conflict, humour, danger and a multitude of colourful characters. Much more than a travelogue, it proves that ordinary people can chase great dreams.

"The power comes from the excellence of the writing"
The Independent

Tea for Two
£7.99

Tim and Polly head to war-torn Assam and follow the 400 miles route taken to enlightenment by the Buddha. The Buddha took six years, but they had six weeks and two bicycles...

A true love story and a great read.

"Polly knows how to wield her pen... This colourful paperback is tailor-made to give armchair adventurers hope"
On Your Bike

www.eye-books.com

Riding with Ghosts
£7.99

An interest in Native American history and a desire to push herself to the limit sees Gwen (a solo woman) try to bicycle the trail from Seattle to Mexico. Her frank and outrageous account of the physical and mental journey she takes is fascinating.

"a beautifully written book which achieves the delicate balance between poetic description, gritty humour and well-paced storytelling."
Manchester Evening News

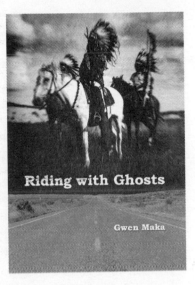

Riding with Ghosts: South of the Border
£7.99

Having ridden, saddle-sore, from Seattle to Mexico, Gwen continues down the Americas to San Jose in Costa Rica. She writes with passion about the pioneers of the South: Columbus, Cortes and Montezuma, whilst describing her journey with her usual courage, candour and humour.

eyeBookshelf

Crap Cycle Lanes
£4.99

Probably the worst bike lanes in the world. This hilarious book names and shames the worst offenders. A brilliant gift for any cyclist.

"It made me laugh out loud, and I can't even ride a bike"
Independent on Sunday

50 Quirky Bike Rides
£9.99

A book detailing 50 quirky things that are uniquely enjoyale by bike: weird places where you can (metaphorically) take your bike downhill skiing, potholing or tightrope walking, or turn it into a pedalo. You'll find delightful oddities like cycling on a motorway or on the right-hand side of the road. Many can be done in a lunchtime; all make an excuse for a day trip, or a three-month tour.

"A cracking good read... probably the funniest guide I've come across"
Herald Review

www.eye-books.com